T0214687

Lecture Notes in Computer Science 11231

Commenced Publication in 1973
Founding and Former Series Editors:
Gerhard Goos, Juris Hartmanis, and Jan van Leeuwen

More information about this series at http://www.springer.com/series/7407

Christophe Debruyne · Hervé Panetto
Wided Guédria · Peter Bollen
Ioana Ciuciu · Robert Meersman (Eds.)

On the Move to Meaningful Internet Systems

OTM 2018 Workshops

Confederated International Workshops: EI2N, FBM, ICSP, and Meta4eS 2018
Valletta, Malta, October 22–26, 2018
Revised Selected Papers

 Springer

Editors
Christophe Debruyne (ID)
Trinity College Dublin
Dublin, Ireland

and

Vrije Universiteit Brussel
Brussels, Belgium

Hervé Panetto (ID)
University of Lorraine
Vandoeuvre-les-Nancy, France

Wided Guédria
Luxembourg Institute of Science
and Technology
Esch-sur-Alzette, Luxembourg

Peter Bollen
Maastricht University
Maastricht, The Netherlands

Ioana Ciuciu
University Babes-Bolyai
Cluj-Napoca, Romania

Robert Meersman
TU Graz
Graz, Austria

ISSN 0302-9743   ISSN 1611-3349   (electronic)
Lecture Notes in Computer Science
ISBN 978-3-030-11682-8   ISBN 978-3-030-11683-5   (eBook)
https://doi.org/10.1007/978-3-030-11683-5

Library of Congress Control Number: 2019930848

LNCS Sublibrary: SL1 – Theoretical Computer Science and General Issues

This Springer imprint is published by the registered company Springer Nature Switzerland AG
The registered company address is: Gewerbestrasse 11, 6330 Cham, Switzerland

General Co-chairs and Editors' Message
for OnTheMove 2018

The OnTheMove 2018 event held during October 22–26 in Valletta, Malta, further consolidated the importance of the series of annual conferences that was started in 2002 in Irvine, California. It then moved to Catania, Sicily, in 2003, to Cyprus in 2004 and 2005, Montpellier in 2006, Vilamoura in 2007 and 2009, in 2008 to Monterrey, Mexico, to Heraklion, Crete, in 2010 and 2011, Rome 2012, Graz in 2013, Amantea, Italy, in 2014, and lastly in Rhodes in 2015, 2016, and 2017 as well.

This prime event continues to attract a diverse and relevant selection of today's research worldwide on the scientific concepts underlying new computing paradigms, which of necessity must be distributed, heterogeneous and supporting an environment of resources that are autonomous yet must meaningfully cooperate. Indeed, as such large, complex, and networked intelligent information systems become the focus and norm for computing, there continues to be an acute and even increasing need to address the software, system, and enterprise issues that are involved and discuss them face to face in an integrated forum that covers methodological, semantic, theoretical, and application issues too. As we all realize, e-mail, the Internet, and even video conferences are not by themselves optimal nor even sufficient for effective and efficient scientific exchange.

The OnTheMove (OTM) International Federated Conference series has been created precisely to cover the scientific exchange needs of the communities that work in the broad yet closely connected fundamental technological spectrum of Web-based distributed computing. The OTM program every year covers data and Web semantics, distributed objects, Web services, databases, information systems, enterprise workflow and collaboration, ubiquity, interoperability, mobility, grid, and high-performance computing.

OnTheMove is proud to give meaning to the "federated" aspect in its full title: it aspires to be a primary scientific meeting place where all aspects of research and development of Internet- and intranet-based systems in organizations and for e-business are discussed in a scientifically motivated way, in a forum of interconnected workshops and conferences. This year's 15th edition of the OTM Federated Conferences event therefore once more provided an opportunity for researchers and practitioners to understand, discuss, and publish these developments within the broader context of distributed, ubiquitous computing. To further promote synergy and coherence, the main conferences of OTM 2018 were conceived against a background of their three interlocking global themes:

- Trusted Cloud Computing Infrastructures Emphasizing Security and Privacy
- Technology and Methodology for Data and Knowledge Resources on the (Semantic) Web
- Deployment of Collaborative and Social Computing for and in an Enterprise Context

Originally the federative structure of OTM was formed by the co-location of three related, complementary, and successful main conference series: DOA (Distributed Objects and Applications, held since 1999), covering the relevant infrastructure-enabling technologies, ODBASE (Ontologies, DataBases and Applications of SEmantics, since 2002) covering Web semantics, XML databases and ontologies, and of course CoopIS (Cooperative Information Systems, held since 1993), which studies the application of these technologies in an enterprise context through, e.g., workflow systems and knowledge management. In the 2011 edition security issues, originally started as topics of the IS workshop in OTM 2006, became the focus of DOA as secure virtual infrastructures, further broadened to cover aspects of trust and privacy in so-called cloud-based systems. As this latter aspect came to dominate agendas in this and overlapping research communities, we decided in 2014 to rename the event as the Cloud and Trusted Computing (C&TC) Conference, and was originally launched in a workshop format.

These three main conferences specifically seek high-quality contributions of a more mature nature and encourage researchers to treat their respective topics within a framework that simultaneously incorporates (a) theory, (b) conceptual design and development, (c) methodology and pragmatics, and (d) application in particular case studies and industrial solutions.

As in previous years, we again solicited and selected additional quality workshop proposals to complement the more mature and "archival" nature of the main conferences. Our workshops are intended to serve as "incubators" for emergent research results in selected areas related, or becoming related, to the general domain of Web-based distributed computing. We were very glad to see that our earlier successful workshops (EI2N, META4eS, FBM) re-appeared in 2018. The Fact-Based Modeling (FBM) <workshop in 2015 succeeded and expanded the scope of the successful earlier ORM <workshop. The Industry Case Studies Program, started in 2011, under the leadership of Hervé Panetto, Wided Guédria, and Gash Bhullar, further gained momentum and visibility in its seventh edition this year.

The OTM registration format ("one workshop or conference buys all workshops and conferences") actively intends to promote synergy between related areas in the field of distributed computing and to stimulate workshop audiences to productively mingle with each other and, optionally, with those of the main conferences. In particular, EI2N continues to create and exploit a visible cross-pollination with CoopIS.

We were very happy to see that in 2018 the number of quality submissions for the OnTheMove Academy (OTMA) noticeably increased. OTMA implements our unique, actively coached and therefore very time- and effort-intensive formula to bring PhD students together, and aims to carry our "vision for the future" in research in the areas covered by OTM. Its 2018 edition was organized and managed by a dedicated team of collaborators and faculty, Peter Spyns, Maria-Esther Vidal, inspired as always by the OTMA Dean, Erich Neuhold.

In the OTM Academy, PhD research proposals are submitted by students for peer review; selected submissions and their approaches are to be presented by the students in front of a wider audience at the conference, and are independently and extensively analyzed and discussed in front of this audience by a panel of senior professors. One may readily appreciate the time, effort, and funds invested in this by OnTheMove and especially by the OTMA faculty.

As the three main conferences and the associated workshops all share the distributed aspects of modern computing systems, they experience the application pull created by the Internet and by the so-called Semantic Web, in particular developments of big data, increased importance of security issues, and the globalization of mobile-based technologies.

The three conferences seek exclusively original submissions that cover scientific aspects of fundamental theories, methodologies, architectures, and emergent technologies, as well as their adoption and application in enterprises and their impact on societally relevant IT issues.

- CoopIS 2018, Cooperative Information Systems, our flagship event in its 26th edition since its inception in 1993, invites fundamental contributions on principles and applications of distributed and collaborative computing in the broadest scientific sense in workflows of networked organizations, enterprises, governments, or just communities.
- C&TC 2018 (Cloud and Trusted Computing 2018), is the successor of DOA (Distributed Object Applications) and focuses on critical aspects of virtual infrastructure for cloud computing, specifically spanning issues of trust, reputation, and security.
- ODBASE 2018, Ontologies, Databases, and Applications of Semantics covers the fundamental study of structured and semi-structured data, including linked (open) data and big data, and the meaning of such data as is needed for today's databases; as well as the role of data and semantics in design methodologies and new applications of databases.

As with the earlier OnTheMove editions, the organizers wanted to stimulate this cross-pollination by a program of engaging keynote speakers from academia and industry and shared by all OTM component events. We are quite proud to list for this year:

- Martin Hepp, Universität der Bundeswehr Munich/Hepp Research GmbH
- Pieter De Leenheer, Collibra
- Richard Mark Soley, Object Management Group, Inc. (OMG)
- Tom Raftery, SAP/Instituto Internacional San Telmo

The general downturn in submissions observed in recent years for almost all conferences in computer science and IT has also affected OnTheMove, but this year the harvest again stabilized at a total of 173 submissions for the three main conferences and over 50 submissions in total for the workshops. Not only may we indeed again claim success in attracting a representative volume of scientific papers, many from the USA and Asia, but these numbers of course allowed the respective Program Committees to again compose a high-quality cross-section of current research in the areas covered by OTM. Acceptance rates vary but the aim was to stay consistently at about one accepted full paper for three submitted, yet as always these rates are subordinated to professional peer assessment of proper scientific quality.

As usual, we separated the proceedings into two volumes with their own titles, one for the main conferences and one for the workshops and posters. But in a different approach to previous years, we decided the latter should appear after the event and so allow workshop authors to eventually improve their peer-reviewed papers based on critiques by the Program Committees and on live interaction at OTM. The resulting additional complexity and effort of editing the proceedings was professionally shouldered by our leading editor Christophe Debruyne - with the general chairs for the conference volume, and with Hervé Panetto for the workshop volume. We are again most grateful to the Springer LNCS team in Heidelberg for their professional support, suggestions, and meticulous collaboration in producing the files and indexes ready for downloading on the USB sticks. It is a pleasure to work with staff that so deeply understands the scientific context at large, and the specific logistics of conference proceedings publication.

The reviewing process by the respective OTM Program Committees was performed to professional quality standards: Each paper review in the main conferences was assigned to at least three referees, with arbitrated e-mail discussions in the case of strongly diverging evaluations. It may be worthwhile to emphasize once more that it is an explicit OnTheMove policy that all conference Program Committees and chairs make their selections in a completely sovereign manner, autonomous, and independent from any OTM organizational considerations. As in recent years, proceedings in paper form are now only available to be ordered separately.

The general chairs are once more especially grateful to the many people directly or indirectly involved in the setup of these federated conferences. Not everyone realizes the large number of qualified persons that need to be involved, and the huge amount of work, commitment, and the financial risk in the uncertain economic and funding climate of 2018, that is entailed by the organization of an event like OTM. Apart from the persons in their roles aforementioned, we therefore wish to thank in particular explicitly our main conference Program Committee chairs:

- CoopIS 2018: Henderik A. Proper, Markus Stumptner and Samir Tata
- ODBASE 2018: Dumitru Roman, Elena Simperl, Ahmet Soylu, and Marko Grobelnik
- C&TC 2018: Claudio A. Ardagna, Adrian Belmonte, and Mauro Conti

And similarly we thank the Program Committee (co-)chairs of the 2018 ICSP, OTMA, and Workshops (in their order of appearance on the website): Wided Guédria, Hervé Panetto, Markus Stumptner, Georg Weichhart, Peter Bollen, Stijn Hoppenbrouwers, Robert Meersman, Maurice Nijssen, Gash Bhullar, Ioana Ciuciu, Anna Fensel, Peter Spyns, and Maria-Esther Vidal.

Together with their many Program Committee members, they performed a superb and professional job in managing the difficult yet essential process of peer review and selection of the best papers from the harvest of submissions. We all also owe a serious debt of gratitude to our supremely competent and experienced conference secretariat and technical admin staff in Guadalajara and Dublin, respectively, Daniel Meersman and Christophe Debruyne.

The general conference and workshop co-chairs also thankfully acknowledge the academic freedom, logistic support, and facilities they enjoy from their respective institutions—Technical University of Graz, Austria; Université de Lorraine, Nancy, France; Latrobe University, Melbourne, Australia – and without which such a project quite simply would not be feasible. Reader, we do hope that the results of this federated scientific enterprise contribute to your research and your place in the scientific network, and we hope to welcome you at next year's event!

September 2018

Robert Meersman
Tharam Dillon
Hervé Panetto
Ernesto Damiani

Organization

OTM (On The Move) is a federated event involving a series of major international conferences and workshops. These proceedings contain the papers presented at the OTM 2018 Federated conferences, consisting of CoopIS 2018 (Cooperative Information Systems), C&TC 2018 (Cloud and Trusted Computing) and ODBASE 2018 (Ontologies, Databases, and Applications of Semantics).

Executive Committee

OTM Conferences and Workshops General Chairs

Robert Meersman	TU Graz, Austria
Tharam Dillon	La Trobe University, Melbourne, Australia
Hervé Panetto	University of Lorraine, France
Ernesto Damiani	Politecnico di Milano, Italy

EI2N 2017 Program Chairs

Wided Guédria	LIST, Luxembourg
Hervé Panetto	University of Lorraine, France
Markus Stumptner	University of South Australia, Australia
Georg Weichhart	Profactor GmbH & Johannes Kepler University Linz, Austria

FBM Program Chairs

Peter Bollen	University of Maastricht, The Netherlands
Stijn Hoppenbrouwers	HAN UAS and Radboud University, The Netherlands
Robert Meersman	T.U. Graz, Austria
Maurice Nijssen	PNA Group, The Netherlands

Industry Case Studies Program Chairs

Hervé Panetto	University of Lorraine, France
Wided Guédria	LIST, Luxembourg
Gash Bhullar	Control 2K Limited, UK

Meta4eS 2017 Program Chairs

Anna Fensel	STI Innsbruck, University of Innsbruck, Austria
Ioana Ciuciu	Babes-Bolyai University, Romania

OnTheMove Academy Dean

Erich Neuhold	University of Vienna, Austria

Publication Chair

Christophe Debruyne   Trinity College Dublin, Ireland

Logistics Team

Daniel Meersman

EI2N 2018 Program Committee

Aasa Fast-Berglund
Agostino Villa
Andres Garcia Higuera
Angel Ortiz Bas
Antonio Abreu
Arturo Molina Gutierrez
Benoit Iung
Birgit Vogel-Heuser
Bruno Vallespir
Christophe Feltus
David Romero
Eduardo Rocha Loures
Eduardo Avles Portella Santos
Erik Proper
Esma Yahia
Franois B. Vernadat
Georg Grossmann
Georg Weichhart
Geza Haidegger
Giuseppe Berio
Hamideh Afsarmanesh
Herve Panetto
Istvan Mezgar
Ivan Lukovi
Janusz Kacprzyk
Janusz Szpytko
Julio Cesar Nardi

Lawrence Stapleton
Li Qing
Llanos Cuenca
Luis Camarinha-Matos
Manel Brichni
Marco Macchi
Marek Wegrzyn
Mario Lezoche
Martin Zelm
Michele Dassisti
Milan Zdravkovic
Mohamed Hedi Karray
Nenad Stefanovic
Ovidiu Noran
Peter Bernus
Rafael Batres
Ricardo J. Rabelo
Ricardo Jardim Goncalves
Richard Soley
Sergio Guerreiro
Stumptner Markus
Ted Goranson
Udo Kannengiesser
Ulrike Lechner
Virginie Goepp
Wided Guedria
Yannis Charalabidis

FBM 2018 Program Committee

Adrian Walker
Baba Piprani
Bas van Gils
Clifford Heath
Cory Casanave
David Cuyler
Dirk vanderLinden
Ed Barkmeyer
Ellen Munthe-Kaas
Erik Proper
Gordon Everest
Hans Mulder
Harald Eisenmann
Inge Lemmens
Jan Vanthienen
Jan-Mark Pleijsant
John Sowa
John Bulles
Jos Vos

Leo Obrst
Mariette Lokin
Mark von Rosing
Martijn Zoet
Martijn Evers
Maurice Nijssen
Paul Iske
Peter Straatsma
Peter Bollen
Peter Spyns
Robert van Doesburg
Robert Meersman
Roel Baardman
Serge Valera
Sjir Nijssen
Stijn Hoppenbrouwers
Terry Halpin
Tom van Engers
Tony Morgan

ICSP 2018 Program Committee

Andrea Persidis
Andres Garcia Higuera
Antoine Lonjon
Arturo Molina
Ben Calloni
Christoph Bussler
Christoph Niedermeier
Daniel Sáez Domingo
David Cohen
Dennis Brandl
Detlef Zühlke
Dimitri Varoutas
Dirk Slama
Dominique Ernadote
Ed Parsons
Eduardo Loures
Eva Coscia
Fabrizio Gagliardi
François B. Vernadat
Francesco Danza
Gash Bhullar
Georg Weichhart

Giancarlo Fortino
Giuseppe Di Fatta
Gottfried Luef
Hans Vandheluwe
Hervé Panetto
Ian Bayley
Jacques Durand
Jean Simao
Jean-Luc Garnier
Joe Salvo
Juan-Carlos Mendez
Kurt Fessl
Lawrence Whitman
Luis Camarinha-Matos
Marc Delbaere
Mark Schulte
Martin Zelm
Mathias Kohler
Mattew Hause
Maximiliano Vargas
Michael Alexander
Michael Ditze

Michele Dassisti
Milan Zdravkovic
Nicolas Figay
Pascal Gendre
Paulo Whitman
Peter Loos
Peter Benson
Peter Gorm Larsen
Piero De Sabbata
Qing-Shan Jia
Ricardo Goncalves

Richard Martin
Richard Soley
Serge Boverie
Sinuhe Arroyo
Sobah Abbas Pertersen
Ted Goranson
Tuan Dang
Vasco Amaral
Vincent Chapurlat
Wided Gudria
Yannick Naudet

META4eS 2018 Program Committee

Adrian Brasoveanu
Ana-Maria Roxin
Andrea Ko
Andres Micsik
Anna Fensel
Özlem Özgobek
Camelia Pintea
Christophe Roche
Cosmin Lazar

Dumitru Roman
Ioana Ciuciu
Jorge Martinez-Gil
Josep Domenech
Kalliopi Kravari
Nick Bassiliades
Peter Spyns
Seongbin Park
Zaenal Akbar

OnTheMove Academy 2018 Program Committee

Christoph Bussler
Claudia d'Amato
Claudia Jiménez
Erich J. Neuhold
Erik Proper
Frédéric Le Mouël
Galia Angelova
Georg Weichhart

Hervé Panetto
Manu De Backer
Maria-Esther Vidal
Paolo Ceravolo
Peter Spyns
Rik Eshuis
Rudi Studer

OnTheMove 2018 Keynotes

Web Ontologies: Lessons Learned from Conceptual Modeling at Scale

Martin Hepp

Universität der Bundeswehr Munich/Hepp Research GmbH, Germany

Short Bio

Martin Hepp is a professor of E-business and General Management at the Universität der Bundeswehr Munich and the CEO and Chief Scientist of Hepp Research GmbH. He holds a master's degree in business management and business information systems and a PhD in business information systems from the University of Würzburg (Germany). His key research interests are shared data structures at Web scale, for example Web ontology engineering, both at the technical, social, and economical levels, conceptual modeling in general, and data quality management. As part of his research, he developed the GoodRelations vocabulary, an OWL DL ontology for data interoperability for e-commerce at Web Scale. Since 11/2012, GoodRelations is the e-commerce core of schema.org, the official data markup standard of major search engines, namely Google, Yahoo, Bing, and Yandex. Martin authored more than 80 academic publications and was the organizer of more than fifteen workshops and conference tracks on conceptual modeling, Semantic Web topics, and information systems, and a member of more than sixty conference and workshop program committees, including ECIS, EKAW, ESWC, IEEE CEC/EEE, ISWC, and WWW.

Talk

Ever since the introduction of the term "ontology" to Computer Science, the challenges for information exchange, processing, and intelligent behavior on the World Wide Web, with its vast body of content, huge user base, linguistic and representational heterogeneity, and so forth, have been taken as a justification for ontology-related research. However, despite two decades of work on ontologies in this context, very few ontologies have emerged that are used at Web scale in a way compliant with the original proposals by a diverse, open audience.

In this talk, I will analyze the differences between the original idea of ontologies in computer science, and Web ontologies, and analyze the specific economic, social, and technical challenges of building, maintaining, and using socially agreed, global data structures that are suited for the Web at large, also with respect to the skills, expectations, and particular needs of owners of Web sites and potential consumers of Web data.

Data Governance: The New Imperative to Democratize Data Science

Pieter De Leenheer

Collibra, USA

Short Bio

Pieter De Leenheer is a cofounder of Collibra and leads the company's Research & Education group, including the Collibra University, which offers a range of self-paced learning and certification courses to help data governance professionals and data citizens gain new skills and expertise. Prior to co-founding the company, Pieter was a professor at VU University of Amsterdam. Today he still serves as adjunct professor at Columbia University in the City of New York and as visiting scholar at several universities across the globe including UC San Diego and Stanford.

Talk

We live in the age of abundant data. Through technology, more data is available, and the processing of that data easier and cheaper than ever before. Data science emerged from an unparalleled fascination to empirically understand and predict societies businesses and markets. Yet there is an understated risk inherent to democratizing data science such as data spills, cost of data exploration, and blind trust in unregulated, incontestable and oblique models. In their journey to unlock competitive advantage and maximize value from the application of big data, it is vital that data leaders find the right balance between value creation and risk exposure. To realize the true value of this wealth of data, data leaders must not act impulsively, but rethink assumptions, processes, and approaches to managing, governing, and stewarding that data. And to succeed, they must deliver credible, coherent, and trustworthy data and data access clearing mechanisms for everyone who can use it. As data becomes the most valuable resource, data governance delivers a imperative certification for any business to trust one another, but also increasingly sets a precondition for any citizen to engage in a trustworthy and endurable relationship with a company or government.

Learning to Implement the Industrial Internet

Richard Mark Soley

Object Management Group, Inc. (OMG), USA

Short Bio

Dr. Richard Mark Soley is Chairman and CEO of the Object Management Group (r), also leading the Cloud Standards Customer Council (tm) the Industrial Internet Consortium (r). Previously cofounder and former Chairman/CEO of A. I. Architects, he worked for technology companies and venture firms like TI, Gold Hill, Honeywell & IBM. Dr. Soley has SB, SM and PhD degrees in Computer Science and Engineering from MIT.

A longer bio is available here: http://www.omg.org/soley/.

Talk

- The Industrial Internet Consortium and its members develop testbeds to learn more about Industrial Internet implementation: hiring, ecosystem development, standards requirements
- The Object Management Group takes real-world standards requirements and develops standards to maximize interoperability and portability
- The first insights into implementation and the first requirements for standards are underway
- Dr. Soley will give an overview of both processes and talk about the first insights from the projects

The Future of Digital: What the Next 10 Years Have in Store

Tom Raftery

SAP/Instituto Internacional San Telmo, Spain

Short Bio

Tom Raftery is a Global Vice President for multinational software corporation SAP, an adjunct professor at the Instituto Internacional San Telmo, and a board advisor for a number of start-ups.

Before joining SAP Tom worked as an independent industry analyst focusing on the Internet of Things, Energy and CleanTech and as a Futurist for Gerd Leonhard's Futures Agency.

Tom has a very strong background in technology and social media having worked in the industry since 1991. He is the co-founder of an Irish software development company, a social media consultancy, and is co-founder and director of hyper energy-efficient data center Cork Internet eXchange – the data centre with the lowest latency connection between Europe and North America.

Tom also worked as an Analyst for industry analyst firm RedMonk, leading their GreenMonk practice for over 7 years. Tom serves on the Advisory Boards of Smart-Cities World and RetailEverywhere.com.

Talk

Digital Transformation, the Internet of Things and associated technologies (block-chain, machine learning, edge computing, etc.) are the latest buzz words in technology. Organisations are scrambling to get up to speed on them before their competitors, or some young start-up gets there first and completely disrupts them.

Right now, these digital innovation systems are, roughly speaking at the same level of maturity as the web was in 1995. So where are these new digital technologies taking us? What is coming down the line, and how will these changes affect my organisation, my wallet, and the planet?

Join Tom Raftery for our OnTheMove keynote as he unpacks what the Future of Digitisation is going to bring us.

Contents

Industry Case Studies Program 2018 (ICSP) 2018

International Workshop on Methods, Evaluation, Tools
and Applications for the Creation and Consumption
of Structured Data for the e-Society (META4eS) 2018

International Workshop on Enterprise Integration, Interoperability and Networking (EI2N) 2018

OTM/IFAC/IFIP EI2N'2018 PC Co-chairs' Message

In 2018 the 13th edition of the Enterprise Integration, Interoperability and Networking workshop (EI2N'2018) has been organised as part of the On The Move Federated Conferences (OTM'2018). This year's workshop took place in Valetta, Malta. The workshop has established itself as a major interactive event for researchers exchanging ideas in the context of organisations and information technologies. This is shown by the long list of groups and committees that support this event since years.

This year, the workshop was co-sponsored by IFAC and supported by IFIP. The main IFAC Technical Committee responsible for this workshop was TC 5.3 "Enterprise Integration and Networking". The workshop also received support from IFAC TC 3.1 (Computers for Control), and IFIP Work Groups TC 5 WG 5.12 on Architectures for Enterprise Integration and TC 5 WG 5.8 on Enterprise Interoperability. Additionally, the SIG INTEROP Grande-Région on "Enterprise Systems Interoperability", the French CNRS National Research Group GDR MACS, and the industrial internet consortium have shown their continuing interest in and support for EI2N.

Today's enterprises have to become S^3 Enterprises: Smart, Sensing and Sustainable Enterprises. These system-of-systems have to adapt in order to be sustainable not only along the environmental but also along economic dimensions. Systems must be able to sense their environment using heterogeneous technologies. The sensed information has to be transferred into knowledge to support smart decisions of systems to adapt. In this context, enterprise integration, interoperability and networking are major disciplines that study how enterprise system-of-systems collaborate, communicate, and coordinate in the most effective way. Enterprise Integration aims at improving synergy within the enterprise so that sustainability is achieved in a more productive and efficient way. Enterprise Interoperability and Networking aims at more adaptability within and across multiple collaborating enterprises. Smartness is required to meet the resulting complexity.

Enterprise modelling, architecture, knowledge management and semantic knowledge formalisation methods (like ontologies) are pillars supporting the S^3 Enterprise.

For EI2N'2018 19 papers have been received. After a rigorous review process, 7 papers have been accepted. EI2N continuous to show high quality by having an acceptance rate of less than 37%! Accepted papers have been made available in pre-proceedings. After the OTM workshops, authors have revised their papers and included feedback from the interactive sessions. This improved the quality of the scientific work, and places emphasis on importance of the interaction in scientific workshops.

With respect to interactivity, EI2N has hosted a highly interactive session called "Workshop Café". This special session has been an integral part of EI2N since many years. The outcomes of these discussions have been reported during a plenary session, jointly organized with the CoopIS and the OTM Industry Case Studies Program. EI2N shared topics and issues for future research with a larger group of experts and scientists. Results have been made available at the IFAC TC 5.3 webpage: http://tc.ifac-control.org/5/3.

The Co-chairs would like to thank the authors, international program committee, sponsors, supporters and our colleagues from the OTM organising team who have together contributed to the continuing success of this workshop.

The EI2N'2018 Workshop Co-chairs

Wided Guédria
Hervé Panetto
Markus Stumptner
Georg Weichhart

Architecture of Integration of Industrialization and Informatization

Qing Li[1(✉)], Yudi Pu[1], Zhiyong Xu[1], Hailong Wei[1], Qianlin Tang[1],
Iotong Chan[1], Hongzhen Jiang[2], Jun Li[2], and Jian Zhou[2]

[1] Department of Automation, Tsinghua University, Beijing 100084,
People's Republic of China
liqing@tsinghua.edu.cn
[2] China Industrial Control Systems Cyber Emergency Response Team,
Beijing 100082, People's Republic of China

Abstract. With the development of information & communication technology (ICT), industrial technology and management technology, manufacturing operation pattern and technology are improving quickly. Two historical processes, informatization and industrialization, are promoted mutually. In order to realize economic transformation and get their national competitiveness, American government proposed Re-industrialization and Industrial Internet, German government announced Industry 4.0, and Chinese government published Made in China 2025 national strategy. Architectures and reference models are systems engineering tools to understand, design, develop, implement and integrate complex systems. In the paper, the new development of ICT and industrial technology are reviewed firstly. Then, architectures and reference models of smart manufacturing, Industry 4.0, intelligent manufacturing, industrial Internet, and Industrial Value Chain are analysed and compared. At the end of the paper, the Architecture of Integration of Industrialization and Informatization is developed.

Keywords: Architecture, smart manufacturing · Framework · Reference model

1 Introduction

With the development of information & communication technology (ICT), industrial technology and management technology, manufacturing pattern and technology are improving quickly. As shown in Fig. 1, two historical processes, informatization and industrialization, are promoted mutually currently.

In the context of integration of informatization and industrialization (iI&I), some developed and developing countries announced their national manufacturing strategies to support their economic transformation and national competitiveness obtaining.

- The United States published *A Framework for Revitalizing American Manufacturing* in December 2009 and *National Network for Manufacturing Innovation: A Preliminary Design* in January 2013.
- Germany published *Recommendation for Implementing the Strategic Initiative INDUSTRIE 4.0* in April 2013.

Published by Springer Nature Switzerland AG 2019
C. Debruyne et al. (Eds.): OTM 2018 Workshops, LNCS 11231, pp. 5–14, 2019.
https://doi.org/10.1007/978-3-030-11683-5_1

- Chinese government announced *Special Action Plan for Deep Integration of Informatization and Industrialization (2013–2018)* in Aug. 2013 and *Made in China 2025* in May 2015.
- Japan announced the *Industrial Value Chain* in June 2015.
- The Government Office for Science and Department for Business, Innovation & Skills of UK sponsored the Foresight project and published *The Future of Manufacturing* serial reports in October 2013.

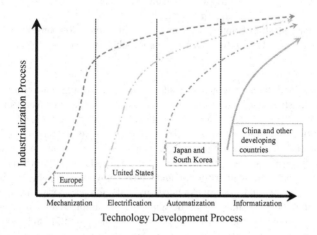

Fig. 1. Industrialization process with technology development process

Above mentioned strategies include different terms: Industry 4.0, smart manufacturing, industrial Internet, intelligent manufacturing, and so forth. Based on comparative studies, all of these terms share the same connotation and can be concluded into one key topic: integration of informatization and industrialization (iI&I).

In order to realize the significance of iI&I, the paper firstly reviews the development of information technology, industrial technology and management technology. Then, architectures and reference models of smart manufacturing, Industry 4.0, intelligent manufacturing, industrial Internet, and Industrial Value Chain are analysed and compared. At the end of the paper, the architecture of iI&I is developed [1].

2 Development of Information, Industrial, and Management Technologies

As shown in Fig. 2, In the past 40 years, ICT develops very quickly and it is integrated with manufacturing activities deeply. There are several dimensions to help us to understand manufacturing technology improvement as well as ICT.

- Computing centre is transferring from machine oriented, to application oriented, and then to enterprise-oriented computing.

- Integration scope is extended from single computer usage, to department application and integration with LAN, to enterprise application and integration with WAN, to inter enterprises application and integration with the Internet, and then to enterprise network collaboration and supply chain network integration.
- Enterprise infrastructure is changing from mainframe, to client/server (C/S), to browser/server (B/S), to SOA (service-oriented architecture) and then cloud computing.

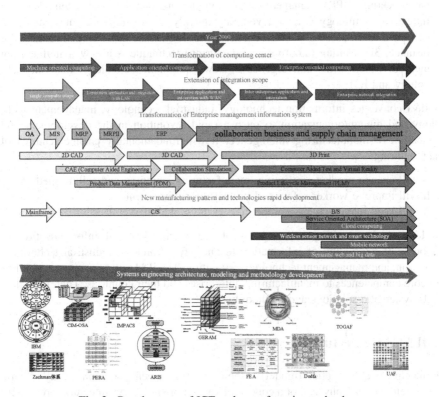

Fig. 2. Development of ICT and manufacturing technology

- The capability of enterprise information system, which evolves from office automation system (OA), to management information system (MIS), to material requirement planning (MRP), to manufacturing resource planning (MRPII), to enterprise resource planning (ERP), and then to collaboration manufacturing/ business and supply chain management, is increasing.
- Computing aided designing tools have emerged to CAD (computer aided design), CAE (computer aided engineering), CAM (computer aided manufacturing), CAPP (computer aided progress planning), PDM (product data management), PLM (product lifecycle management), collaboration simulation, virtual reality (VR) and so forth.

- Service Oriented Architecture (SOA), cloud computing, wireless sensor network and smart technology, mobile network, IoT, semantic web, big data, 3D printing technology, CPS, artificial intelligence and so forth, these new emerged technologies are integrated with manufacturing more and more deeply and quickly.
- Manufacturing patterns transform from craft manufacturing, mass production, computer integrated manufacturing (CIM), lean production, agile manufacturing, next generation manufacturing (NGM), to smart manufacturing, Industry 4.0 and industrial Internet. Including total quality management (TQM), business process reengineering (BPR), management technologies are also developing quickly.
- Industrial technology is also developing quickly. New equipment, new material, new production process and new energy technology make many breakthroughs. For instance, 3D printing (additive manufacturing) technique is a new manufacturing method, which is the convergence of new equipment technology, material technology and ICT.

iI&I converges information technology, industrial technology, management technology and human/organization to push a rapid revolution in the development and application of manufacturing intelligence. It will fundamentally change features of manufacturing.

- It will change products inventing, manufacturing, shipping and selling methods.
- It will improve worker safety and protect the environment.
- It will keep manufacturers competitive in the global marketplace.

iI&I stands on the junction point of industrialization and informatization, it embodies of integration of information technology revolution, industrial technology revolution, and management technology revolution. The iI&I will take new capabilities and core competences to manufacturing enterprises and their countries. Therefore, iI&I needs systematic solutions and methodologies.

3   iI&I Architecture

Architecture is a description (model) of the basic arrangement and connectivity of parts of a system (either a physical or a conceptual object or entity). Architectures are widely used to describe top structures and internal relationships of complex systems. There are several iI&I related architectures developed by different industrial organizations.

- Smart Manufacturing Ecosystem (SME) [2], developed by NIST;
- Reference Architecture Model Industrie 4.0 (RAMI4.0) [3], developed by Industrie 4.0;
- Intelligent Manufacturing System Architecture (IMSA) [4], developed by Ministry of Industry and Information technology of China (MIIT) and Standardization Administration of China (SAC);
- Industrial Value Chain Reference Architecture (IVRA) [5], developed by IVI;
- Industrial Internet Reference Architecture (IIRA) [6], developed by industrial internet consortium (IIC);

- Framework for Cyber-Physical Systems (F-CPS) [7], developed by Cyber-Physical Systems Public Working Group, Smart Grid and Cyber-Physical Systems Program Office, and Engineering Laboratory, published by NIST;
- Internet of Things Architectural Reference Model (IoT-ARM) [8], developed by IoT-A project.

NIST describes the SME that encompasses manufacturing pyramid with three dimensions – product, production, and business.

- Product. The product lifecycle is from design, process planning, production engineering, manufacturing, use & service, to EOL & recycling.
- Production. The production system lifecycle is from design, build, commission, operation & maintenance, to decommission & recycling.
- Business. The supply chain cycle is from plan, source, make, deliver to return, which mainly addresses the functions of interactions between supplier and customer.
- Manufacturing pyramid. This dimension is based on the IEC/ISO 62264 model - enterprise level, manufacturing operations management (MOM) level, supervisory control and data acquisition (SCADA) level, device level and cross levels, which is the vertical integration of machines, plants and enterprise systems.

RAMI4.0 includes three dimensions to define the domains of industry 4.0.

- Layers: from asset, integration, communication, information, functional, to business. It includes asset layer representing the real, physical world and also a virtual map of the physical installation of a system.
- Life cycle & value stream: from development to maintenance/usage which is defined by IEC 62890.
- Hierarchy levels: from product, field device, control device, station, work centres, enterprise, to connected world defined by ISO/IEC 62264 and IEC 61512.

IMSA includes 3 dimensions - Life Cycle, System Level, and Smart Functioning. For instance, the scope of industrial robot within the model is presented in the building block formed by resource factors, equipment, and manufacture, indicating that industrial robot technology affects production process within the product lifecycle dimension, belongs to device and control level within the system level dimension, and can be seen as a resource for performing smart function.

IVRA observes manufacturing units from 3 views:

- Asset view. The view shows assets valuable to manufacturing enterprises. Four classes of assets (personnel, process, product and plant) are distinguished.
- Activity view. The activity view is composed of the cycle of "Plan", "Do", "Check" and "Action", which is the core methodology of total quality management and business process continuous improvement.
- Management view. The management view shows targets of management. Quality, cost, delivery accuracy, and environment are included.

IIRA includes 3 dimensions: Viewpoints, Lifecycle Process and Industrial Sectors. Management fields are the core consideration of IIRA.

Above mentioned architectures have aroused worldwide attention, and there are several papers compare and research these architectures. Takahashi, Ogata and Nonaka use 4 aspects to compare these architectures: logical, physical, lifecycle and comprehensive [9], whose goal is to develop a Unified Reference Model for smart manufacturing, which follows the framework of UML and SysML. Papazoglou and Heuvel propose an architecture and knowledge-based structures for smart manufacturing networks [10]. The structure focuses on smart manufacturing system components and their relationships, which is a technical realization scheme. Mohsen, et al. investigate the IIRA and RAMI4.0's commonalities, limitations and architectures in order to identify the existing technological gaps and make some recommendations for next-generation enterprises [11].

Based on comparative analysis we can conclude that the construction of all these architectures are based on following principles:

- Decomposition. All architectures are described as multi dimensions diagrams.
- Focalization. Not all elements and concepts of advanced manufacturing are included in these architectures. All architectures focus on their own core concepts. For instance, SME only includes layers of ISA 95/IEC/ISO 62264, and life cycles of business, production and product. IVRA emphasizes the important role of P (Plan), D (Do), C (Check), A (Action) cycle, which comes from total quality management.
- Strategic consistency. These architectures embody related national manufacturing strategies. SME embodies application areas of smart manufacturing. IMSA emphasizes new technical areas, such as PLC, industrial robot, which need further research and development investment. The lack of core technologies has always been a short board for the development of Chinese manufacturing.

As discussed above, current advanced manufacturing technology and system development is the convergence of information technology, industrial technology and management technology, and aims to take new capabilities and core competences to manufacturing enterprises. Although above analysed architectures share some common ideas and similar concepts/elements, it is necessary to develop a general architecture and reference model of iI&I with related smart manufacturing, Industry 4.0, intelligent manufacturing, industrial value chain, industrial Internet, and so forth, to realize interoperation among these architectures and models.

Summary above discussed architectures, as well as framework of IoT, CPS and so forth, we can get the result as shown in Table 1.

Currently, we are facing three technological revolutions: industrial technological revolution, information technological revolution and management technological revolution.

- Information technology is developing in different layers and directions. Information systems are coupled tightly with design process. From this viewpoint, CAD, CAE, CAM, CAPP, PDM/PLM are integrated into digital mockup. Infrastructure transforms from C/S, B/S, SOA to cloud computing. Database technology improves from local database, distributed database, cloud data storage, to big data cloud storage. Network technology develops from LAN, WAN, Internet, mobile Internet, to IoT. These directions are all important for iI&I.

Table 1. Dimensions and sub-dimensions of iI&I related architectures and reference models

Dimension	Sub-dimensions	SME	RAMI4.0	IMSA	IVRA	IIRA	F-CPS	IoT-ARM
Business/management (domains, technology revolution)	System hierarchy	x	x	x	x	x		
	Product lifecycle	x	x	x	x	x	x	x
	Business (supply chain) lifecycle	x	x	x	x	x	x	x
	Production lifecycle	x	x	x	x	x	x	x
	Manufacturing mode development							x
Industrial technology revolution	New equipment		x	x	x			
	New manufacturing process techniques		x	x	x		x	
	New energy				x			
	New materials				x			
Information technology revolution	Function layers	x	x	x			x	x
	Communication technology development		x	x	x	x	x	x
	Network technique development		x	x	x	x		x
	Data storage technology development					x		x
	Database technology development		x	x				x
	IT infrastructure development		x	x	x	x		x
	CAX/simulation technology development	x	x					
Human/organization promotion	Organization management scope	x	x					
	Human resource talent levels				x			
	Capability/performance	x			x			

- Industrial technology is also developing quickly. Currently, new equipment, new manufacturing process techniques, new energy and new material get great achievements. For instance, 3D-print involves new print device, new materials and new information applications.
- Management technology is also developing quickly. SME, RAMI4.0, and so forth all consider management processes from different viewpoints. Product lifecycle, production lifecycle, and supply chain are described in these architectures. Management layers are also included in these architectures. New manufacturing patterns are also springing up.

- The target of iI&I is to achieve new capabilities and core competences. IVRA emphasizes personnel improvement and enterprise culture development. Time, quality, cost, and environment is defined as core management performance indicators by IVRA. In SME, the key smart manufacturing enabling capabilities are classified into productivity, agility, quality and sustainability.

As shown in Fig. 3, core viewpoints of iI&I are defined based on above analysis. iI&I covers fields of industrial fields, information technology fields and management fields. At the same time, iI&I tries to improve performances of enterprises. Therefore Fig. 3 has 4 dimensions: industry, information, management and human/organization. The 4 dimensions also show technology development and revolution directions.

Fig. 3. Core viewpoints of iI&I

As mentioned above, in the context of iI&I, every dimension can be decomposed into several sub-dimensions. All of these sub-dimensions present detailed technology development directions. Sub-dimensions shown in Fig. 3 can be extended as necessary.

Different from SME, RAMI4.0, IVRA and IIRA, Fig. 3 embodies the situation of most developing countries. Because their manufacturing enterprises locate in Industry 1.5 to Industry 3.0, these countries are integrating the two progresses, industrialization and informatization.

iI&I is currently standing on the junction point of ICT revolution, industrial technology revolution and management technology revolution. Because iI&I is a long developing progress, with the development of information technology, industrial technology and management technology, enterprise performance will improve continuously, and iI&I will spiral up.

Based on Figs. 3 and 4 shows the architecture of iI&I. In Fig. 4, the four spirals come from the four dimensions in Fig. 3 which embody the interaction of ICT development, industrial technology development, management technology development and enterprise performances improvement. The interaction is also the driving force for smart manufacturing, industrial internet, intelligent manufacturing, Industry 4.0 and so forth.

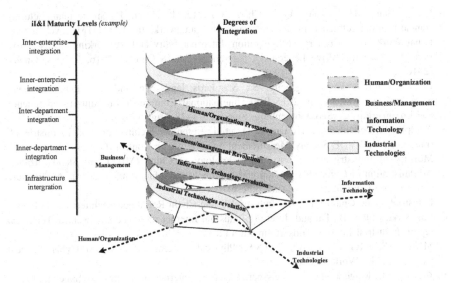

Fig. 4. iI&I architecture

4 Summary and Conclusion

iI&I is a systematic solution for manufacturing industries updating, which relates to ICT, industrial technology and management technology. NIST, DIN, MIIT&SAC and so forth published architectures and reference models for iI&I related smart manufacturing ecosystem, Industry 4.0, industrial Internet, industrial value chain and so forth. Based on comparing and analysis of these architectures and reference models, the iI&I architecture is developed in the paper.

iI&I architecture includes four dimensions: information technology, industrial technology, management technology and human/organization. The four dimensions can further be decomposed into some sub-dimensions and sub-domains, which present detailed technology development routines.

Based on iI&I architecture, manufacturing enterprises have a guidance in recognizing, organizing and implementing related technology and standards. At the same time, technology and standard researchers shall focus on integration of information technology, industrial technology and management technology.

Acknowledgements. This work is sponsored by the China High-Tech 863 Program, No. 2001 AA415340 and No. 2007AA04Z1A6, the China Natural Science Foundation, No. 61174168 and 61771281, the Aviation Science Foundation of China, No. 20100758002 and 20128058006, the 2018 Industrial Internet innovation and development project.

References

1. Li, Q., Jiang, H.Z., Tang, Q.L., Chen, Y.T., Li, J., Zhou, J.: Smart manufacturing standardization: reference model and standards framework. In: 11th OTM/IFAC International Workshop on Enterprise Integration, Interoperability and Networking (EI2N'2016), Part of the on the Move Federated Conferences, 24–28 October 2016, Rhodes, Greece (2016)
2. Lu, Y., Morris, K.C., Frechette, S.: Standards landscape and directions for smart manufacturing systems. In: 2015 IEEE International Conference on Automation Science and Engineering (CASE), Gothenburg, Sweden, 24–28 August 2015
3. Adolphs, P., Bedenbender, H., Dirzus, D., et al.: Reference architecture model industrie 4.0 (rami4. 0). VDI/VDE Society Measurement and Automatic Control (GMA) (2015)
4. Ministry of Industry and Information technology of China (MIIT) and Standardization Administration of China (SAC): National Intelligent Manufacturing Standards Architecture Construction Guidance (2015). (in Chinese)
5. Industrial Value Chain Initiative: Industrial Value Chain Reference Architecture (IVRA)
6. Lin, S.W., Miller, B., Durand, J., et al.: Industrial Internet reference architecture. Technical report, Industrial Internet Consortium (IIC) (2015)
7. MJB, KAS, ERG: Framework for Cyber-Physical Systems - Release 1.0, Cyber Physical Systems Public Working Group. 2016
8. De Loof, J., Magerkurth, C., Meissner, S., et al.: Internet of Things–Architecture IoT-A Deliverable D1. 5–Final architectural reference model for the IoT v3. 0 (2013)
9. Takahashi, K., Ogata, Y., Nonaka, Y.: A proposal of unified reference model for smart manufacturing. In: 2017 13th IEEE Conference on Automation Science and Engineering (CASE), Xi'an, China, 20–23 August 2017, pp. 964–969 (2017)
10. Michael, P., van den Heuvel, W.J., Mascolo, J.E.: A reference architecture and knowledge-based structures for smart manufacturing networks. IEEE Softw. **32**, 61–69 (2015)
11. Moghaddam, M., Kenley, C.R., Colby, J.M., et al.: Next-generation enterprise architectures: common vernacular and evolution towards service-orientation. In: 2017 IEEE 15th International Conference, Industrial Informatics (INDIN), Emden, Germany (2017)

Big Data Architecture and Reference Models

Qing Li[1(✉)], Zhiyong Xu[1], Iotong Chan[1], Shaobo Yang[2], Yudi Pu[1],
Hailong Wei[1], and Chao Yu[1]

[1] Department of Automation, Tsinghua University,
Beijing 100084, People's Republic of China
liqing@tsinghua.edu.cn
[2] Systems Engineering Research Institute,
China State Shipbuilding Corporation, Beijing 100094,
People's Republic of China

Abstract. The emergence of big data provides opportunities for both academic and industrial area and changes the way people solve complex problems and evaluate the value of data. However, there is a lack of studies on architecture frameworks and modelling methods in the context of big data, which is the key to support the analysis, design, implementation and evaluation phases of big data applications. The paper proposes a Big Data Architecture (BDA) to support the top-level design of enterprise information integration applications in big data environments. Moreover, reference models of performance, business, application, data, infrastructure and security views are discussed.

Keywords: Big data · Enterprise architecture · Enterprise modelling

1 Introduction

Data sources such as the Internet, the mobile Internet, the Internet of things, the Internet of cars, security monitoring systems, and telecommunication infrastructures are producing data at all times. The emergence of massive data promotes the development of a new generation of information technology and business innovation, changing people's understanding of data value and the thinking mode of human scientific research [1]. The "big data era" is coming [2].

In order to solve a series of business, data, application, technology, security and efficiency problems faced by big data analysis and commercial application, the research of big data technology needs more and more support from model-based systems engineering technology which is based on architecture, methodology and system modelling. At present, many standardization organizations are carrying out the research on big data systems, as shown in Table 1. The latest edition of the big data interoperability framework has been released in 2017 by the NIST. A reference architecture for big data interoperability is proposed in the document [3]. This model divides a big data system into system coordinator, data provider, data application provider, data framework provider, and data consumer from the perspective of system role division. Security, privacy and management run through the five components. The Chinese academy of electronic technology standardization has released a white paper on big

C. Debruyne et al. (Eds.): OTM 2018 Workshops, LNCS 11231, pp. 15–24, 2019.
https://doi.org/10.1007/978-3-030-11683-5_2

data standardization in 2018 [4] and proposed a big data standardization architecture, identified existing standards related to big data, also provided a standard classification method.

Table 1. Standardization organizations' researches on the BDA

Organizations	Standard	State
ISO	ISO/IEC AWI TR 20547-1 Information technology - big data reference architecture - part 1 framework and application process	Under study
	ISO/IEC TR 20547-2:2018 Information technology - big data reference architecture - part 2 use cases and derivative requirements	Released in January 2018
	ISO/IEC DIS 20547-3 Information technology - big data reference architecture - part 3 reference architecture	Under study
	ISO/IEC AWI 20547-4 Information technology - big data reference architecture - part 4 security and privacy	Under study
	ISO/IEC TR 20547-5:2018 Information technology - big data reference architecture - part 4 standardization roadmap	Released in February 2018
NIST	NIST big data interoperability framework: volume 2 data classification tables	Released in September 2015
	NIST big data interoperability framework: volume 3 use cases and general requirements	Released in September 2015
	NIST big data interoperability framework: volume 4 security and privacy	Released in September 2015
	NIST big data interoperability framework: volume 6 reference architecture	Released in September 2015
	NIST big data interoperability framework: volume 7 standardization roadmap	Released in September 2015
China institute for electronic technology standardization	White paper on big data standardization (data standardization architecture)	Released in March 2018

Based on the review and analysis of current big data architecture (BDA), some problems can be concluded:

- At present, researches of BDA are still at initial stage, which lack complete achievements of BDA;

- Most researches on BDA have strong dependence on relevant application fields, lack of universality, and are difficult to generalize and popularize;
- Most of BDA researches focus on data processing processes and technical systems, ignore elements on business level, data level and safety level, and lack integrity.

Based on principles of enterprise architecture (EA), this paper proposes the framework of BDA which focuses on key issues of data processing technology, data quality, data infrastructure, data security and privacy in big data environments, and builds reference models for different views of the BDA.

2 Big Data Architecture

In big data environments, enterprises need to face a series of problems including data security and privacy, infrastructure, data quality, big data analysis, big data application utility evaluation, etc. [5–10], as shown in Table 2. It is necessary to modify the existing enterprise system framework specifically and establish the system framework applicable to big data environments to meet the processing needs of new concerns of the big data system.

Table 2. The focus of enterprise information integration in big data environments

Classification of concerns	The main focuses
Data security and privacy	(1) Legitimacy of data acquisition and use (2) Security of data storage technology (3) Security of data transfer technology (4) Laws and regulations on data privacy (5) Data security related standards
Infrastructure	(1) Distributed data storage and computing architecture (2) Big data related database technology (3) The use of cloud services (4) Multi-source heterogeneous data integration technology (5) Storage and computing resource scalability
Data quality	(1) The credibility of the data source (2) Data and business relevance (3) Availability of data (4) Data integrity (5) Data accuracy (6) Data acquisition cost
Big data analysis	(1) The logic of data analysis (2) Data analysis process (3) Data driven system design method (4) Data analysis algorithm
Big data application utility evaluation	(1) Evaluation method of big data application (2) Evaluation index of big data application

With the rapid development of information technology and system complexity, people need a set of structured and systematic methods to understand, analyze and design complex systems [11]. The Model Based Systems Engineering (MBSE), is the key methodology for analysing and designing sophisticated systems. MBSE uses standardized modelling languages to support requirements definition, design, analysis, and validation activities of systems' full life cycles [12]. EA is the core component of MBSE, providing modelling tools and structural approach for system design, analysis and implementation [13, 14].

This paper constructs the architecture of big data analysis, which has adopted the construction logic and basic framework of FEAF (Federal Enterprise Architecture Framework). Based on that framework, the BDA framework is divided into performance view, business view, application view, data view, infrastructure view and security view. Each view is supported by corresponding reference models, as shown in Fig. 1. The architecture framework also provides detailed modelling methods for business requirements definition, data modelling and application design processes in big data environments.

- Performance reference model mainly focus on big data analysis targets, evaluation indicators and evaluation methods;
- Business reference model focuses on big data analysis in aspects of business requirements, business logic and business models;
- Application reference model focuses on big data analytics involved in the application domain classification, data processing technology, and related algorithms;

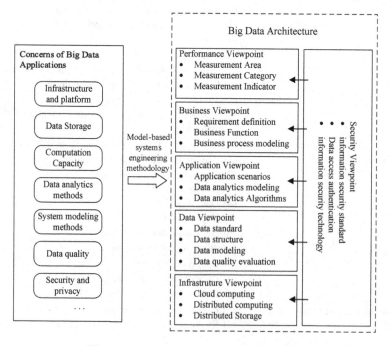

Fig. 1. Composition of the BDA framework

- Data reference model focuses on the degree of data structure, data processing, real-time requirements, data standard and big data related data evaluation;
- Infrastructure reference model mainly focuses on that acquisition of operational resource and storage resources, distributed storage and computing architecture, and data security technology;
- Security reference model focuses on the information security requirements at multiple levels, the corresponding data security and data privacy standards.

3   Big Data Analysis Reference Models

From the perspective of performance, business, application, data, infrastructure and security, the big data architecture describes the key problems and processing methods of big data systems. We need to build the corresponding reference model from these perspectives, providing an important guiding method for the development of big data analysis processes.

The big data performance reference model describes targets and evaluation methods of big data analysis from a performance perspective, as shown in Fig. 2. Due to the implementation of big data in business, enterprises focus on costs and benefits. Evaluating targets is about economic performance, customer conversion performance, business performance, retail performance, and so on. It's based on the performance of people, things, organizations and processes that are involved in the big data analysis. Such as customer performance analysis, evaluation indicators include the customer full life cycle value and average acquisition cost. By constructing indicator and acquiring data, the performance evaluation during the implementation of big data can be calculated.

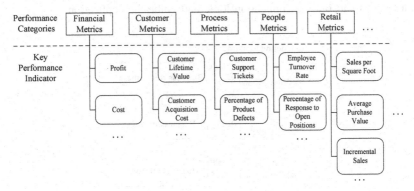

Fig. 2. BDA performance reference model

The big data business reference model focuses on business requirements, business logic and business models of big data analysis at the business level, as shown in Fig. 3. Business requirements drive the implementation of business processes. The real process of enterprise big data business implementation is described mainly through the corresponding enterprise process modelling method. The functional requirements and functions of enterprise big data business are described mainly through functional modelling method. Through such a complete process, we can describe business processes from the perspective of business requirements, implementation processes and business logic of enterprises.

The reference model of big data application is shown in Fig. 4, which is mainly based on the idea of classification, and describes the application field of big data, application process of big data, application technology of big data and algorithm, so as to guide the application of big data and facilitate implementation.

- Application field: As the application business is supported by data analysis application, especially complex application scenarios often require the support of multiple data analysis applications. Then the corresponding analysis process is designed in the practical application process. Typical applications of big data analysis include social network computing, biological information, finance, astronomy, public services, etc. [15];
- Big data processing technology: such as natural language processing, image recognition, voice recognition, etc. [16], among which there are a large number of mature processing theories and algorithm models, such as classification, clustering, regression, association rule mining, and data feature extraction, which provide important reference for data analysis applications;
- Data analysis process: driven by the demands and supported by technology and algorithms, the standard data analysis process generally includes data collection, data cleaning, feature extraction, data analysis and data visualization. This process can help us sort out the application logic and guide the application.

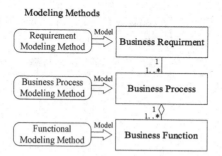

Fig. 3. BDA business reference model

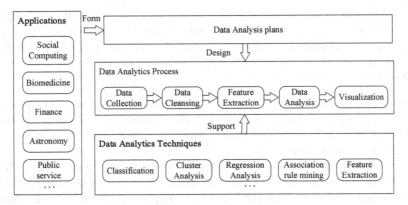

Fig. 4. BDA application reference model

The data reference model of big data is shown in Fig. 5, which is mainly used to describe data processing requirements and data standards, in order to realize data evaluation.

- Data processing requirements: processing demand is mainly used for real-time assessment data processing and storage requirements, both reflect data analysis application in the structural characteristics of the data and processing requirements of events. So the data can be divided into structured, semi-structured, and unstructured data, and the real-time processing requirements are divided into batch and real-time processing;

- Data standards: based on the previous focus on big data applications and the evaluation standards, this paper analyse data from eight dimensions including data availability, data relevance, data timeliness, data authorization scope, data clarity, data accuracy, data integrity and data consistency. We can use them to measure and evaluate the quality, value, usage range, etc. of the data of multi-source heterogeneous, different scene and field.

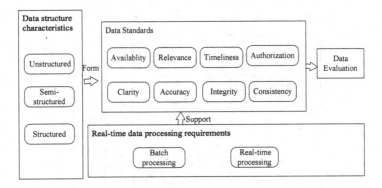

Fig. 5. BDA data reference model

The reference model of big data infrastructure is shown in Fig. 6, which mainly focuses on the acquisition of computing resources and storage resources, distributed storage and computing architecture, and data security technology. Divided into cloud services layer, distributed storage technology, distributed computing, data mining and distributed resource management layer.

- Cloud service layer: Due to the advantages of easy expansion, on-demand use of resources and low maintenance costs [17], cloud services include public cloud and private cloud, respectively providing software as service, platform as service and infrastructure as service,
- Distributed storage technology layer: distributed storage technology layer includes distributed file storage system technology and database technology. The distributed file storage system provides the basic file storage support, while the distributed database technology provides users with fine-grained data operation and management services to improve the data processing efficiency;
- Distributed computing technology layer: distributed computing technology layer is able to realize distributed computing and solve large-scale computing tasks. It can realize distributed processing logic such as task disassembly, calculation task assignment and calculation task result synthesis, which can also be divided into three computing frameworks: batch processing, flow processing and mixed processing;
- Data mining technology layer: a collection of data mining techniques used to meet different data analysis requirements, including machine learning technology, statistical analysis, natural language processing technology, data visualization technology, etc.;
- Distributed resource management layer: running through the cloud service layer, distributed storage technology layer and distributed computing technology layer, the distributed resource management layer is a bridge for the collaborative work of technology at three levels, responsible for providing resource management and task scheduling services for big data system.

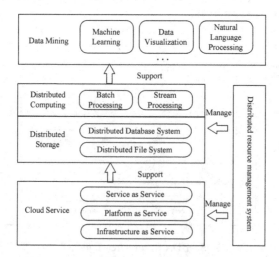

Fig. 6. BDA infrastructure reference model

Big data information security reference model is shown in Fig. 7, which is from the performance level, business level and application level, the data level and infrastructure level. The model is put forward to ensure data security and privacy requirements, through the corresponding information security standard and laws and regulations. A data collection strategy phase requires a consideration of the legality of the data source, and the need to implement the necessary data removal process for the raw data, and to prevent the analysts from leaking privacy-sensitive data, to strengthen data access control and supervision. We should ensure that data storage and data transmission technologies meet the requirements of network security and data cloud storage security when refer to big data issues.

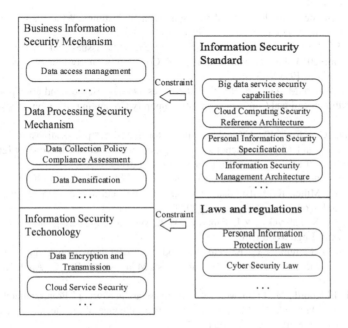

Fig. 7. Big data architecture security reference model

4 Summary and Conclusion

Based on a series of problems refer to big data analysis and commercial application, which are shown at business, data, application, technology, safety, efficiency levels, the paper uses model driven systems engineering method to propose a big data analysis architecture.

Starting from performance view, business view, application view, data view, infrastructure view and security view, this paper constructs a complete big data analysis architecture and solves the top-level design problems in big data analysis field. Each view is also supported by a corresponding reference model. This paper presents a specific reference model of performance, business, application, data, infrastructure and security in the framework of the system, which is of great significance to the analysis, application, integration and evaluation of big data.

Acknowledgements. This work is sponsored by the National Natural Science Foundation of China, No. 61174168 and 61771281, the 2018 Industrial Internet innovation and development project.

References

1. Kitchin, R.: Big data, new epistemologies and paradigm shifts. Big Data Soc. **1**(1) (2014). https://doi.org/10.1177/2053951714528481
2. Lohr, S.: The age of big data. New York Times **11**(2012) (2012)
3. NBD-PWG, et al.: NIST big data interoperability framework, pp. 1500–1506. Special Publication (2015)
4. China electronic technology standardization research institute. White paper on big data standardization (2018). http://www.cesi.cn/201803/3709.html
5. Kaisler, S., Armour, F., Espinosa, J.A., et al.: Big data: issues and challenges moving forward. In: 2013 46th Hawaii International Conference on System Sciences (HICSS), pp. 995–1004. IEEE (2013)
6. Katal, A., Wazid, M., Goudar, R.: Big data: issues, challenges, tools and good practices. In: 2013 Sixth International Conference on Contemporary Computing (IC3), pp. 404–409. IEEE (2013)
7. Boyd, D., Crawford, K.: Critical questions for big data: provocations for a cultural, technological, and scholarly phenomenon. Inf. Commun. Soc. **15**(5), 662–679 (2012)
8. Crawford, K., et al.: Six provocations for big data (2011)
9. Jacobs, A.: The pathologies of big data. Commun. ACM **52**(8), 36–44 (2009)
10. Michael, K., Miller, K.W.: Big data: new opportunities and new challenges [guest editors' introduction]. Computer **46**(6), 22–24 (2013)
11. Blanchard, B.S., Fabrycky, W.J., Fabrycky, W.J.: Systems Engineering and Analysis, vol. 4. Prentice Hall, Englewood Cliffs (1990)
12. Ramos, A.L., Ferreira, J.V., Barceló, J.: Model-based systems engineering: an emerging approach for modern systems. IEEE Trans. Syst. Man Cybern. Part C (Appl. Rev.) **42**(1), 101–111 (2012)
13. Shah, H., El Kourdi, M.: Frameworks for enterprise architecture. IT Professional **9**(5) (2007)
14. Crawley, E., De Weck, O., Magee, C., et al.: The influence of architecture in engineering systems (monograph). Citeseer (2004)
15. McAfee, A., Brynjolfsson, E., Davenport, T.H., et al.: Big data: the management revolution. Harvard Bus. Rev. **90**(10), 60–68 (2012)
16. Russom, P., et al.: Big data analytics. TDWI Best Practices report, fourth quarter, vol. 19, no. 4, pp. 1–34 (2011)
17. Armbrust, M., Fox, A., Griffith, R., et al.: A view of cloud computing. Commun. ACM **53**(4), 50–58 (2010)

Introduction to Personalisation in Cyber-Physical-Social Systems

Bereket Abera Yilma[1,2(✉)], Yannick Naudet[1], and Hervé Panetto[2]

[1] Luxembourg Institute of Science and Technology (LIST),
Esch-sur-Alzette, Luxembourg
bereket.yilma@list.lu
[2] Université de Lorraine, CNRS, CRAN, Nancy, France

Abstract. In this paper we introduce the notion of personalisation in Cyber-Physical-Social Systems (CPSS). A CPSS is an extension of Cyber-Physical systems involving cyberspace and physical space, in which humans, machines and objects interact adding to the complexity of the system, especially due to the dynamics of human behaviour that is not yet fully understood. We propose Personalisation to address this complexity. Since the development of CPSS is still at its infancy, we first cover a brief overview on the existing conceptualizations of CPSS and present the perspective we take for our work. Then we discuss the benefits of introducing Personalisation in CPSS and formalize the notion. The discussion further illustrates research challenges for Personalisation in CPSS with examples on possible use cases, taken from preceding works as well as future ones.

Keywords: Personalisation · Recommender system · Cyber-Physical Social-Systems · Cobotics

1 Introduction

From a general perspective, CPSS is a system comprising three intertwining subsystems: the Cyber, the Physical and the Social systems. The European Commission contributed a major part for the emergence of the Internet of Things (IoT) paradigm from a computer science perspective, which played an indispensable role for the orchestration of the physical and cyber systems with the goal of making tools and services intelligent by connecting tools and electronic equipments to the Internet so as to develop a network of computers and objects that are capable of self configuration [19]. On the other hand the US National Science Foundation (NSF) initially supported the notion of CPS derived from an engineering perspective, with the objective of controlling and monitoring physical environments and phenomena via the integration of sensing, computing, and actuating devices [20]. Despite their initial philosophical difference, IoT and CPS share many similarities hence they have been used interchangeably without a clearly

© IFIP International Federation for Information Processing 2019
Published by Springer Nature Switzerland AG 2019
C. Debruyne et al. (Eds.): OTM 2018 Workshops, LNCS 11231, pp. 25–35, 2019.
https://doi.org/10.1007/978-3-030-11683-5_3

defined demarcation. There is however a fundamental difference that should be highlighted: the fact that a CPS refers to a particular system explicitly, while IoT refers at the same time to the concept, the system formed by all the connected devices and a particular system of interconnected objects. As a system, a CPS typically collects and controls information about phenomena from the physical world through networks of interconnected devices, in order to achieve its objective. Originally, humans are assumed as external entities interacting with the system. Over the years the increasing use of smart phones and the tight link with their users has lead CPS systems to exploit the large number of such users as a multifaceted source of information, i.e. human sensors. Subsequent research studies have then recognized the importance and perspectives open by a new, Human-in-the-Loop (HitL) CPS paradigm [2], where humans are intrinsic actors of the system. Different techniques have then been used to introduce human actors in CPS, paving the way for the foundation of Cyber-Physical-Social Systems(CPSS). The development of CPSS, where *social* refers to the human aspects, is still in its infancy, especially because it often faces inevitable system instabilities, mainly due to the fact that human's actions and behaviour are the result of individual preferences, cognition, motivation and other natural or/and environmental factors. Moreover, each person is unique and might not follow system's rules that are not aligned with his way of thinking, convictions, etc. Indeed, the human behaviour is driven by complex phenomena that we do not fully understand and are still difficult to predict and manage compared to machines and softwares which are made by humans and usually prone to errors. To ensure a good functioning of CPSS, means are needed, to some extent, to have more control on the human system, while keeping individuals' freedom to operate. We think that the personalisation might be a solution; personalisation of IT services and devices, or more generally of Human-Machine Interaction. Our postulate is that personalisation provides a way to have more control over CPSS in such a way human behaviour does not interfere with the system's functioning, that is optimized for individual's satisfaction by adapting to individual's characteristics, needs, capabilities and preferences. There are several opportunities where the CPSS would benefit from, both for a better functioning of the system (the CPSS) and the user experience. The purpose of this paper is to make a first step in introducing the notion of personalisation in Cyber-Physical-Social Systems by discussing its added values, capabilities, applications, and by examining the associated issues and scientific challenges. The rest of this paper is organized as follows. Section 2 covers a brief literature review on CPSS, highlighting the common views and the widely accepted current conceptualizations of a CPSS. Section 3 presents the concept of personalisation in CPSS, and the problems and opportunities that personalisation brings when applied to CPSS. Section 4 presents illustrative Use-cases, their associated issues and scientific challenges for personalisation in CPSS. Section 5 proposes a concluding discussion.

2 Cyber-Physical-Social Systems

CPSS encompass Cyber, Physical and Social systems. Recent foundational works [6,7] presented it as an evolution of the preexisting notion of Cyber-Physical system (CPS) where Socio-technical aspects are added. In the following section we present a brief overview of the main conceptualizations of CPSS that appear in the literature.

2.1 State-of-the-Art

In this section we present a brief literature review on CPSS, organized in two main categories. In the first category we introduce the different *ways* researchers define CPSS, whereas in the second we present the two main *views* conceptualizing the social aspect in CPSS.

A common understanding, shared by most of the works in the literature or constituting at least a common ground, is that **CPSS** is a system comprising three intertwining subsystems *(i) The human-based system* which refers to the social system containing human actors and their interconnected devices/agents and/or social platforms providing human-based services, *(ii) The software-based system* that refers to the cyber world providing software-based services including the underlying infrastructures and platforms, either on-premise or in the Cloud and *(iii) The thing-based systems* referring to the physical world that includes sensors, actuators, gateways and the underlying infrastructures [1,3,5,7,9–12].

Different definitions have also been proposed. Particularly, in [4] CPSS has been defined as the integration of **CPS** and **CSS** (Cyber-Social System) to enable smart interaction between cyber, physical and social spaces, where **CPS** includes communicators, multimedia entertainment and business processing devices, etc. and **CSS** refers to social networks such as Facebook, Twitter, Youtube, etc. In [4] CPSS has also been described as the extension of IoT/CPS in the presence of humans interacting with CPS and other users.

In [8] and [18], the following definition is used: "CPSS is a system that captures a synergetic interaction between computing and human experience while providing holistic computational solutions encompassing the PCS (Physical, Cyber and Social) dimensions." Some works have tried to analyze the social aspect further by subdividing it further into *Social space* and *thinking space*. [10] introduces the acronym CPST (Cyber-Physical-Social-Thinking hyperspace), a system established through the emergence of the new dimension of thinking space in the CPS space. The *thinking space* is related to high-level thoughts or ideas raised during intellectual activities.

The way of defining CPSS is clearly use-case dependent and not homogeneous. However, despite the existence of various definitions, all agree on the presence of humans as an integral part of the system. Depending on the meaning they associate to the social aspect of CPSS, most works adopt one of the two views discussed below.

1. *Human as a sensor*: [5–7,12] conceptualize the social aspect by considering humans as information sources, *i.e.* sensors. This view of conceptualization

primarily focuses on fusing various information originating from the social space (humans and their observations) with cyber-systems and physical-systems in order to accommodate various application needs.

2. *Human as a system part*: [1–3,8,11] On the other hand most of the recent works intend to conceptualize the social aspect of CPSS not only by considering humans as social sensors but also as co-creators being an integral part of the system. It is also known as the human-centric way of conceptualizing CPSS [8]. This way of conceptualization considers humans as full members of the CPSS, involving observations, experiences, background knowledge, society, culture and perceptions (i.e. human intelligence and social organizations (e.g. Communities)) in order to co-create products and services together with the CPS. Here, humans play the role of resources in that they provide information, knowledge, services, etc., which at the same time they consume, thus becoming users of the CPSS. Hence, the human aspect is at the center of the system design, to provide user centered services.

2.2 Definitions

Following the state of the art analysis, we propose to adopt a definition and conceptualization for CPSS that is grounded on the generic framework provided by the theory of systems. From this systemic perspective, a CPSS can be understood as an environment, or system, where humans and machines evolve in both the physical and the virtual world, interacting all together. As illustrated by Fig. 1, the elements of a CPSS are its three interconnected systems, the Cyber, the Physical and the Social, which we represent as CPS and Social System, which interact in an environment composed by the physical and the virtual spaces. In an effort to a generic and uniform understanding of CPSS, we propose the following three definitions.

Definition 1: *CPSS.* *A system strictly composed of a CPS, a Social System, a virtual space and a physical space, in which the systems components interact,* where CPS and Social System are defined respectively as follows.

Definition 2: *CPS.* *A system encompassing all the systems and subsystems of Cyber and Physical Systems, their components and the interaction between them, as well as integrations of computation with physical processes* [2,4,6,10].

Definition 3: *Social System.* *A system that comprises interacting individuals, having each their own cognition, preferences, motivation and behaviour.*

In the following subsection we briefly cover Crowd systems which to a certain extent can be considered as a CPSS.

2.3 CPSS and Crowd Systems

Crowd systems are systems where a large group of people interact with an information system either in virtual or physical spaces towards the fulfillment of

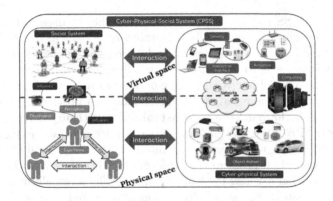

Fig. 1. Elements of a Cyber-Physical and Social System

the system's objective [15]. As it is the case in CPSS, the complexity of crowd systems arises from the existence of a human factor which can never be fully controlled. As a result, certain inconsistencies and systemic instabilities always remain in crowd systems. Examples of such systems are crowd-sourcing platforms, but also Wikis, or museums equipped with smart guidance systems. As a CPSS some crowd systems also involve CPS and Human systems interacting in Virtual and physical spaces, therefore to a certain extent, crowd systems can be considered as CPSS. However due to the fact that the interaction do not always involve physical spaces, not all crowd systems can be considered as a CPSS. Nevertheless, personalisation has been recently proposed in [15] as a tool to mitigate the inconsistencies arising from the human involvement in crowd systems, so as to improve system performance and provide better services. We build on this proposal to extend this idea to the domain of CPSS, since similar challenges are shared, but in a broader context involving physical spaces.

3   Personalisation in CPSS

Personalisation, broadly known as customization, refers to tailoring a service or a product in a way that it fits to specific individuals' preferences, cognition, needs or capabilities under a given context. In some cases, it also targets a group of people sharing a common context. Strategies of personalisation primarily depend on the a-priori knowledge and understanding of the target individual or group so as to build a user model and latter apply the related customization. We strongly believe that it can be used in CPSS to mitigate challenges imposed by the human behaviour, cognition and preferences. In the following, we provide a high-level formalization of personalisation in CPSS, defined as an optimization problem.

3.1   Problem Formalization

In general inconsistencies imposed by user's behaviour and preferences, together with constraining factors and other co-existing possibly divergent systemic objectives make the CPSS rather complex. Therefore, efficient means are needed to keep the CPSS equilibrium by fulfilling objectives respecting its constraints while at the same time fulfilling the objectives and interests of humans inside. Personalisation in CPSS needs to take into account all the constraints from the environment but the main objectives are those of the user (e.g. matching interests or preferences) and of the application (i.e. personalisation provider). This particular scenario can be formalized as a **constrained multi-objective optimization problem.** Providing that a personalized service generally implies making the best possible trade-offs between user interests and the general objectives. A classical personalisation problem can be formalized [21] as a function of a user u, the IT application a which implements the specific personalisation objective pursued and a context c (a set external elements) related to u or a which can have an influence on the personalisation objective (e.g. rules regarding the kinds of users, regulations, etc.), written as $P_u^{(classic)} = f(u, a, c)$. In a *CPSS*, there exist multiple coexisting objectives, influencing each other and constrained by different factors from the external environment and adding to the complexity of the personalisation problem. The user evolves in a physical space, with other persons. His behaviour is constrained by the first, while influencing and being influenced by the later. Additionally, the physical space has itself a given purpose, calling for expected specific behaviours of people inside. This particular context leads to formulate the personalisation problem differently, as a function of the user u, the physical space s, the crowd of other persons in the physical space cr, the IT application implementing personalized services a and the global context c, the latter being feed typically by sensors' observations written as:

$$P_u^{(CPSS)} = f(u, s, cr, a, c) \tag{1}$$

To illustrate this function, we can take the case of Personalized recommendations, which is a particular case of personalisation. In CPSS, with Eq. (1) rewritten as $PR_u^{(CPSS)} = f(u, I, s, cr, a, c)$, it can be defined as the problem of finding the subset $Irec_u \subset I$ that an application a can suggest to a user u, under the set of constraints $CO = CO_u \cup CO_s \cup CO_{cr} \cup CO_c$ induced by u, the space s in which he evolves, the crowd cr to which he belongs and the influencing context c, and fulfilling at best the set of objectives $O = O_u \cup O_s \cup O_a$ linked to u, s and a.

4   Illustrative Use-Cases

In the following sections we illustrate the notion of personalisation in CPSS through different use cases with the goal of opening a new perspective for building personalized IT services in future physical spaces designed as CPSS.

4.1   Personalized Guidance in Exhibition Areas

Exhibition areas are normally composed of a large number of items to be visited commonly refereed as points of interest (POI). They exist in the physical space, containing visitors having different visiting style and preferences and carrying their sensor-enabled smart devices, all together in one environment: a **CPSS**. In such sites visitors usually miscalculate their available time and spend wondering around exhibition sites, sometimes following different recommendations biased by many sources without visiting items that would have been interesting to them. Introducing personalized services in such environments guiding visitors to their presumed POIs delivers a great deal of benefits to both the exhibition center and the visitors. However doing so is far from trivial not only because of the inconsistencies imposed by humans behaviour and preferences but also the existence of the IT services and the visitors together in a physical environment by itself brings additional constraints such as congestion around popular exhibits, the size of the museum and the number of items to be visited which is normally subject to available time of visitors. Apart from exhibition center's general objective of reducing congestion and increasing visitor satisfaction there might also be an objective of making less popular items to be visible. Another important scenario in exhibition areas is the case of personalized recommendation for a group visit, where each group comprises individuals having their own interests, but behaving as a single entity, the group. This is the typical scenario of the *Social Choice* problem, that a group of people arrive at a saddle point where a group-wise recommendation has to be provided that satisfies some notion of consensus among the group. Incorporating all these aspects in making a personalized guidance is a complex problem which has not yet been fully addressed. Some experimental results from preceding works indicated that personalized path recommendations increased the perceived visitor satisfaction and reduced congestion [13–15] in exhibition areas like Museums. Nevertheless personalisation in physical spaces is rare due to the existence of multiple objectives and numerous constraining factors. We believe the formulation of the problem as a constrained multi-objective optimization could open a new perspective and bring us a step forward in introducing personalisation to the domain of exhibition areas for providing a better visitor experience.

4.2   Personalisation in Cobotics

Industry 4.0, often refereed to as the 4th industrial revolution is a terminology for the emerging advent in manufacturing and automation technologies which includes CPS and humans interacting in a physical environment which could be seen as a typical CPSS. Our interest in this particular domain is the increasing trend of using Cobots in such manufacturing and automation facilities. The term cobotics is formed by joining the terms *collaborative* and *robotics* to imply the direct interaction between humans and robots [16]. A Cobot is defined as *a robot that has been designed and built to collaborate with humans in various application domains such as industrial, domestic, medical, military, etc. for performing specific tasks such as, moving and carrying objects, transporting, assembling, surface processing, welding, cutting engraving, etc.* [17]. Even though the Cobots are designed to perform a desired task, their duty in collaborating with humans might not be a satisfying experience to the human users. Despite the collaborating humans are assumed to possess similar set of skills and qualification towards the desired goal, their individual preference, cognition, motivation and other natural factors could result in an unenjoyable collaboration experience. This could lead to reduced system performance and worst case scenario failure to achieve the desired objective. In this particular scenario the main source of systemic instability comes from the complexity imposed by human nature. In addition the various industrial objectives and their constraining factors add up to this complexity. We believe introducing personalisation in this domain could greatly benefit the overall system performance and also user experience by customizing the system according to one's preference, cognition and behaviours.

4.3   Issues and Challenges of Personalisation in CPSS

Personalisation in CPSS is subject to a number of challenges arising from the four components of CPSS in addition to the classical issues like, e.g. cold start, user profiling and situation identification. Since it is a broad subject which covers and tries to bring together concepts from different research areas mainly *personalisation, Social systems, Cognitive science, Recommender systems, CPSS and CPS*, it is vulnerable to different issues and challenges originating from these fields. The orchestration of various concepts from different fields by itself constitute a challenge adding to the complexity of the problem. In the following, we highlight some of these issues and challenges specific to *Personalisation in CPSS*.

Interoperability Challenges: As the personalisation in CPSS is a broad notion encompassing various systems, subsystems, their components and different devices, efficient interoperability is an indispensable requirement for satisfying the overall Personalisation objectives. Indeed, different challenges arise with the orchestration of these components. For instance communication related challenges, tool selection challenges and data related challenges are among the main ones. Personalized recommendations mainly relies on data gathering about the users of personalized services, which is collected through different sensing sources (devices). Furthermore the question of which tools or sensing sources to employ, which data features to use and which techniques (algorithms) to adopt in different use cases is left for the personalisation engineer to decide. This as clearly an impact on the personalisation quality. Hence at the heart of Personalisation in CPSS, smart and context-aware interoperability is a prerequisite.

Privacy and Compliance Challenges: Providing personalized services in CPSS essentially requires the acquisition of Personal data of users. However it is compulsory to follow privacy rules by being completely transparent. There are a number of regulatory restrictions on tracking user's behaviour and accessing personal data of users. In this regards different countries have different rules. Users of personalized services expect service providers to know their preferences and needs. Therefore introducing personalisation in CPSS also faces a challenge to find a proper balance between the satisfaction of users with personalized offerings and organizational objectives, while keeping data secure. The data protection regulations are an important component of the context in a personalisation problem (the generic context c in Eq. (1)), which generate constraints and objectives that need to be taken into account.

Human Complexity Challenges: Human behaviour is a complex piece of the puzzle that is not yet fully understood. Providing personalized offerings to individuals, as such, impacts the CPSS where the individuals evolve. This in turn drives or limits their actions. Additionally human's actions and behaviour are demonstrations induced by individual preferences, cognition, motivation and other natural or/and environmental factors. On top of this, social choice scenarios like the personalized group tour recommendation, where a group comprises individuals having their own interests, but behaving as a single entity requires making group-wise decision that satisfies some notion of consensus among the group through deep and complex analysis of different preferences. Personalisation requires the modelling of human behaviour, accounting for the multiple kinds of interactions people have with the components of a CPSS. This is the main prerequisite to be able to use personalisation as a tool for building more efficient, more stable or more smart CPSS.

5 Conclusion

In this introductory paper we proposed an approach to introduce the notion of personalisation in CPSS which opens an interesting perspectives for the evolution and improvement of CPSS. Our approach primarily intends to provide a way for controlling the complexities caused by human behaviour in CPSS. We formalized the notion as solving a constrained multi objective optimization problem for the future to work on modeling and experimentally analyzing use cases involving physical spaces designed as CPSS. The perspective contributes both to the fields of CPSS, and personalisation/User Modelling/Recommender Systems where application to the physical world have gained momentum. This also brings opportunities to contribute to new Crowd Management approaches, matching the objectives of both the environment and the individual users.

References

1. Liu, Z., Yang, D., Wen, D., Zhang, W.: Cyber-physical-social systems for command and control. IEEE Intell. Syst. **26**(4), 92–96 (2011)
2. De, S., Zhou, Y., Larizgoitia Abad, I., Moessner, K.: Cyber-physical-social frameworks for urban big data systems: a survey. Appl. Sci. **7**, 1017 (2017)
3. Candra, Z.C.M., Truong, H.L., Dustdar, S.: Cyber-physical- social systems. In: IEEE World Congress on Services (SERVICES), San Francisco, California, USA, pp. 56–63 (2016)
4. Zeng, J., et al.: A survey: cyber-physical-social systems and their system-level design methodology. Future Gener. Comput. Syst. (2016). https://doi.org/10.1016/j.future.2016.06.034

5. Su, Z., Qi, Q., Xu, Q., Guo, S., Wang, X.: Incentive scheme for cyber physical social systems based on user behaviours. IEEE Trans. Emerg. Topics Comput., to be published. https://doi.org/10.1109/TETC.2017.2671843

6. Wang, F.-Y.: The emergence of intelligent enterprises: from CPS to CPSS. IEEE Intell. Syst. **25**(4), 107–110 (2010)

7. Gharib, M., Lollini, P., Bondavalli, A: Towards an approach for analyzing trust in cyber-physical-social systems. In: IEEE System of Systems Engineering Conference (SoSE) (2017)

8. Sheth, A., Anantharam, P., Henson, C.: Physical-cyber-social computing: an early 21st century approach. IEEE Intell. Syst. **28**(1), 79–82 (2013)

9. Smirnov, A., Levashova, T., Shilov, N., Sandkuhl, K.: Ontology for cyber-physical-social systems self-organisation. In: Proceedings of the 16th Conference of Open Innovations Association FRUCT, Oulu, Finland, pp. 101–107, 27–31 October 2014

10. Zhu, Y., Tan, Y., Li, R., Luo, X.: Cyber-physical-social thinking modeling and computing for geological information service system. In: Proceedings of the 4th International Conference on Identification, Information, and Knowledge in the Internet of Things (IIKI 2015), Beijing, China, October 2015

11. Wang, S.G., Zhou, A., Yang, M., Sun, L., Hsu, C.-H.: Service composition in cyber-physical-social systems. IEEE Trans. Emerg. Topics Comput. (2017). https://doi.org/10.1109/TETC.2017.2675479

12. Huang, C., Marshall, J., Wang, D., Dong, M.: Towards reliable social sensing in cyber-physical-social systems. In Proceedings of the 2016 IEEE International Parallel and Distributed Processing Symposium Workshops (IPDPSW), Chicago, IL, USA, 23–27 May 2016

13. van Hage, W.R., Stash, N., Wang, Y., Aroyo, L.: Finding Your Way through the Rijksmuseum with an Adaptive Mobile Museum Guide. In: Aroyo, L., et al. (eds.) ESWC 2010. LNCS, vol. 6088, pp. 46–59. Springer, Heidelberg (2010). https://doi.org/10.1007/978-3-642-13486-9_4

14. Naudet, Y., Lykourentzou, I., Tobias, E., Antoniou, A., Rompa, J., Lepouras, G.: Gaming and cognitive profiles for recommendations in museums. in Proceedings of the 8th International Workshop on Semantic and Social Media Adaptation and Personalisation (SMAP2013), pp. 67–72 (2013)

15. Lykourentzou, I., et al.: Improving museum visitors quality of experience through intelligent recommendations: a visiting style-based approach. In: Museums As Intelligent Environments (MasIE), Workshop co-located with the 9th International Conference on Intelligent Environments - IE 2013, Athens, Greece, 16–19 July 2013

16. Surdilovic, D., Schreck, G., Schmidt, U.: Development of collaborative robots (COBOTS) for flexible human-integrated assembly automation. In: 41st International Symposium on Robotics, ISR (2010)

17. Seban, T.M., Salotti, J.M, Claverie, B., Bitonneau, D.: Classification of cobotic systems for industrial applications i towards a framework for joint action (2018)

18. Murakami, K.J.: CPSS (cyber-physical-social system) initiative-beyond CPS (cyber-physical system) for a better future. In: Keynote Speech, The First Japan-Egypt Conference on Electronics Communication and Computers JEC-ECC, Egypt (2012)

19. Nunes, D.S., Zhang, P., Silva, J.S.: A survey on human-in-the-loop applications towards an Internet of all. IEEE Commun. Surv. Tutor. **17**(2), 944–965 (2015). Secondquarter

20. Koubâa, A., Andersson, B.: A vision of cyber-physical Internet. In: Proceedings of the Workshop RTN, pp. 1–6 (2009)
21. Naudet, Y., Yilma, B.A., Panetto, H.: Personalisation in cyber physical and social systems: the case of recommendations in cultural heritage spaces. In: Proceedings - 13th International Workshop on Semantic and Social Media Adaptation and Personalization, SMAP 2018 (2018). https://doi.org/10.1109/SMAP.2018.8501890.

Sustainability Assessment of Manufacturing Organizations Based on Indicator Sets: A Formal Concept Analysis

Yasamin Eslami[1(✉)], Michele Dassisti[1], Hervé Panetto[2], and Mario Lezoche[2]

[1] Department of Mechanical, Mathematics and Management DMMM, Politecnico di Bari, Bari, Italy
yasamin.eslami@poliba.it
[2] Université de Lorraine, CNRS, CRAN, Nancy, France

Abstract. Organizations are struggling to survive in today's competitive market. They are mostly obliged to meet customers' expectations and demand for sustainable products from one side and comply with governmental rules and regulations regarding energy, resources, materials, etc. on the other side. Therefore, measuring their sustainability performance and trying to keep up with the competitors is essential for their future development. Consequently, organizations' perception of operational sustainability can reveal their strategies on how to be sustainable, endeavouring the three pillars of economic, environmental and social. The present work investigates the role of indicators' choice and their meaning for sustainability assessment of manufacturing organizations. To this point, an analysis is conducted on the sustainability assessment of 100 manufacturing organizations using GRI indicators for assessing their sustainability state. A Formal Concept Analysis was run to look over the indicators and their interpretations to reach a given degree of sustainability of the organization.

Keywords: Sustainability assessment · Sustainable organization · Indicator-based sustainability assessment · Formal Concept Analysis

1 Introduction

Companies across the world are facing with elevated expectations of customers on one hand and increasing prices for materials, energy and compliance on the other. Therefore, the sustainability target seems to become a vital opportunity and has changed face from a show-off achievement to a competitive imperative and a must-have in today's market. However, the pressure made the manufacturing organizations think about ways, tools and methodologies to assess the level of sustainability in the whole manufacturing system. Therefore, it is safe to say that Sustainable Assessment of manufacturing operations is one of the essentials of sustainable development in an organization. The concept of sustainability assessment is introduced to offer new perspectives to impact assessment geared toward planning and decision making on sustainable development [1].

© IFIP International Federation for Information Processing 2019
Published by Springer Nature Switzerland AG 2019
C. Debruyne et al. (Eds.): OTM 2018 Workshops, LNCS 11231, pp. 36–44, 2019.
https://doi.org/10.1007/978-3-030-11683-5_4

Sustainability assessment is defined as a methodology that can help decision-makers and policy-makers decide what actions they should take and should not take in an attempt to make society more sustainable [2]. Sustainability Assessment (SA) is known to be a complex task and conducted for supporting decision making and policy in a broad environmental, economic and social context [3]. Various methods of assessment have been accomplished through the literature so far, trying to find a way for companies to assess their sustainability state, help the companies choose between sustainable solutions, define and solve problems on the way to sustainability and identify potential solutions. Among all methods, assessment through adopting indicators are increasingly recognized and it is known to be a tool for policymakers to convey performance information in environmental, economic, social and development field [4]. Sustainable development indicators, in general, can serve to assess and evaluate the performance, provide trends on improvements plus warnings in case the corporate is facing a drop off in features of sustainability and provide information to decision makers [5, 6]. Therefore, the choice of indicators inside organizations can represent the priorities of the organization and to define strategic and political goals as well as its objectives [7]. Accordingly, the aim of this study is to get deep into the definition of the indicators applied for sustainability assessment to pave the path to the comparison of organizations on their strategies toward assessing their sustainability status. To serve this purpose, an analysis has been conducted on the sustainability reports of 100 manufacturing organizations and a Formal Concept analysis (FCA) was run on the results to get deep into the definition and choice of indicators by the organizations. The rest of the paper will discuss the analysis procedure and its sample. Furthermore, the FCA results will be discussed. Finally, the conclusion and the future work is presented.

2 Analysis

The abundance of the sustainability indicators created a huge confusion for manufacturers when it comes to indicators selection and sustainability assessment [8]. In order to increase the reliability and effectiveness of the indicators, several standard sets, guidelines and frameworks have been introduced by international initiatives. To serve the purpose of the study, an analysis on sustainability reports of organizations which use a defined and standard set of indicators needs to be run. A study of the existing sets of indicators is here performed to clarify the differences between the sets and raising the awareness on the applicability and adjustability of the indicators. The study, as represented in the following, will be led to choosing a standardized set of indicators.

2.1 Review of the Standard Sets of Indicators

In the literature, standard sets of indicators are presented. For the present work, the sets were studied and analysed according to the fulfilment of the following criteria: (**1**) **Level of Application:** As the aim of the study clearly stated, the assessment needs to be done throughout the whole organization. Therefore, the tools which are not applicable or adaptable for the factory levels were excluded from the study. **(2) Cross-Industry Comparison:** The chosen set of indicators needs to have generic applicability to enable the decision makers to make a comparison between various organization without limitation. Thus, the product/process- specific sets limit the general use of the proposed study. **(3) Holistic View over Sustainability:** as mentioned before, the assessment of progress toward sustainable development should consider the well-being of social, ecological, and economic sub-systems, the tools which are specified on just one feature, i.e. environmentally focused ones, might limit the assessment in the proposed study and will not be considered.

Table 1. Indicators' set review

Indicator set	Description	Reference	Level of Application	Holistic View			Cross-Industry Comparison
				Social	Environmental	Economic	
GRI	Global Reporting Initiatives	[14]	Organization Level	Y	Y	Y	●
DJSI	Dow Jones Sustainability Index	[15]	Organization Level	N	N	Y	▲
ISO 14031		[16]	Organization Level	Y	Y	Y	○
IChemE	The institution of Chemical Engineering	[17]	factory Level	Y	Y	Y	○
LCSP	The Lowell Centre for Sustainable Production	[18]	Organization level	Y	Y	Y	●
UNCSD	UN Commission on Sustainable Development	[19]	Country Level	Y	Y	Y	●
FPSI	Ford of Europe's Product Sustainability Index	[20]	Product Level	Y	Y	Y	○
GM MSM	General Motors Metrics for Sustainable Manufacturing	[21]	Product Level	Y	Y	Y	▲
NIST	National Institute of Standard and Technology Sustainable Manufacturing Indicator Repository	[22]	Organization/Process/Product Level	Y	Y	Y	●
OECD	Organization for Economic Co-Operation and Development (OECD) Sustainable Manufacturing Toolkit	[23]	organization level	N	Y	N	●

Note: Y=YES; N=NO; ● = Covered; ▲= Covered with the limitation ; ○ = Not Covered

As shown in Table 1, tools like GRI, NIST and LCSP appear to meet all our needs. However, NIST is not an open source set of Indicator anymore and LCSP considers a limited and generalized assessment. Therefore, GRI seemed to be an effective selection of standard indicators based on the needs of the study. Indicators of GRI which are related to the three dimensions of sustainability are available through the website (https://www.globalreporting.org/standards/gri-standards-download-center/).

2.2 The Sample of 100 Organizations

Among the verified sustainability assessment reports available on the website (https://www.globalreporting.org/reportregistration/verifiedreports#), the first 100 manufacturing ones related to the years 2016 and 2017 were chosen regardless of the size, country and the field of activity. The reports were all inspected for GRI indicators they encompass in three traditional sustainability dimensions: economic, environmental and social.

2.3 FCA on GRI Indicators

As previously indicated, the organization's reports were studied and the GRI indicators related to the three traditional sustainability dimensions were scrutinized. Then, each dimension was analysed separately with the help of Formal Concept Analysis (FCA). Formal Concept Analysis (FCA) as a clustering technique was chosen to assist the interpretation of the indicators used for sustainability assessment within the organizations. FCA is a branch of lattice theory [9] and it is best used for knowledge representation, data analysis and information management. It detects conceptual structures in data and consequently extraction of dependencies within the data by forming a collection of objects and their properties [10, 11]. FCA is able to visualize and represent knowledge by exploring the relationship between objects and is known to be effective for data analysis and association rule extraction [12, 13].

Based on the set of data given by FCA, GRI indicators were categorized in a formal context in which the regularity of the indicators' choice by the organizations was shown. Having Access to these kinds of result, made it possible to analyses the tendency of the organizations toward the definition of sustainability knowing what indicators have been adopted the most and with what frequency in each dimension. Consequently, the most practiced combinations of the indicators were shown. However, for only one dimension like environmental, more than 15000 combinations were exposed. The wide range in the formal context and the limitation of the space, restricted the present study only upon results of the application of the indicators alone and in two-indicator combinations that are shown in Figs. 1, 2 and 3.

In each figure, solo indicators are shown as circles whose size varies based on the number of the organizations that have applied them in the analysis. Therefore, the bigger the circles are, the more frequent the indicators appeared in the analysis. The scale of the size of the circles is fixed, therefore all indicators in all three dimensions are comparable. On the other hand, if the indicator was applied in the sustainability report of the organization in company with another indicator, the two were connected with a line. The thickness of the line shows the frequency of the application of the two

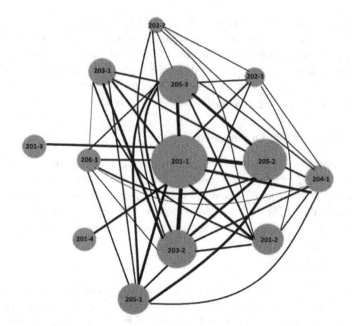

Fig. 1. Economic GRI indicators

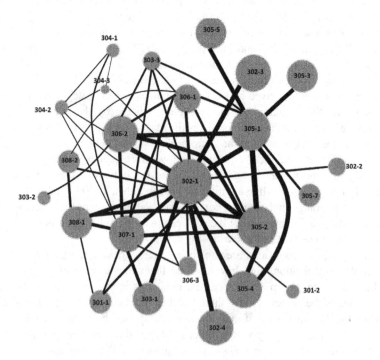

Fig. 2. Environmental GRI indicators

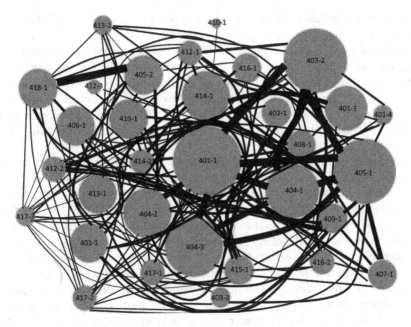

Fig. 3. Social GRI indicator

indicators in comparison with the rest of the two-combination indicators in the same dimension. In better words, the thicker the connection line is, the more the two connected indicators were used in the assessment process of the organizations. The position of the circles and the length of the connection lines speak for no meaning and are fully accidental.

2.4   Results and Discussion

Looking through the economic dimension (Fig. 1), the indicator "direct economic value generated and distributed" (201-1), was ranked as the first with a significant difference from the second one. However, the vast meaning of the indicator can be a justification of its highly ranked application since it contains all three aspects of direct economic value generated (revenues), economic value distributed (operating costs, employee wages and etc.) and economic value retained. On the other hand, the rest of the economic indicators are practiced with smaller differences in frequency of the application which can be the representative of the tendency toward interpreting economic sustainability as costs and profit. In addition, the second-most-used indicator was surprisingly "Communication and training about anti-corruption policies and procedures" (205-2) which is known as both a social and economic value in sustainability definition and it was employed more than "Significant indirect economic impacts" (203-2). The other two anti-corruption indicators, (205-3, 205-1) come next and before "other indirect economic impacts" or "procurement practices" that can be a sign of propensity of organizations toward the concept of anti-corruption. Nonetheless, indicators related to "market presence" which seemed to be an interesting topic were positioned at the end of the ranking list. As concerns the combinations, it is clear that the combinations with the indicators related to "direct economic value" and "anti-corruption" (all its three indicators) be the ones with the highest position among all. However, the two-indicator combination of (201-1 and 205-2) stood first with an evident difference from the second one which is the combination thought to be the first: direct and indirect economic value (201-1, 203-2). The observation reconfirms the importance of anti-corruption when it comes to economic sustainability in an organization.

Considering the environmental dimension of sustainability (Fig. 2), "Energy Consumption within the organization" which is represented by the indicator (302-1) stood out while the "GHG emission" with two indicators of (305-2) and (305-1) came closely after. However, the difference between the third place (305-1) and the fourth (307-1) and forward is clearly notable. On the other hand, it is observed that most of the indicators at the top of the ranking are the ones related to topics of "energy" (energy consumption, energy intensity, reduction of energy consumption, etc.) and "GHG emissions" (Direct and Indirect GHG emission, GHG intensity, Reduction of GHG emission, etc.) which displays the most representative concepts of environmental sustainability in the organizations. Indicators covering "waste management" like (306-2), (306-1) and the ones for the "water" like (303-1) were among the highest ranked ones which put an emphasis on the importance of this categories on the concept of environmental sustainability in an organization. However, indicators like (301-2), (304-1), (304-3) relating to the categories of "material" and "biodiversity" were placed at the bottom of the list but it does not imply a lack of importance or their ineffectiveness toward sustainability since the shortage can be related to the field of the organizations participated in the analysis. The combination of direct and indirect GHG emissions and their combination with energy consumption within the organization were the most used ones as it was expected. However, although waste management was not the at the top of the list of solo indicators, its combination with GHG emission came rather high in the ranking.

Inspecting the social dimension (Fig. 3), the most noticeable fact is the closeness of the frequency of the indicators and also how repetitive the thickness of the lines is which itself can express that how selective the social dimension is, and the choice can thoroughly differ based on the objective of an organization. However, it is seen that three indicators which deal with "employees", "diversity and equal opportunities" and "injuries" were the ones with the most concentration on with negligible differences. Nevertheless, the indicator (401-1) which stood at the top of the list, covers the new employees and their turnover, gender, age and region, so it is relatively vast in terms of what it covers regarding the characteristics of employees. The same goes for the next indicator, (403-2), which examines the "occupational health and safety" inside the organization and it encompasses types of injury, injury rate (IR), occupational disease rate (ODR), lost day rate (LDR), absentee rate (AR), and work-related fatalities, for all employees, with a breakdown by gender and region. On the other hand, the next topic with a bit of difference in frequency is "training and education". Yet, these prominent topics reveal the importance of the employees, their safety and health and non-discrimination in terms of employment in reaching sustainability from a social point of view. In addition to these topics, indicators representing social screening of suppliers (414-1), incidents of non-compliance with laws and regulation (419-1), and operations with local community engagement (413-1) also attracted a good deal of attention to themselves. Subsequently, looking through the combination of the indicators, it can be detected that employees and their related issues are the ones that are the most depictive of social sustainability in an organization.

As seen above, the economic and environmental indicators, seem to be more straightforward than the social ones. In other words, unlike economic and environmental, no indicator can be strictly called as the representative of the social dimension. all indicators have been chosen to reach sustainability in the manufacturing organization while the difference in the frequency of the choice is almost negligible. The approach the organizations took toward social sustainability, can speak for the irregularity in defining sustainability from the social point of view while the other two dimensions are mostly approached the same.

3 Conclusion and Future Work

The paper focuses on indicator-based sustainability assessment in manufacturing organizations and tries to scrutinize the meaning of the choice of indicators by the organizations. The study starts with a survey on available indicators set provided for sustainability assessment to choose the most responsive one according to the defined criteria. Among all sets, GRI was elected as the indicator source of the assessment throughout the organizations. Furthermore, 100 organizations were inspected on their choice of GRI indicators for assessing their sustainability status. The result of the analysis was then interpreted by Formal Concept Analysis (FCA) to investigate the strategies of the organizations toward sustainability and help decision makers define a more sustainable strategy for the organization considering the trends. Nevertheless, the future work of the present study can focus on comparing the painted picture of sustainability by the manufacturers to the assumed concept of sustainability delineated in the literature.

References

1. Hacking, T., Guthrie, P.: A framework for clarifying the meaning of triple bottom-line, integrated, and sustainability assessment. Environ. Impact Assess. Rev. **28**, 73–89 (2008). https://doi.org/10.1016/j.eiar.2007.03.002
2. Hardi, P., Zdan, T.: The Bellagio principles for assessment. In: Assessing Sustainable Development: Principles in Practice (1997)
3. Sala, S., Ciuffo, B., Nijkamp, P.: A systemic framework for sustainability assessment. Ecol. Econ. **119**, 314–325 (2015). https://doi.org/10.1016/j.ecolecon.2015.09.015
4. Nardo, M., Saisana, M., Saltelli, A., Tarantola, S.: State-of-the-art report on simulation and indicators. D7 (2005)
5. Lundin, M.: Indicators for measuring the sustainability of urban water systems - a life cycle approach (2003). http://publications.lib.chalmers.se/publication/421-indicators-for-measuring-the-sustainability-of-urban-water-systems-a-life-cycle-approach

6. Mayer-Spohn, O.: Sustainable development indicators within the German water industry: a case study. Chalmers tekniska högskola (2004)

7. Corbire-Nicollier, T., Blanc, I., Erkman, S.: Towards a global criteria-based framework for the sustainability assessment of bioethanol supply chains: application to the Swiss dilemma: is local produced bioethanol more sustainable than bioethanol imported from Brazil? Ecol. Ind. **11**, 1447–1458 (2011). https://doi.org/10.1016/j.ecolind.2011.03.018

8. Joung, C.B., Carrell, J., Sarkar, P., Feng, S.C.: Categorization of indicators for sustainable manufacturing. Ecol. Ind. **24**, 148–157 (2013). https://doi.org/10.1016/j.ecolind.2012.05.030

9. Wille, R.: Restructuring lattice theory: an approach based on hierarchies of concepts. In: Rival, I. (ed.) Ordered Sets. ASIC, vol. 83, pp. 445–470. Springer, Dordrecht (1982). https://doi.org/10.1007/978-94-009-7798-3_15

10. Mezni, H., Sellami, M.: Multi-cloud service composition using formal concept analysis. J. Syst. Softw. **134**, 138–152 (2017). https://doi.org/10.1016/j.jss.2017.08.016

11. Wajnberg, M., Lezoche, M., Massé, B.A., Valtchev, P., Panetto, H.: Complex system tacit knowledge extraction through a formal method. INSIGHT – Int. Counc. Syst. Eng. (INCOSE) **20**, 23–26 (2017). https://doi.org/10.1002/inst.12176

12. Li, D., Zhang, S., Zhai, Y.: Method for generating decision implication canonical basis based on true premises. Int. J. Mach. Learn. Cybern. **8**, 57–67 (2017). https://doi.org/10.1007/s13042-016-0575-2

13. Yan, H., Zou, C., Liu, J., Wang, Z.: Formal concept analysis and concept lattice: perspectives and challenges. Int. J. Auton. Adapt. Commun. Syst. **8**, 81–96 (2015). https://doi.org/10.1504/IJAACS.2015.067710

14. Global Reporting Initiative (GRI): Sustainability Reporting Guidelines. https://www.globalreporting.org/resourcelibrary/G3.1Guidelines-Incl-Technical-Protocol.pdf. Accessed 15 Jan 2018

15. Dow Jones Sustainability Index (DJSI): Index Family Overview. http://www.sustainability-index.com/dow-jonessustainability-indexes/index.jsp. Accessed 1 Dec 2018

16. ISO (International Organization for Standardization): Environmental Management-Environmental Performance Evaluation-Guidelines, ISO14031:1999(E), Geneva, Switzerland

17. Labuschagne, C., Brent, A.C., van Erck, R.P.G.: Assessing the sustainability performances of industries. J. Clean. Prod. **13**, 373–385 (2005). https://doi.org/10.1016/j.jclepro.2003.10.007

18. Veleva, V., Ellenbecker, M.: Indicators of sustainable production: framework and methodology. J. Clean. Prod. **9**, 519–549 (2001). https://doi.org/10.1016/S0959-6526(01)00010-5

19. UN-CSD (the United Nations Committee on Sustainable Development): Indicators of Sustainable Development: Guidelines and Methodologies, 3rd edn. The United Nations, New York. Accessed 16 Jan 2018

20. Schmidt, W.-P., Taylor, A.: Ford of Europe's product sustainability index. In: 13th CIRP International Conference on Life Cycle Engineering, p. 6 (2006)

21. Dreher, J., Lawler, M., Stewart, J., Strasorier, G., Thorne, M.: GM metrics for sustainable manufacturing (project report). Laboratory for Sustainable Business, MIT (2009)

22. Thompson, K.D.: Sustainable Manufacturing Indicator Repository (SMIR). https://www.nist.gov/services-resources/software/sustainable-manufacturing-indicator-repository-smir. 14 Jan 2018

23. OECD sustainable manufacturing indicators – OECD. https://www.oecd.org/innovation/green/toolkit/oecdsustainablemanufacturingindicators.htm

Information Systems for Steel Production: The Importance of Resilience

Elmar Steiner[1]([⊠]), Georg Weichhart[2], and Andreas Beham[3]

[1] voestalpine Stahl Donawitz Gmbh, Leoben, Austria
elmarpeter.steiner@voestalpine.com
[2] PROFACTOR Gmbh, Steyr, Austria
georg.weichhart@profactor.at
[3] HEAL: FH-OÖ, Hagenberg, Austria
andreas.beham@fh-ooe.at

Abstract. In this initial research work we show the industrial need to analyze production systems with respect to their resilience. In the LOISI project enterprise models will be developed to support the analysis and management of resilient production processes for half-finished steel products. We describe the software models currently developed and the conceptual integration. We briefly reflect on challenges to be met in a demanding industrial setting.

Keywords: Production process · Discrete-time simulation · Operations research · Logistics · Industry case

1 Introduction

In this paper we report on initial considerations of the research project LOISI (LOGISTICS OPTIMIZATION IN STEEL INDUSTRY). LOISI has started in October 2016 and runs for 3 years. The overall goal of the project is to support the modelling, analysis and design of resilient production logistics processes.

In the project multiple and intertwined models are developed as no single model can capture all aspects, which are of relevance [13]. The developed models are focusing on the logistics sub-system of a steel production system, to support the analysis of the system's behaviour in various settings with respect to *resilience*.

Resilience can be generally defined as the ability of a system to (proactively) resist disruptive events, returning to its equilibrium state. In production and logistics contexts, typical disruptions refer to a breakdown of a machine, a material handling device respectively. Consequently and since *"the question on 'how to assess the supply chain resilience' still has no answer"* [2, p. 19] the project aims to formalize requirements for resilient operations for the given logistics system and to provide tools that support the analysis of the system's behaviour with respect to to-be-defined key performance indicators (KPIs).

© IFIP International Federation for Information Processing 2019
Published by Springer Nature Switzerland AG 2019
C. Debruyne et al. (Eds.): OTM 2018 Workshops, LNCS 11231, pp. 45–54, 2019.
https://doi.org/10.1007/978-3-030-11683-5_5

This in turn requires to build and interconnect information systems that support adaptation and minimization of the reaction time for meeting exceptional situations despite the growing complexity of production processes, due to the increasing flexibility and product variety.

The paper is structured as follows. First, the industrial application domain and its challenges are briefly described. Then the solution approach and the developed models are discussed in detail. Finally, we conclude the current developments of this initial research work.

2   LOISI Industrial Challenges

In this section we introduce the motivating industry case, its challenges, and describe the relevance of resilience, as well as its potential, in industrial application fields.

To retain the production of semi-finished steel products in high-wage regions steel companies specialize in production of a wide variety of high quality products. The considered system starts at the continuous caster and ends when products are leaving the facility. The metallurgical details are out of scope, we focus on information systems for production processes, including intra-logistics, storage and cooling.

Every product type may be produced using one of multiple alternative processes and process routes. Alternatives include additional work-steps for rework, re-classifications of products (downgrading products with properties out of quality-parameter limits). The term *process route* is used to emphasize that besides having different process steps, which are required to meet or change desired quality parameters, different process routes also result in different physical flows.

2.1   Industry Case

Higher quality steel production results in more stringent process requirements for processing, transport and storage of (semi-finished) products. Process control ensures to keep the production for each product type within well defined parameter boundaries (e.g. weight percentage of alloy). Additionally, the wide variety of product types results in a high variety of process routes. These two factors lead to disproportionately high volatility and dynamic process changes. Ad-hoc changes of process routes are required, if products do not meet the quality-parameter limits. Steel quality is measured along a multi-dimensional chemical analysis with steel type and product-quality level dependent sets of limits for the chemical composition/parameters. The quality is further influenced by surface conditions and the micro-structure of the material.

Typical, frequent changes include additional surface treatments and inspections. Of importance to the work here are controlled storage and cooling procedures. The time of cooling and the temperature of the surrounding environment in hot-storage places influences the quality, and can be used to improve the parameters of the products.

The execution of alternative process routes may not only be triggered by steel quality issues, but by a high number of disruptions such as failing machines, overfull storage areas, broken transport means or shifting demands of customers.

2.2   Resilience of Production Systems

From a logistics point of view, dynamic change of process routes constitute a disruption since additional machines' or material handling devices' capacities are used. Processes of warehouse and intra-logistics not only interconnect the continuous production with customer demands. Moreover, the internal logistics in this context has to support resilient behaviour and becomes the crucial factor of competitiveness for a resilient production.

The impact of disruptive events on the performance of the enterprise is depicted in Fig. 1 below. This figure shows the throughput over time as it experiences some form of spontaneous disruption. In the graph, the event becomes visible as a sudden drop of the key performance indicator (KPI) *throughput*. Over time, due to recovering activities, it returns to the value that the system had attained before the disruption event. In this figure a single performance indicator (*throughput*) is used. However, the principle holds true for the overall Performance Measurement Systems (PMS) with multiple dimensions of KPIs, developed in LOISI.

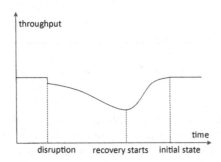

Fig. 1. Impact on throughput of a production system after disruption [6]

Figure 2 gives an impression of small events impacting multiple performance indicators used along a production process. Different performance indicators will react differently to the same event. Additionally the same event will show up in multiple places of the PMS along the process.

Due to the magnitude of the performance indicator change, the triggering event is easily detectable and the performance measurement system needs to be analyzed only for a short timer-period to learn about the event.

This figure implicitly highlights, that short-time extreme events are easier to detect than long-time trends. That has implications for resilience related activities that aim at retaining or sustaining normal performance. If the performance measurement system allows identifying the event's source, the underlying reason in the performance change can be addressed immediately.

For long-term trends a long period of time, likely being cluttered by a number of extreme and not extreme events, needs to be analyzed. In addition to being hard to detect, there is often not a single cause for long term trends. Selecting the right strategy for resilience is much harder. A strategy, or a set of strategies, need to be applied for no obvious reason and their suitability/success and also negative consequences are much harder to estimate as consequences get not visible immediately.

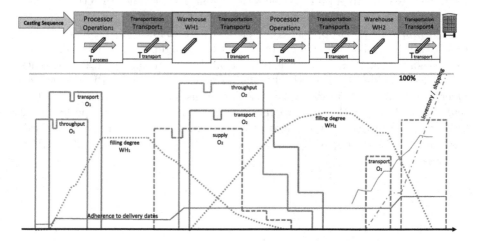

Fig. 2. Time dependent performance of multiple indicators, exemplifying contradicting reactions to events.

However, due to the system's complexity and not fully transparent interdependencies, some events may have severe impact on entirely different and unexpected processes or resources. There are effects, which result in a slow deviation of the measured performance from the normal level, that cannot easily be detected. This implies, that focused activities to establish "normal" performance levels cannot simply be started if the reason for the performance change is not clear.

On abstract level, resilience may be reached through robust (e.g. by using buffer), and flexible (e.g. more means for transport, alternative paths), adaptive processes (e.g. transport route optimization, based on the current situation).

2.3   Modelling Resilience

Multiple approaches exist to model resilience of production systems. Analytic models of the system are using either discrete-time or continuous-time Markov

Chains (see [5]). Other approaches use system dynamics models [9]. That approach incorporates a general formulation of resilience (i.e. for all kind of systems) and includes three measurements of resilient systems [4]:

- amount of change the system can undergo and still remain in the same configuration (same system state)
- degree to which the system is capable of self-organization
- degree to which the system can build the capacity to learn and adapt.

With respect to the development of a performance measurement system for resilience, there are two key questions: what system state is being considered (*resilience of what*) and what disturbances are of interest (*resilience to what*) [4]. Especially the former is of high interest for any enterprise as long as the system is in a favorable *configuration*. Configuration refers to a diversity of system states that are possible under a particular regime of actors, processes and functions. As a result resilience often requires the need to change configurations.

3   LOISI for Resilient Production

In this section we discuss in more detail, how we analyze and model resilient production processes in the steel industry.

3.1   Resilience in LOISI

In the project reported here, we develop a performance measurement system (PMS) that allows us to capture the *steady-state*, the mentioned disturbances and the resulting exceptional performance along multiple dimensions.

In LOISI we have decided to use simulation, not only to evaluate different strategies for improving resilience (dispatching rules for logistics decision - see below), we also use it to determine performance measurement values describing the steady-state within a statistical range of indicator values.

We have defined a system configuration describing the usual amount of space available for storage, the usual manipulation rates of handling devices, transport duration and number of vehicles available, customer order mix (steel in different qualities) and demand (amount).

Having defined a set of performance indicators (around five indicators per dimension and five dimensions) we observe the overall system and "normal" variations in performance indicators for some time. We divide these indicators into the following five dimensions:

- of a warehouse
- of a machine
- of means of transport
- of a handling device
- or related to customer satisfaction.

3.2 Simulation of Resilient Production Processes

To have an integrated model of the relevant part of the enterprise system, we use *discrete event simulation*. This type of simulation environment allows to follow discrete parts along their individual production and logistics processes. Environments also allow to introduce some statistical distribution of e.g. failure or some variations in the order mix/order sequence. The model for analyzing the production system's behaviour with respect to resilience is implemented using Tecnomatix Plant Simulation Software.

The simulation environment enables us to use this configuration as a baseline by running the scenario without any extreme events and without any trends that bring the system into a unstable state. This establishes what is "normal" in terms of performance indicators.

The values of the performance measures are also examined over certain period of time after a disruptive events and also global trends. The simulation allows us to determine the delta of the performance and hence makes it easier to spot long-term deviations from normal performance.

The LOISI team has analyzed a real-world steel production system to produce a list of analyzed sub-systems that are relevant for modelling. For each of these (sub-)systems we have described their normal function, duration for applying the function, amount of steel to which this function can be provided, etc. For each of these, we have also described possible failure events, and some distribution of failure impact and failure probability.

By introducing defined sets of (failure) events, it is possible to understand causal relationships between the events and values of performance indicators. The reproducibility of simulation runs, allows analyzing short-term (extreme) events and long-term trends which are discussed in more details in the following.

3.3 Resilience to Short-Term Events

As indicated above, a common and important event in the "extreme, short-term" category is the breaking of a sub-system (e.g. transport vehicles). The simulation will use a statistical distribution of how long such a break down will take and when it occurs.

Another common event is, that the product quality parameters of the steel are not met. Again, using a statistical distribution, the severity will be determined.

Dependent on the type of event a number of measures to increase the resilience of production have been created. For sub-system break downs, where the casting process is stopped, special procedures are in place. This concerns the sub-systems close to the caster. Any breakdown here will impact procedures of the basic oxygen steel-making. Here a LD-Converter will blow oxygen through molten pig iron to convert a charge of iron (several dozen tons) into steel in less than 40 min. For these melted tons of steel care has to be taken (e.g. alternative production route and/or different processing in secondary metallurgy), if further processing is stopped.

The simulation environment allows to elaborate and quantify the effects of different alternative procedures to increase resilience. This is particularly important in situations, as described above, where failure tolerance is not low.

At the other end of the spectrum of severity level, are events where repair takes only few hours and no particular measurement is required.

For the events in between, the project team has elaborated resilience procedures. These include alternative process routes, modification of production sequences and increasing production capacity by introduction of additional shifts.

The identified procedures and measurements do not take inter-dependencies in the complex system into account, nor is it possible to provide a performance quantification of effects in alternative scenarios/configurations. The simulation will allow to elaborate different procedures and will indicate the changes of performance using the identified performance measurement system. It allows determining different procedures in different system configurations and with different events.

3.4   Resilience to Long-Term Trends

The situation is different with long term trends. The first difference is that, due to the missing event character, these are only visible by taking a look at long-term developments of the performance measurement system values. Known trends include an increase in customer orders with higher steel quality (as mentioned above). That implies an increase in "high quality" procedures which have longer and more controlled cooling phases.

Currently, only a rough bottleneck analysis can be made for the future production system with changed order mix. By using the controlled simulation environment it is possible to elaborate on alternative scenarios for the developments of customer orders.

Of importance to long-term resilience are alternative process-routes. As mentioned above the term process-route is used to indicate that any production process has an important physical component, where the steel half-finished goods have to be routed differently through the shop floor.

The usage of alternative routes for certain product types results in a different system load when still meeting the desired quality standards and fulfilling operational constraints (such as landing at the correct loading point). An alternation of a production sequence is likewise resulting in changed usage of resources which may affect customer satisfaction. The enhancement of the system capacity can be obtained by enlargement of storage area. However, this is facing the disadvantage of increase of handling effort and being limited by spacial constraints.

To conquer the challenge of these developments, an optimization tool called HeuristicLab [11,12] is used to optimize the process routes. This optimization supports users by choosing the best route dependent on the product's state and the overall state of the production system.

Another way to enhance resilience (in particular for long term trends), is that the overall production system configuration is altered. Typically production system functionality is improved by applying changes and re-executing the model and analyzing the disturbance effect again. Mathematical optimization of certain input parameters (production plan etc.) or policies appears to be a promising tool for remaining in favorable domain or changing the domain if any disruption occurs.

By using simulation models and automatized decision-making in operational planning through mathematical optimization we expect a better utilization of the logistical system as well as more stability of the system with respect to disruptive events, and long term trends. This is realized (also) by providing simulation models and optimization models [1, 3].

Needless to say, short-time events and long-term trends will be analyzed together and effects of bottle-neck sub-system breakdowns will be explored.

3.5 Modelling Considerations

Enterprise Modelling (in general) is used for integration and knowledge transfer [13]. In this project, simulation is used to provide a behaviour oriented enterprise model. The simulation model, build in LOISI, allows to gain better understanding of (future) scenarios, with particular systems configurations like number of transport vehicles, amount of steel that can be stored and the overall conception of interconnected material flows.

For users of the developed models, the knowledge gain lies in the results of the analysis of impacts of events and trends on the performance of the enterprise system and its subsystems. Besides this, the developed performance measurement system will have to prove its usability in the scenarios and will then be integrated in the running information systems.

In order to develop the models, we have defined objective functions and identified appropriate degrees of abstraction that help to reach our targets while allowing to model as simple as possible. The selection of proper abstraction level is a general question for the analyses of any behavioural aspect of a system (cf. [10]). There is no general answer as it is depending on the goal.

In any case we face the challenge that the degree of abstraction is neither particularly obvious nor a static factor, but changing and adapting throughout the project. Some initial research on business process modelling focuses on support for the process and less on the results [7].

However, this support for the process, with respect to resilience, has not been researched in full detail. In one approach the authors additionally carried out a study to evaluate the concept of resilience in general, and they proposed a *resilience analysis method* [9]. The effect of varying abstraction levels on the validity of the resulting quantification of resilience of any state has not been addressed in the steel production processes. A driving fact for a higher degree of abstraction might always be the generality of a model for applying it to difference scenarios or even in different domains. On the contrary a very detailed model might serve better for observing detailed performance indicators in the specific manufacturing system.

4   Conclusion

In LOISI we are building multiple models (simulation, performance measurement system, optimization) to support analysis and decision making with respect to resilient production and intra-logistic processes.

The engineered models will consequently be used in corporate information systems as well as in business intelligence tools to provide decision-support in real world systems. The development of the models supports users in gaining a common understanding [8]. The understanding is needed so that the independent models (conceptually) fit together.

This common understanding is also of importance for being able to articulate future trends that need to be handled in the production system. It includes the derivation of knowledge about the characterization of the systems state by quantification of its behaviour, the formulation and the evaluation of alternative utilization concepts to sustain in a favorable configuration that is efficient and robust to disruptions. Furthermore, we expect insights how to translate the trends adequately into probable scenarios which requirements in some form exceed the production systems capacities.

Challenges we will address in the (near) future, include the interfaces to real world information systems. The challenge lies in making the different models inter-operable with the existing systems to properly process information or data as well as redistribute it accordingly.

This challenge is already addressed partially. On conceptual level all models take the same point of view. On technical level, the provider of the real world information system is part of the project team. Part of the PMS is already implemented in the software.

Acknowledgement. The research described in this paper has been funded by the Governments of Upper Austria, Styria and the FFG: FFG Project "Logistics Optimisation in Steel Industry (LOISI)" Contract nr.: 855325.

References

1. Affenzeller, M., et al.: Simulation-based optimization with HeuristicLab: practical guidelines and real-world applications. In: Mujica Mota, M., De La Mota, I.F., Guimarans Serrano, D. (eds.) Applied Simulation and Optimization, pp. 3–38. Springer, Cham (2015). https://doi.org/10.1007/978-3-319-15033-8_1
2. Barroso, A., Machado, V., Carvalho, H., Machado, V.C.: Quantifying the supply chain resilience, Chap. 2. In: Applications of Contemporary Management Approaches in Supply Chains. IntechOpen, Rijeka (2015). https://doi.org/10.5772/59580
3. Beham, A., Kofler, M., Wagner, S., Affenzeller, M.: Coupling simulation with HeuristicLab to solve facility layout problems. In: Winter Simulation Conference, pp. 2205–2217 (2009)
4. Carpenter, S., Walker, B., Anderies, J.M., Abel, N.: From metaphor to measurement: resilience of what to what? Ecosystems 4(8), 765–781 (2001)

5. Gu, X., Jin, X., Ni, J.: Resilience measures of manufacturing systems under disruptions. In: Proceedings of the ASMA 2014 International Manufacturing Science and Engineering Conference, MSEC 2014 (2014)
6. Lee, S., Gu, X., Ni, J.: Stochastic maintenance opportunity windows for unreliable two-machine one-buffer system. Expert Syst. Appl. **40**, 5385–5394 (2013)
7. Oppl, S.: Evaluation of collaborative modeling processes for knowledge articulation and alignment. Inf. Syst. e-Bus. Manag. **15**(3), 717–749 (2017). https://doi.org/10.1007/s10257-016-0324-9
8. Oppl, S.: Supporting the collaborative construction of a shared understanding about work with a guided conceptual modeling technique. Group Decis. Negot. **26**(2), 247–283 (2017). https://doi.org/10.1007/s10726-016-9485-7
9. Rydzak, F., Chlebus, E.: Application of resilience analysis in production systems - Bombardier transportation case study. Technical report. Centre for Advanced Manufacturing Technologies, Wroclaw University of Technology, Wroclaw, Poland (2007). https://www.researchgate.net/profile/Edward_Chlebus/publication/25245 3880_Application_of_Resilience_Analysis_in_Production_Systems_-_Bombardier_Tra nsportation_Case_Study/links/543bce220cf204cab1db3718.pdf
10. Vasudevan, K.: Selecting simulation abstraction levels in simulation models of complex manufacturing systems. In: Proceedings of the 2011 Winter Simulation Conference, pp. 2268–2277 (2011)
11. Wagner, S., Affenzeller, M.: HeuristicLab: a generic and extensible optimization environment. In: Ribeiro, B., Albrecht, R.F., Dobnikar, A., Pearson, D.W., Steele, N.C. (eds.) Adaptive and Natural Computing Algorithms, pp. 538–541. Springer, Vienna (2005). https://doi.org/10.1007/3-211-27389-1_130
12. Wagner, S., et al.: Architecture and design of the HeuristicLab optimization environment. In: Klempous, R., Nikodem, J., Jacak, W., Chaczko, Z. (eds.) Advanced Methods and Applications in Computational Intelligence. TIEI, vol. 6, pp. 197–261. Springer, Heidelberg (2014). https://doi.org/10.1007/978-3-319-01436-4_10
13. Weichhart, G., Stary, C., Vernadat, F.: Enterprise modelling for interoperable and knowledge-based enterprises. Int. J. Prod. Res. **56**(8), 2818–2840 (2018). https://doi.org/10.1080/00207543.2017.1406673

Collaborative Platform for Urban Transport Engineering, Praia Case Study

Carla Mericia Monteiro Tavares[✉] and Janusz Szpytko

AGH University of Science and Technology, Av. A. Mickiewicza 30,
PL 30-059 Krakow, Poland
{tavares, szpytko}@agh.edu.pl

Abstract. The present paper proposes a design of a collaborative platform for urban transport exploitation. The platform is built based on the combined use of web services and statistical analysis to have an integration of maintenance activities within the fleet operation. The solution is developed taking into consideration the available resources and infrastructure of a bus fleet operating in Praia city in Cape Verde. The target is the development of an e-platform for cooperative information of buses based transport system to improve the exploitation efficiency. The development of the paper, demonstrate the potential of the use of smart devices to aggregate the data, and interact with other physical objects/devices by the use of the telematics technology and internet of things, to support the improvement of bus fleet exploitation process.

Keywords: Fleet exploitation platform · Transport engineering · Maintenance

1 Introduction

In this paper exploitation process of the urban transport is defined as the operation and maintenance performance to support the needs. Transport exploitation process is associated with the mechanical structure, routine, control, and bureaucracy [1].

The intensity of business competition has significantly increased, and the knowledge is the primary organizational resource able to generate competitive advantage through innovation [2, 3]. Maintenance management is changing its potential thanks to the Information Communication Technology (ICT) development [4]. Maintenance, is not merely preventive, although this aspect is an essential ingredient. It has long been recognized as extremely important in the reduction of maintenance cost and improvement of equipment reliability [5]. Maintenance has been transformed, regarding its mission, from a prevalently operational activity of repair to a sophisticated management system, oriented more than anything else towards the prevention of failures, this is not an easy passage, as it implies a considerable cultural change in management in general and maintenance in particular [6]. Advanced support today is related to data processing and communications technologies. Currently, progress in the field of Information Technology (IT) allows acquisition of data in real time and analysis of the information. The technological development, currently achieved, enables an empowered distribution of control and monitoring of activities in production plants and machinery [4].

C. Debruyne et al. (Eds.): OTM 2018 Workshops, LNCS 11231, pp. 55–64, 2019.
https://doi.org/10.1007/978-3-030-11683-5_6

In this paper is proposed a platform for cooperative information on buses for the development of an e-platform to improve the exploitation efficiency of buses operating in Praia city in Cape Verde. In the city, in the past 40 years three bus fleet has been working, nowadays only one bus fleet still operate after an extended period of decay [7]. The poor management together with poor maintenance support destroyed the others buses fleet operating in the city. To decrease maintenance and operation costs simultaneously, companies have to perform maintenance at least cost without loss of system reliability [8]. In bus transportation companies, buses are regularly maintained in a fixed time or mileage intervals [9]. The paper presents an ongoing work with purpose to solve a persistent problem in the urban bus transportation in Praia city due to lack of sufficient and efficient fleet exploitation approach. The proposed enterprise platform uses the internet of things (IoT) architectures. Elements of the platform are equipped with optical, machine-readable, representation of data, and computing devices so they can communicate with each other. The existing solution is developed without any systematic approach, enterprise integration, interoperability and networking, and is based only on available human and technological resources.

2 Problem Definition

The present paper has as a case study a bus fleet operating in Praia city in Cape Verde. The country is defined as a small island developing states (SIDS), that are a distinct group of developing countries facing specific social, economic and environmental vulnerabilities [10]. The bus fleet under study has been growing in recent years. There is a substantial investment in improving the fleet management and support for users. The bus fleet has a total of 73 buses, and 69 is in operation, they support a total of 12 different lines in the city with different routes [11]. All buses of the fleet are equipped with telematics units and applications for the users and to support the fleet management. There are many persistent and urgent problems related to maintenance and conservation of buses, and this has brought many negative consequences to the fleet operation. For the case study, the following has been noticed: The bus fleet operates with busses from two different brands which is available some instructions for the preventive replacements; The fleet has no maintenance management strategy or actions defined; The maintenance is view as a simple act of correction when a malfunction occurs (Fig. 1 shows the example of the existing maintenance sheet which is filed in handwriting); The today available staff is composed of professionals that work according to the experience gained with the time "learning by doing"; The busses of the fleet operate from 6 am to 22 pm with some breaks (not fixed); There is a lack of maintenance professionals and tools to perform the required actions. Currently, the fleet has some buses in which is out of operation due to lack of proper maintenance action, and some buses are degrading due to inadequate and insufficient maintenance actions.

It is clear that the bus fleet faces an urgent need to solve the existing problems and enhance the existing exploitation process strategy. The improvement of the fleet exploitation process efficiency will improve the availability of buses that can improve the economic capabilities of the fleet. The solution for the defined problems above must be designed according to the available resources and business needs.

Fig. 1. Bus fleet existing malfunction sheet

3 Bus Fleet Exploitation Platform

In this chapter is presented the proposal for the bus fleet exploitation platform including the required functions and architecture of the system. The platform will have monitoring and control capabilities: it will allow the communication between IT-Based systems to support the integration of maintenance activities within the fleet operation to improve the fleet exploitation process activities.

Before defining the type of web services is necessary to identify the kind of information's essential to gather to evaluate the existing practice, and organize de data for further analyses and manipulations. The data necessary is divided into three main sections as shown in Fig. 2 [12]. The "Bus Data" contains all basic technical information's related to each device of the fleet (buses). "Bus Maintenance" gather information's related to maintenance procedure, including the occurrence of failure and others related. "Bus Operation" gather information related to the operation of the device, this includes the operating line, the conservations state of the devices, as well as information regarding the driver. The defined structure is designed to analyze existing practice to develop a solution able to adapt to the business needs.

To collect and organize the necessary data shown in Fig. 2, a platform has been developed through the use of PostgreSQL database and phpPgAdmin software, working in operating system Linux. With this work is intended through the analyses of the data to identify what, how and where to improve the services and manage the transport devices exploitation. The results of the studies are used as fundament to design the transport devices exploitation solution.

For the data collection, and to allow the real-time monitoring of data, is used PostgreSQL database and application for a website and mobile devices interface, this solution is used for evaluation of the existing practice and proposal of a new solution. The platform is used as support to enhance maintenance services provision within

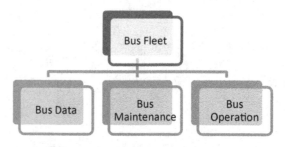

Fig. 2. The bus fleet data block scheme [12]

transport devices operation. As mentioned before the case study has available 69 buses distributes in 12 different lines across the city with different destinations (Table 1).

Table 1. Distribution of busses in different lines

	Fleet, bus distribution												Total
Line	2	3	4	5	6	7	8	9	10	11	12	13	12
N. buses	4	6	6	5	7	3	6	4	12	5	5	5	69

The data related to operation and maintenance of buses are introduced in the platform through the use of smartphone or tablet with an Android operating system, for this, a bar code is generated for every element of the system under analysis (buses). The computer is used to host the platform and to communicate with other devices. For the communication between devices an application is developed for a website and mobile devices interface that is connected to the dedicated database, this has the task to read write and analyze data as demanded. Is also necessary a dedicated web server to store all applications, access to data and keep all applications online, this is in a particular place, is a virtual machine that has a power supply from many sources, support for battery, many internet connections, as a precaution the data are continuously stored. Figure 3 represents the hardware architecture of the system.

4   Algorithm for Fleet Exploitation Evaluation

To develop a solution for the assessment of the bus fleet exploitation, the model presented by Faccio et al. [13] has been used. The bus fleet is considered as a system composed of n = 12 subsystems (bus lines) working in parallel; each subsystem has N elements working in series (buses operating in each line). Let us consider a series-parallel system, where each element is evaluated for the mission m. In this case, we can define the subsystem elements Bij, where:

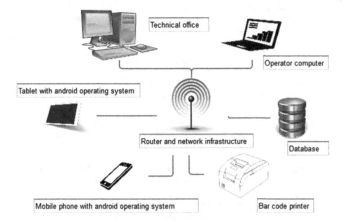

Fig. 3. The hardware architecture of the system

$$i = \{1, 2, 3, \ldots 12\} \ \ and \ \ j = \{1, \ldots Ni\} \tag{1}$$

$$Xij(m) = \begin{cases} 1, & \text{if Bij is functioning at the end f the mission m} \\ 0, & \text{otherwise} \end{cases} \tag{2}$$

$$Xij(m+1) = \begin{cases} 1, & \text{if Bij is functioning at the end f the mission m} + 1 \\ 0, & \text{otherwise} \end{cases} \tag{3}$$

The system evaluation focus on the calculation of the effectiveness of the bus system, this depends on the availability, reliability and maintainability analyses. Taking as reference the model presented by Szpytko and Kocerba [14] and adapted to the case study. Figure 4 represents the diagram for the system exploitation evaluation approach (the system is continuously monitored).

The effectiveness of the system is measured through the formulas (4, 5), where: *Ess* is the indicator of the effectiveness of the system and is represented in percentage. *Es* is the coefficient of the effectiveness of the operating system, *TMT* is the total time of the system maintenance, and A is the availability, R the reliability, and M the maintainability of the system under analysis.

$$Ess = Es/TMT \tag{4}$$

$$Es = A \cdot R \cdot M \tag{5}$$

The Availability is measured as the probability that the system is operating without failure when it is required for use. Reliability is the probability of the system to perform the necessary function for the desired period without failure, accounts the time that will take to fail, does not consider for the repair action. Maintainability deals with the duration of maintenance outage. The parameters A, R, M, are calculated as the following formulas [14–16].

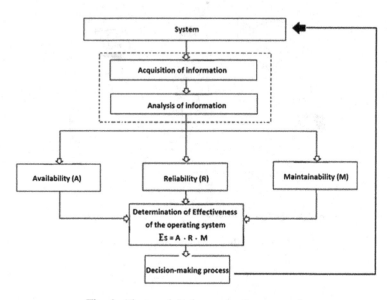

Fig. 4. Fleet exploitation evaluation approach

$$A = \frac{MTBF}{MTBF + MTTR} \tag{6}$$

$$R = Exp\left(-\frac{t}{MTBF}\right) \tag{7}$$

$$M = 1 - Exp\left(-\frac{t}{MTTR}\right) \tag{8}$$

MTBF represents the mean time between failure, and it measures the mean exposure time between consecutive failure of an element. Is defined as the total operating time divided by the total number of failure. MTTR is the mean time to repair, is the total time of the maintenance. T is the operating time and the length of repair.

The calculation of the effectiveness will give a better picture of how effectively the system is running, and it makes easy to track improvements over time. The effectiveness calculation is helpful for understanding benchmarks, past, present, and future status of the system. After the acquisition of information and data as presented in the previous chapter, analyses are performed, the bus conditional exploitation system is defined. After the evaluation of the bus operating system is identified what where and how to improve the system, and after the implementation of the required actions, the same analyses are performed with newly collected data. To improve the bus exploitation system is possible to adjust the maintenance strategies and relocation of system components in different subsystems to improve the availability.

5 Illustrative Example

In this chapter is demonstrated an example of the use of web services and statistical analyses based on real data of an operating system to evaluate the exploitation efficiency of a bus fleet. The illustrative example has been prepared only as demonstrative, some functionalities of the platform are still under development. Figure 5 demonstrates the data acquisition process and the data manipulation of the developed solution. For the illustrative example will be used data of one operating day where one operating line has been selected. When a bus goes under maintenance, all data related to the maintenance performance is collected. All buses are connected with a barcode, with the use of a tablet and mobile phone with an Android operating system and interface to access to the platform, the data is introduced in the project database.

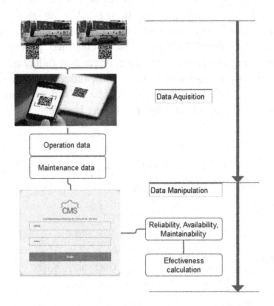

Fig. 5. Data procession and information flow

Table 2 demonstrates the effectiveness evaluation for one operating line using collected data of one working day. In the selected line, two buses have been registered in the maintenance workshop. The 'time in' indicates the time the bus entered the maintenance workshop for necessary repair, and the 'time exit' indicates the time after the conclusion of the maintenance actions.

Table 2. Effectiveness evaluation of one operating line, in one operating day

Bij	Time in	Time exit	A	R	M	TMT (min)	Ess
B2,12	10:00	11:30	0,77	0,14	0,99	90	0,08
B2,17	15:10	16:00				50	

Using the equations presented in the previous chapter (Eqs. 4, 5, 6, 7 and 8) and considering: Operating time 960 min, TMT 140 min, MTBF = 480 min, MTTR = 140 min. Table 2 represents the value of the calculation of the parameters A, R, M, and Ess.

From the data presented in Table 2, is possible to observe in one day, in one operating line, that has four buses operating, two of them has been in maintenance, which mean that in that day the line was unable to fulfill the need. The proposed evaluation will be made through the use of the platform for each bus and each operating line to identify the existing problem and design a solution that better fit to the case.

To improve the efficiency of the fleet exploitation, it is essential to have an efficient and sufficient plan of maintenance. The application of a precise method to ensure the safety of employees and passengers also can contribute to achieving the bus fleet objectives, and the work of the company is developed at its full capacity.

To improve the today exploitation solution, practice an efficient application of a planned preventive maintenance is suggested, starting to transform the today practice of maintenance for corrective maintenance and scheduled preventive maintenance (with the aim of reducing the probability of occurrence of failures). Also is proposed the control of the stock to support an efficient maintenance performance and avoid the non-use of vehicles due to lack of components. The prosed structure is based on the evaluation of the existing exploitation solution of the bus fleet, is presented in Fig. 6.

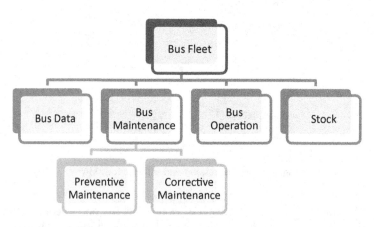

Fig. 6. Bus fleet, the proposal for improvement

To apply the proposed new strategy, the buses will be divided by brands, and systems, creating maintenance teams capable of preparing the planned maintenance of transport devices (preventive maintenance). The maintenance will be planned according to the operation time so as not to affect the operation of the fleet. The solution will be developed and implemented as a cooperation between the research team and the bus fleet maintenance team.

6 Conclusion

The presented enterprise platform is used as the primary tool to evaluate the existing exploitation solution to support the proposal for improvements of the maintenance performance that will enhance the bus fleet efficiency. The platform will support the identifications of what, how and where to improve the services and manage the transport devices exploitation. The business requirements drive the selection of functions supported by the platform, the selection of the technologies to support the interoperability and local remote operations take in consideration the available technologies in the country and IT devices already in use in the bus fleet.

With the elaboration of this work, will be possible to improve the business efficiency and people satisfaction, also will be possible to create a more sustainable transportations system. This work uses the smart devices with the capability to aggregate the data and interact with other physical objects/devices by the use of the internet.

The presented solution will allow the bus enterprise to be more smart, efficient and also to be more sustainable, improving the exploitation efficiency by reduction of maintenance cost and improvement of buses reliability. The work proposes an enterprise platform that uses the Internet of things architectures. The solution will help the business to share and access to information. It creates networking with the ability to exchange and make use of information flow to improve business strategy. A solution that will allow the enterprise to communicate and coordinate more efficiently, and to adapt to today technology needs.

Acknowledgment. The work has been financially supported by the Polish Ministry of Science and Higher Education in the year 2018.

References

1. Holmqvist, M.: Experiential learning processes of exploitation and exploration within and between organizations: an empirical study of product development. Org. Sci. **15**, 70–81 (2004)
2. Grant, R.M.: Toward a knowledge-Based theory of the firm. Strateg. Manage. J. **17**, 109–122 (1996)
3. Torugsa, N.A., O'Donohue, W.: Progress in innovation and knowledge management research: from incremental to transformative innovation. J. Bus. Res. **69**, 1610–1614 (2016)
4. Fumagalli, L., Macchi, M.: Integrating maintenance with the production process through a flexible E-maintenance platform. IFAC Papers Online. **48**(3), 1457–1462 (2015)
5. Lindley, R., Higgins, P.E.: Maintenance Engineering Handbook, 5th edn. McGraw-Hill Inc., New York (1995)
6. Monteiro, T.C., Szpytko, J.: Vehicles emerging technologies from maintenance perspective. IFAC-PapersOnLine. **49**, 67–72 (2016)
7. Monteiro, T.C., Szpytko, J.: Selected problems of control the urban transport system. Cape Verde case study. Logistyka. **4**, 4977–4983 (2015)
8. Sittithumwat, A., Soudi, F., Tomosovic, K.: Optimal allocation of distribution maintenance resources with limited information. Electr. Power Syst. Re. **68**, 208–220 (2004)

9. Zhou, R., et al.: Bus maintenance scheduling using multi-agent systems. Eng. Appl. Artif. Intell. **17**, 623–630 (2004)
10. UN-OHRLLS: Small Island developing states. One United Nations Plaza, **1**, 2–28 (2011)
11. SolAtlantico home page. https://solatlantico.cv
12. Monteiro, T.C., Szpytko, J.: Developing innovation thought data collection and analyses. J. KONES. **24**, 1231–4005 (2017)
13. Fraccio, A.M., et al.: Industrial maintenance policy development: a quantitative framework. Int. J. Prod. Econ. **147**, 85–93 (2014)
14. Szpytko, J., Kocerba, A.: Availability as the indicator of the operation reliability (Gotowość jako wskaźnik niezawodności eksploatacyjnej). Polish Academy of Sciences, pp. 325–333 (2008)
15. Velasquez, R., Lara, J.: Reliability, availability and maintainability study for failure analysis in series capacitor bank. Eng. Failure Anal. **86**, 158–167 (2018)
16. Borba, E., Tavares, E.: Stochastic modeling for performance and availability evaluation of hybrid storage systems. J. Syst. Softw. **134**, 1–11 (2017)

International Workshop on Fact Based Modeling (FBM) 2018

FBM 2018 PC Co-chairs' Message

The FBM 2018 workshop gives insight into the professional application of Fact Based Modeling in government and business practice. Our main theme for this workshop is Conceptual Thinking and Information Modelling at the Core of the Information Economy. For FBM 2018, 11 high quality papers were selected for presentation. We congratulate the authors of these contributions.

FBM 2018 will once again be centered around the presentation of practice reports and theoretical papers on Fact Based Modeling. The focus of this year's workshop will be on conceptual thinking at the core of the information economy in a broad range of domains, i.e. financial and insurances services, engineering, governmental agencies and business transactions.

The first session of the workshop will start with an invited talk on a concerns based analysis of the Fact based modeling approach. The first paper in the first session will illustrate how the power of the crowd interacts with information modeling.

The second session of the first day of the workshop will be entirely devoted to permissioned block-chain technology and how conceptual thinking in tandem with the power of examples has facilitated the creation of documentation on this new subject that is accessible to a broad audience.

The first day of the workshop will be concluded by two papers on FBM and Agile.

The first presentation session of the 2nd day of the workshop will be on FBM in a wider context.

In the second paper session of the second day, four papers on FBM applications will be presented.

The 2nd day of the workshop will be concluded by an open discussion on the future of Conceptual Modeling chaired by Maurice Nijssen.

November 2018   Peter Bollen

Proof of Concept on Time Travelling and Assertions Generating an Assertions Administration Using FBM

John Bulles[1]([⊠]), Ralph Mak[1], and Diederik Dulfer[2]

[1] PNA, Heerlen, The Netherlands
{john.bulles,ralph.mak}@pna-group.com
[2] Belastingdienst, Apeldoorn, The Netherlands
dph.dulfer@belastingdienst.nl

Abstract. The Dutch Tax Office processes millions of tax assessments containing assertions from tax payers. These assertions are compared with assertions from data registers and third parties like employers, banks, etc. The tax office has to combine all these assertions into a consistent set of facts about the tax payer on which necessary calculations are performed. These facts often change in time as well. Currently different approaches and systems are implemented to deal with these challenges.

In the "Proof of Concept Gegevens" a pattern is developed for handling these challenges in a generic and repeatable manner. This includes the development of a meta model for defining conceptual data models. This meta model uses parts of the FBM meta model [1], but also extends the FBM meta model with concepts for time granularity and multi-reality.

The defined data model is automatically transformed into an administration handling assertions and time travelling facts.

Keywords: Fact Based Modeling (FBM) · Assertions · Time travelling · Multi-reality

1 Introduction

Each year more than 8 million tax assessments are processed by the Dutch Tax Office. A tax assessment for the income tax can lead to more than 100 assertions for fact types about a tax payer. Furthermore data is retrieved from data registers and third party organisations like employers, banks and pension funds. The total set of assertions about a tax payer can be huge.

In the process of, for example, deriving the tax return for the income tax of a tax payer, these assertions are processed into facts. But to process these assertions, one must take into account all different assertions about a tax payer, but also already existing facts. This complex process is handled at the tax office in multiple different implementations, all with their own way of handling the challenges that come with such a complex set of assertions and facts.

The complexity increases even more, if the changes of the facts in time are taken into account as well. At any time, the tax office must be able to determine what facts are

© Springer Nature Switzerland AG 2019
C. Debruyne et al. (Eds.): OTM 2018 Workshops, LNCS 11231, pp. 67–76, 2019.
https://doi.org/10.1007/978-3-030-11683-5_7

valid at a certain point in time, but also at what time these facts came available and from where they originate. A fact can originate from an assertion, but also from a derivation. At any time, the tax office needs to be able to derive what basis is used for a certain derivation.

Since a few years the Tax Office is developing a new way of working [7], which will help them to become more agile and flexible in carrying out their tasks. In the developed ways to handle multi-reality and time travelling, often only a part of the generic problems of multi-reality or time travelling is tackles. The Dutch Tax Office has started a proof of concept, the "PoC Gegevens" in which the goal is to develop a generic and reusable pattern of handling these kind of administrations. In this PoC, the Tax Office hopes to develop a generic approach for these kind of issues. Another goal of the PoC Gegevens is to develop a tool kit which will be able to generate a lot of the necessary code and scripts for supporting an administration which has to deal with multi-reality and time traveling.

The starting point of such an administration is a conceptual data model. For defining this data model, a subset of the FBM meta model is selected. In the PoC Gegevens the concept of multi-reality is of importance. Multi reality is the possibility to have multiple statements about a particular fact type which might be inconsistent. Furthermore the PoC Gegevens has to support three time axis. Therefore the used subset is extended with some concepts to define additional metadata for the fact types.

After defining the conceptual data model, the logical and physical data models are generated. The logical data model is an application view on the conceptual model, extended with entities for all necessary metadata about the assertions and derivations. The physical data model is a DB2-datamodel in the flavour Linux or Z/OS [2]. Where system time and business time are implemented in the physical data model [3].

In Sect. 2, the concepts assertions, facts, multi-reality and time travelling will be explained in more detail. Section 3 describes the developed meta model. The actual creation of the assertion administration is described in Sect. 4.

2   Assertions Versus Facts

An assertion is a statement claimed by a certain party. Such an assertion is not necessarily true and therefore not necessarily a fact. A fact on the other hand is a proposition taken to be true. The parties that can do assertions are the tax payer himself, but also public data registers, like the "Gemeentelijke Basis Administratie" (Dutch register of all municipalities containing a.o. the data about who lives where) or third parties like banks, employers, pension funds, etc. Because one or more different parties can do assertions on the same fact type for the same tax payer in the same time period, with the support of assertions automatically multi-reality is supported. Based on certain rules or manual judgement an assertions can be approved. This action will change the status of an assertion, but also will create a fact. For traceability of these actions, it is necessary to store these assignments as well as the input used to do the manual judgement (and, if present the rules applied).

Typically for the administrations like the Tax Office, the created facts are input for further processing, mainly in derivation rules to calculate for example the amount of tax to be paid. The output of such a derivation also creates facts and also for these facts it is necessary to have a trace to the derivation performed and the input of this derivation.

Possibly facts about the tax payer already exist in the fact base and thus new assertions which are assigned as true, can influence the period these facts are valid. As example we take an assertion of a tax payer himself in which he states that he was in the military from February 1st 2017 till June 1st 2017. If this assertion is approved, a fact representing the same proposition will be inserted in the fact base (Fig. 1).

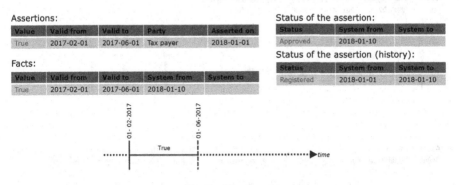

Fig. 1. Situation 1

In this example, the period the assertion is valid, is represented by the "Valid from" and "Valid to" fields, the fields "System from" and "System to" point out the period in which the assertion is registered in and deleted from the administration. When a fact is deleted, it will remain in the administrations history tables, so that all data which ever was present, can be assessed.

Then a new assertion is made by the Ministry of Defense, in which is stated that the tax payer was not in the military from April 1st 2017 till September 1st 2017. A tax officer will evaluate this new assertion, taken the fact base and other assertions into account. If he approves this new assertion as well (without withdrawing the old fact), both facts will exist in the fact base, but the newer assertion will overwrite a part of the period in which the first fact is valid. This results in a "time dependent fact" which has different values in different timeframes (without overlap) (Fig. 2).

If the tax payer asserted an assertion before the Ministry did and this is registered and approved after the approval of the fact of the Ministry, this new assertion would create a fact, but will not affect the fact created from the assertion of the Ministry (Fig. 3).

In the example above, the three used time axis are used. One is for the business time, when is which fact valid. The second time axis is for system time, when did we register a fact or assertion. At any time a tax officer must be able to travel back in time to a certain time in the past (or sometimes even in the future), to see what data was available (known) at that time. This is necessary because changes can be asserted

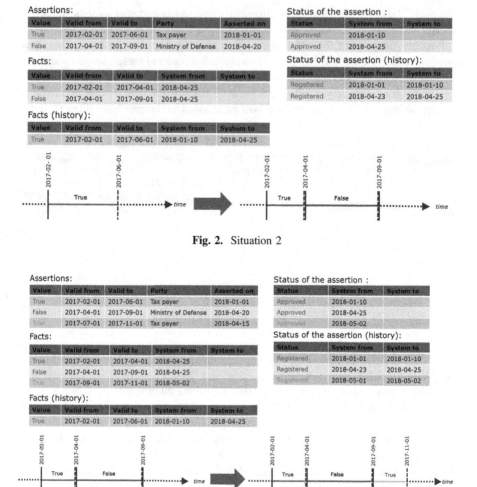

Fig. 2. Situation 2

Fig. 3. Situation 3

which are retroactive. For example, if a derivation was done before the assertion of the Military department was registered, it must be possible to determine why a derivation done at that time results in a different amount than a derivation done after that the assertion of the military department was registered (and approved). The third time axis is used to determine in which order the assertions are done. Often assertions are sent to the Tax Office digitally (online forms, web services, etc.), but also a lot of assertions are still sent using paper forms in the post mail. Because of this, the possibility arises that a assertion done by mail is registered later than an assertion done in an online application, but the date on which the paper form was sent is before the date on which the online form was sent. Only looking at registration times would then give a wrong view on the actual order of assertions.

3   The Developed Meta Model

The base of the developed meta model is the meta model of the FBM Meta model, working draft 08 [1]. Because of the current purpose and scope, not all concepts of the meta model are necessary. For example, most constraints are left out of scope. These will be subject of future development. For now, the check on these constraints must be done manually or rules which are defined outside the scope of the PoC.

The meta model is in this paragraph displayed in conceptual structures, as described in [4]. Because of the size of the meta model, not every part of the meta model is displayed, but is limited to the differences only.

The first section displayed is about fact types (Fig. 4).

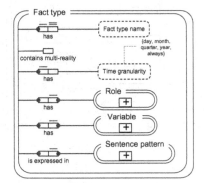

Fig. 4. Fact type

Additional to the meta model of FBM, of a fact type can be registered whether the fact type can contain multi-reality assertions. Only fact types that contain multi-reality will be used to generate the part of the administration that contains the assertions. All fact types are subject of generation in the part of the administration that contains the actual facts. For example, facts which are always derived will not be in the assertions administration but will be in the administration of the actual facts. Fact types used to define the identification of entity types will often also not be subject of assertions in most administrations, these facts will be available from other systems, which are only for this identification purposes.

Another addition in the PoC Gegevens is the time granularity of a fact type. This time granularity will define what periods of business time are valid for a certain fact type. In the current way of working at the Dutch Tax Office, facts are often declared for a period of a whole year or a quarter. In some approaches, daily changing facts are also present. Some facts are supposed to be valid forever and therefore only totally over-writing these facts is possible.

Not different as in the FBM meta model, a fact type can be expressed in roles and in variables and sentence patterns are used to express the fact type.

Because the most of the focus of the PoC Gegevens is in defining the data structures of the conceptual data model, currently no difference in sentence patterns for facts of roles are made. The sentence pattern of expressing the actual facts in the fact base is (for now) generated from the sentence patterns based on the roles of the fact type and the sentence pattern of the fact type from which the entity type is a objectification.

Another difference in the meta model of the PoC in comparison with the FBM meta model is with respect to the entity types (Fig. 5).

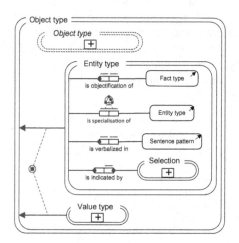

Fig. 5. Entity type

For simplification of the implementation of the current meta model in a domain specific language, it is chosen not to express a data type as an object type, therefore the concept of domain object type is not needed between object type and entity and value type. Furthermore, it is decided to limit the idea of subtyping to only entity types. Within the Dutch Tax Office, subtyping is often referred to as subject of programming. Therefore is chosen to talk about specialization instead of subtyping.

Another difference with the FBM meta model is the addition of selection. Within the Tax Office, identification is used to identify the subjects of assertions, for example a Social Security Number for a tax payer. But such a tax payer can also be selected from the set of tax payers with the use of first name, last name, address and birth date. If this is not unique within the total set of tax payers, an employee of the tax office must point out which tax payer in the administration, is the tax payer of the assertion based on this information. To indicate the roles of the fact types which can be used to select an instance of a certain entity type, in the meta model the concept of selection is created. For the current (first) implementation this selection is always identical to the identification (Fig. 6).

As explained earlier, the other difference is, that only a part of the FBM meta model is used. Only the uniqueness constraints are used. All other constraints will be subject of further development outside the scope of the current PoC.

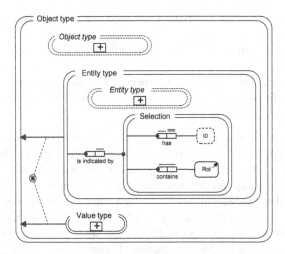

Fig. 6. Selection

4   Creating an Assertion Administration

When creating a new assertion administration, at first the conceptual data model must be defined. This is done in natural language in MPS [5, 6] with the use of a developed domain specific language in line with the described meta model. For a small example, this looks like (Fig. 7):

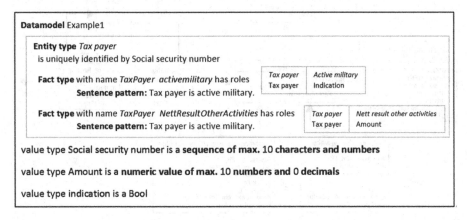

Fig. 7. Example conceptual data model

Then, after defining the conceptual model, this automatically is transformed into a logical model. This logical model is composed of three different parts:

1. A part generated from the fact types to store the values for a fact type for possible assertions
2. A part generated from the fact types to store the values for a fact type for the time dependent facts
3. A part which is added for storing the metadata of the assertions, additional information about the assignation of assertions as assigned and additional information about performed derivations.

In the logical data model, all fact types are grouped into a poly entity, which could be seen as a super type with all its subtypes contained within the super type and not the subtypes as separated elements. This is done for assertions and for facts. Possibly some fact types have no multi-reality and therefore will only be present in the poly entity for facts.

The physical data model, generated from the logical data model transforms the poly entity into separate tables. Also history tables are created for all tables which store the actual facts. Assertions do not have history tables, assertions cannot change in time. Only the status of an assertion can change. Therefore for the assertions only the assertion status table has a history table (Fig. 8).

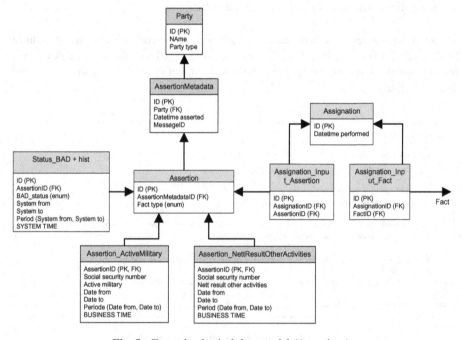

Fig. 8. Example physical data model (Assertions)

The physical data model is used to generate a database, currently a DB2 database within the project. Besides the database also services to access the database are generated. To be able to process assertions to facts, a stored procedure is generated that ensures that the facts are correctly created with respect to the time travelling aspect as explained in Sect. 2. The physical data model would, for the example presented above, be as displayed below. To keep the example readable, it is represented in two figures which relate to each other (Fig. 9).

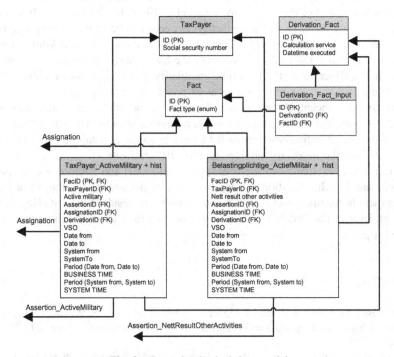

Fig. 9. Example physical data model

5 Future Development

The upcoming year some functional and technical issues have to be tackled. Performance is an important issue. First tests are hopeful, but extensive tests on the infrastructure of the Tax Office should prove the performance of the chosen technology. Also the evolution of a conceptual model must be handled. A conceptual model will in time evolve, for example fact types will be added, changed or deleted. The generated administration must be able to handle this without any loss of data etc.

Other future development is analyzing and implementing issues coming from the General Data Protection Regulation, the Tax Office internal security documents and the Dutch law about archiving processed data.

Furthermore, actual projects for departments of the Tax Office must prove this approach as useful.

6 Summary

In the PoC Gegevens, the Tax Office develops a generic approach for administrations dealing with the complexity of multi-reality and time traveling. The meta model of PoC Gegevens is a subset of the current meta model of FBM, but it also extends this meta model with a few concepts. Because fact types need to support time travelling, a time granularity is added to the fact type. This time granularity defines what kind of periods can be used to define the validity of a fact of the fact type (for example a lot of data of the Dutch Tax Office currently has a time granularity of a year). Another added concept is whether a fact type can have assertions as population or only facts.

The created conceptual data model is, with some additional data structures transformed into a logical and from there on into a physical data model. The physical data model is expressed in database scripts for a DB2 bi temporal database. Also Java code is generated for the necessary services on this DB2-database.

Performance, evaluation of the conceptual data model and additional concepts for European and Dutch regulation and internal security documents are subject of further development in the upcoming year. Of course, using the result of the PoC Gegevens in actual projects at the Dutch Tax Office will really prove whether this approach has reached it goals.

References

1. Fact Based Modeling: Fact-Based Modelling Metamodel (version WD08) (2014). http://www.factbasedmodeling.org/Data/Sites/1/media/FBM1002WD08.pdf. Accessed 29 Aug 2018
2. Goksu, M.C., McFeely, C., McKellar, C., Wang, X.H.: Managing Ever-Increasing Amounts of Data with IBM DB2 for z/OS. IBM Corporation, Armonk (2015)
3. Johnston, T., Weis, R.: Managing Time in Relational Databases. Elsevier, Amsterdam (2010)
4. Lemmens, I.: Integrating modelling disciplines at conceptual semantic level. In: Ciuciu, I., et al. (eds.) OTM 2015. LNCS, vol. 9416, pp. 188–196. Springer, Cham (2015). https://doi.org/10.1007/978-3-319-26138-6_22
5. JetBrains: MPS: Domain-Specific Language Creator (2004). https://www.jetbrains.com/mps/. Accessed 29 Aug 2018
6. Dulfer, D., Boersma, M.: MPS Community Meetup 2018 – Challenges of the Dutch Tax and Customs Administration (2018). https://www.youtube.com/watch?v=_-XMjfz3RcU. Accessed 29 Aug 2018
7. van Zanten, G.V., Nissink, P., Dulfer, D.: Fact based legal benefits services. In: Ciuciu, I., et al. (eds.) OTM 2015. LNCS, vol. 9416, pp. 178–187. Springer, Cham (2015). https://doi.org/10.1007/978-3-319-26138-6_21

Towards Key Principles of Fact Based Thinking

Stijn Hoppenbrouwers[1,2(✉)], Henderik A. Proper[3,4],
and Maurice Nijssen[5]

[1] HAN University of Applied Sciences, Arnhem, The Netherlands
`Stijn.Hoppenbrouwers@han.nl`
[2] Radboud University, Nijmegen, The Netherlands
[3] Luxembourg Institute for Science and Technology,
Esch-sur-Alzette, Luxembourg
`E.Proper@acm.org`
[4] University of Luxembourg, Luxembourg, Luxembourg
[5] PNA Group, Heerlen, The Netherlands
`Maurice.Nijssen@pna-group.com`

Abstract. In this paper, we present ten principles that, in our view, underlie and define the practice and science of 'Fact Based Thinking'. In itself, Fact Based Thinking underpins Fact Based Modelling (FBM) in all its forms. FBM has been around for decades, and has brought forth a number of meta-models and formalizations. The principles as discussed in this paper focus on Fact Based Thinking rather than on matters of representation and precise semantics, which have been elaborately discussed elsewhere. The principles presented are deliberately worded for broad use and inspirational purposes, rather than worked out in detail. As such, this paper suggests the initialization of further work rather than presenting a final result. The sketch of the principles presented aims to express the basics of Fact Based Thinking in a way that most members of the FBM community can feel at home with.

Keywords: Fact Based Modelling · Fact Based Thinking ·
Conceptual modelling · Knowledge engineering · Information systems

1 Introduction

Fact Based Modelling (FBM) has been around since the nineteen seventies, and though it has never become mainstream, it has been influential in education and research (in particular in Europe and Australia) and has both directly and indirectly helped in shaping current thinking about data, information, and knowledge as well as, of course, information and knowledge systems. One of the major achievements has also been a structural impact on the creation of the SBVR [13] standard for business rules.

In the history of FBM, a key role has been played by the ORM (Object Role Modelling) workshops, which in 2015 were renamed FBM workshops. Though a whole range of FBM related topics was addressed in these workshops (and in other, related ones, such as the EMMSAD workshops), there has been a strong emphasis on

© Springer Nature Switzerland AG 2019
C. Debruyne et al. (Eds.): OTM 2018 Workshops, LNCS 11231, pp. 77–86, 2019.
https://doi.org/10.1007/978-3-030-11683-5_8

the meta model, representations, formalisations, verbalisations etc., of the various FBM flavours; the broadly known ones including NIAM [1], ORM [2], FCO-IM [3], DOGMA [27] and cogNIAM (which integrates process and rules aspects fully on an FBM grounding).

While this work is invaluable for the FBM practice and community, the various specific representations and techniques have all been modestly successful in terms of practical adoption in "mainstream industry". This set aside, most FBM enthusiasts, when asked, will tell us that they like and use the *way of thinking* of FBM even if in their professional practice they do not use (or are not facilitated to use) one of its actual techniques (and/or one of the tools supporting them, like cogNIAM Analyser, NORMA, or CaseTalk). In particular through the thousands of information and IT experts that have gotten to know FBM and FBM thinking in their academic or professional higher education, the perspective and ideas of FBM seem to be very much alive, even if they are relatively covert and "internalised".

In line with the latter, the current paper takes the 'Fact Based Thinking' perspective and sums up what we believe to be the chief principles that make up the Fact Based Thinking core of FBM. They are put forward here as suggestions, to start further discussion. The general idea is that, at least to a reasonable extent, all FBM supporters, adepts, teachers and users will recognize the principles as key features of Fact Based Thinking underlying FBM in all its rich variety. After all, the thinking may underlie the modelling, but the models are the chief and vital, tangible end product of the application of FBM.

Why advocate these principles? Because they are key to the whole FBM effort and its ideas, and have been underemphasized in comparison with the details and pros and cons of meta-models and representations of separate FBM techniques/methods. Even more, when modellers are required to use, for example, the UML class diagram or ER notation, they can still follow Fact Based Thinking when developing the model [3, 4].

The principles underlying Fact Based Thinking are generally known within the FBM community, but have not been very clearly communicated as such in a comprehensive, manifesto-like way – which we believe is an interesting and useful thing to do. Arguably, the principles (possibly in a more mature form than the one presented in the current paper) are the most important part of what FBM is, and constitute its main impact on the world of conceptual modelling, information systems, and knowledge engineering. As such, this paper is also the result of a fundamental discussion on the future of FBM, as started during the OnTheMove conference FBM workshop in 2017.

The status of the principles put forward in this paper, is that they have been proposed by, and discussed among, a small group of 'first generation' FBM experts, while some comments on them have been received from a wider circle of FBM experts. We emphasise that the current set does not yet reflect a widely shared, explicit agreement among the FBM community at large. Instead, we hope this initial proposal may eventually lead to such established, explicitly phrased common ground. We aim to obtain further feedback on the current version of the principles and discuss them during this year's FBM workshop, expecting to further develop and finalize this set of principles. The goal is to develop these into a proper Fact Based Thinking manifesto, which should then not only identify the key principles, but also provide evidence for the added value of using Fact Based Thinking in real world situations.

In the remainder of this paper, we will first present the current set of principles. We will then continue with a brief reflection on the consequences of these principles on the modelling method and associated tooling.

2 Principles of Fact Based Thinking

2.1 P1: Facts Are First Citizens

Facts are central to Fact Based Thinking and FBM. As a consequence, actual/example instances are "first citizens" in Fact Based Thinking. Facts, or "instance level statements", are an integral and crucial part of dealing with and describing the structures of the domain (in terms of [6]: the universe of discourse) being modelled. This principle is directly related to a basic and rather universal approach to abstraction: taking concrete examples from a domain (typically, verbalized expressions or statements) and creating a set of categories (type level concepts; not unlike a 'signature' as used in mathematical logic) and constraints (comparable to axioms) structuring the domain and providing coherence and cross-conceptual, type-level meaning for the domain. It is not only related to basic abstraction in logic, but also to notions of abstraction in cognition and language. Note that whether some concept is seen as instance level ('concrete') or type level ('abstract') is essentially a context-specific choice [7, p. 291-2].

2.2 P2: Models Should Be Evidence Based

In line with treating facts as first citizens, Fact Based Thinking is "evidence based" in the sense that it requires underlying evidence in terms of facts that express (f)actual observations about the domain to be modelled. Note that this is irrespective of the question whether this pertains to an existing domain, or an "imagined" (future) one. This works in a bi-directional fashion in that it is allowed for modellers to conceptualise in two directions, either: (1) from example facts to fact types (deriving/abstracting fact types from facts), or (2) from fact types to example facts (validating fact types through facts). In Fact Based Thinking, a good model is, once finished, always grounded in examples from the domain. This is important for both the conceptualisation process (a basis for well founded, manageable abstracting, and cognitive grounding in instances) as for meaningfulness and quality of results (models, descriptions). It provides not just "descriptive meaning" (intensional definition) but also an example set substantiating the description; "example meaning" (extensional definition[1]).

2.3 P3: Models Should Reflect the Communication About a Domain

In Fact Based Thinking, a model should reflect the communication about the domain being modelled. In other words, it "abstracts away" from communication medium specific considerations, such as technological platforms, etc., used for communication.

---

[1] See https://en.wikipedia.org/wiki/Extensional_and_intensional_definitions.

It also considers information and meaning to be present in communication between humans (or possibly other sentient beings), and not an objective representation of "reality" (whatever that may be). In line with Ogden and Richards [5], meaning involves referents; i.e. interpreting beings.

2.4 P4: Models Should Embed and Use the Language Used by Domain Experts

Fact Based Thinking not only reflects the communication about a domain, it more specifically reflects the language used (naturally) by the domain experts (knowledgeable members of the domain community). Both fact structures and terms used in fact types need to reflect the languages used to communicate about the domain. As a result, fact based models are sometimes referred to as "information grammars", capturing the communication structures by domain experts in communicating about the domain. For a model to be an information grammar specifically does not mean that the model would be a model of the *communication about the domain*. The model will still have to be a model of the actual *domain*.

The use of the domain expert's language is very explicitly reflected in the systematic and precise use of *verbalizations* in expressing FBMs (both at instance and type level), in particular in order to make validation of models possible without exposing domain experts to specialist diagrams. This principle can be effectively used even of non-FBM representations are used, like ER[2].

2.5 P5: The Use of Elementary Facts Is Strongly Favoured

An important part of the way Fact Based Thinking deals with linguistic statements (sentences and phrases) concerns the urgent preference for focusing on and working with Elementary Facts. Traditionally [1], the difference between a 'fact' and an 'elementary fact' is that an elementary fact cannot be simplified without loss of meaning. This should always be based on evidence (sample facts) from the domain. However, in line with principle P4, it remains up to the domain experts if they want to split a fact type or not. Nevertheless, this should always be a deliberate and conscious decision.

2.6 P6: Domain Knowledge Representation Is the Primary Use

The primary use for Fact Based Thinking is to produce *knowledge representations*; knowledge about the domain being modelled. Other uses, like database design, are also important but can be seen secondary to and derived from the independent, rational (i.e. logical) representation of information structures. Knowledge representation, usually classified as a branch of artificial intelligence, is the art and science that underlies all forms of (conceptual) modelling, and is heavily embedded in disciplines like data engineering, software engineering, knowledge engineering and, indeed, artificial intelligence. It can also be used, in various levels of formality, in information

---

[2] See https://datavaultusergroup.de/wp-content/uploads/Hannover2017jpzwart.pdf.

management and knowledge management. Knowledge representation combines well established insights from fields like logic, mathematics, cognition, linguistics, and philosophy.

2.7 P7: No A-Priori Conceptualisation of Attributes

Fact Based Thinking does not include a-priori attribution of concepts (i.e. it does not use attributes as sub-items of entities, like for example UML and ER do). It considers such entity-attribute distinction to be arbitrary and driven by representation choices, and therefore not part of "pure" conceptual modelling. Instead Fact Based Thinking focuses on expressing all items in terms of facts, and the objects playing a role in these facts.

2.8 P8: Modelling Language and Procedure Are Two Sides of the Same Coin

In Fact Based Thinking, modelling language and modelling procedure are considered as two sides of the same coin. Fact Based Thinking integrates a structure (language, notation, metamodel) with a procedure: a stepwise process for creating a structure. The procedure serves as a set of guidelines for modellers and can be used for instruction and training. However, in its stricter form and use it is a protocol that safeguards the quality of the resulting model and the repeatability of the procedure (rendering the same results).

2.9 P9: Term Definitions Are an Integral Part of Models

Definition of terms, i.e. of the names of concepts/relations, are an integral part of a fact based models. In line with principle P3 and P4, Fact Based Thinking implies the use of terms from natural (domain) language, while combining such elements into fact statements. The meanings of the (individual) terms, as used in domain context, are essential building blocks for the meanings of composed models/structures. Therefore, description of those terms (in natural language, in the context of the domain) is a crucial and inherent part of Fact Based Thinking.

2.10 P10: Variation Between Specific Situations of Use

Fact Based Thinking is used in many different contexts, with differing goals. Every situation requires a situation-specific use. In other words, no "one-size-fits-all" notation, process, etc., but rather options and variations that balance effectiveness and efficiency for each specific situation of use, tuning the precise concepts, representations, procedures and tools used to specific goals and contexts of use.

3   Consequences for Fact Based Modelling Methods

Given the above suggested principles of Fact Based Thinking, we now reflect on their consequences towards FBM methods and tools. Of course, in formulating the candidate principles, we made sure that the existing FBM variations largely meet the stated principles. Nevertheless, it is still relevant to reflect on these consequences for at least two key reasons. Firstly, when using FBM in practice, one may be "forced" to use modelling languages and tools that were not created from a Fact Based Thinking perspective [4]. In such cases, it will be beneficial to know the (minimum) requirements needed for Fact Based Thinking, to best utilise the means at hand. Secondly, it will also allow us to clarify and motivate why an "ideal" FBM modelling language and procedure, has to provide the ability to be precise and specific in modelling. In discussing the consequences, we have clustered the principles in terms of related consequences.

3.1   Situational Variety and Methodological Integrity

As principle 10 states, Fact Based Thinking requires the ability to vary between specific situations of use. This means that a specific FBM flavour can still be dedicated to a specific class of situations, e.g. ontology engineering [8], or conceptual database design [2]. It does, of course, require these variations to be explicit about their intended purpose/scope, as well as offering options for situational adoptions, in the vein of situational method engineering [9].

Principle 8 refers explicitly to the need to have an integrated perspective on the modelling language used, and the modelling procedure. This "methodological integrity" between language and procedure, would suggest all FBM variations to at least provide a core description of a suitable modelling process as well as an associated modelling language. In cases where one is "forced" to combine Fact Based Thinking with the use of other modelling languages, an existing FBM procedure will have to be used, while elements such as example facts may have to be "stored" separate from the model and associated tool. The latter would also suggest that the development of a generic Fact Based Thinking modelling process and associated modelling concepts (i.e. a core common meta-model) could be beneficial as well.

3.2   Fact Based Evidence

Principles 1, 2 and 5 clearly point towards the need to be able to express example facts, and keep these as an integral part of a FBM model. As far as we know, most FBM variations indeed support this. However, when indeed using other notations (e.g. UML class diagrams), one may be forced to store such information separately. This is, of course highly undesirable. At the same time, there is an increasing awareness that the motivation of a model (in terms of e.g. purpose, intended audience, etc.), as well as the way it has been created, should be an integral part of a model (as a purposely created artefact) [10, 11] as well. As such, adding evidence and domain knowledge to a model in terms of concrete example facts may also be beneficial in other than FBM contexts.

3.3   Rich Verbalisations and Definitions in the Language of the Domain Experts

Principles 3 and 4, result in the need to be able to use rich verbalisations, expressed in the language of the domain experts, in FBM models. Again, as far as we know, all FBM variations support this, while languages such as ER and UML class diagrams provide no real obstacles in this regard and can be enhanced to fit this purpose. Example mappings from ORM to UML and cogNIAM to UML class diagrams also support this [2].

Principle 9 leads to the need to be able to include definitions of key terms, as a kind of a dictionary, in FBM models. This is not generally supported by all FBM variations. Most tools, however, do allow the addition of at least some extra explanation for fact types and/or object types. In future, however, it would be recommendable to make this into an explicit structure in modelling language(s) used for FBM.

An open question with regard to the use of verbalisations in the language of domain experts, is the level at which insights from the modelling process should actually lead to changes in the language used by the domain experts. For example, insights into the question whether a fact is elementary or not, knowledge about the existence of homonyms and/or synonyms within the group of domain experts, but also more fundamental ontological insights that may be concluded when using guidance from e.g. a foundational ontology [12]. However, in line with principles 3 and 4, such a choice has to remain in the hand of the domain experts, using evidence in terms of facts observed in the modelled domain (principles 1 and 2). At the same time, in the context of database design, there may be good arguments to more normatively manage elementarity of facts, as well as synonyms and homonyms [2].

3.4   Attribution and Decomposition

As stated in principle 7, Fact Based Thinking does not require an a-priori conceptualisation of attributes. There is no a-priori attribution of object types; no identifying one object type as being conceptually subordinate to another object type. Fact Based Thinking considers attribution to be arbitrary and driven by representation choices, and therefore not part of "pure" conceptual modelling. When having to combine Fact Based Thinking with a modelling language that traditionally uses attribution, one can simply refrain from using this.

A possible advantage of attribution is of course that the resulting models look, at first glance, simpler than FBM models traditionally do. After all, attribution enables the use of graphical abbreviations for the identified attributes. This is, indeed, a representational consideration.

As has been studied in the FBM community, attribution as provided by e.g. (standard) ER and UML does not scale well, in the sense that it does not enable a recursive, i.e. stepwise, decomposition of a complex domain into more detailed parts. This would require a recursive use of attribution [14, 17] to develop (purpose specific) recursively decomposed views on top of flat conceptual models.

In the context of e.g. enterprise architecture modelling [15], a clear distinction is made between views and (core) models, where views are tuned to the communicative/representational needs in specific situation [16]. This distinction would also enable FBM to make a clear distinction between the (flat) conceptual model, and (purpose/audience specific) derived views with attributions.

Where principle 7 clearly states that attribution is considered to be non conceptual and in general arbitrary and driven by representation choices, there is a need to further underpin/nuance this. For example, work on foundational ontologies [12] may provide guidance to identify "natural" attributions. The work reported in [14] also aimed to provide objective heuristics to use constraint patterns to identify natural attributions.

3.5   Expressiveness for Knowledge Representation

Principle 6 states that the primary use for Fact Based Thinking is knowledge representation. This implies that the modelling languages used for FBM should be expressive enough to express, for a given domain, all conceptually relevant knowledge. For FBM, this has resulted in logic based [18] as well as set-theory based [19], and even category-theory based [20] formalisations of the semantics of FBM models, including associated query and constraint language(s) [21, 22]. Principles 3 and 4, also have implications for the non-graphical query and constraint languages. In the context of FBM, this has resulted in a number of alternatives [21–23], essentially leading up to the SBVR standard [13]. These languages, embodying principles 3 and 4, are in a stark contrast to e.g. UML's OCL [24], which remains a sugared version of set theory at best.

The need for FBM to be expressive, in particular also in terms of graphical constraints, also leads to models that have a (apparent) high level of graphical complexity. Simply put, "people" (and sometimes even reviewers) argue against FBM by stating that UML and ER diagrams look much simpler. Here, it would be advisable for FBM to explicitly embrace the use of simpler views (diagrams) depicting the core fact structure, with fewer graphical constraints. In addition, it would also need to be clarified that when one wants to add more knowledge about a domain, the diagrams will (have to) become more complex. The latter is supported by Moody's work [25], stating that a graphical model needs to reflect the complexities of the domain being modelled, which he motivates in terms of Shannon and Weaver's information theory [26], in the sense that a model will need to reflect all information one wants to capture from a domain (given a modelling purpose).

4   Conclusion and Next Steps

In this paper, we presented ten candidate principles that collectively aim to define the essence of the practice and science of 'Fact Based Thinking', in order to underpin FBM in all its forms. We also discussed possible consequences on methods and tool development for FBM, based on these principles. Of course, the existing FBM flavours largely meet these requirements. However, especially when a dedicated FBM modelling language and/or tooling, cannot be used, these requirements can provide guidance in using available languages and tools.

The presented principles have deliberately only been sketched, as their elaboration and adoption should be part of a broader discussion in the FBM community. We hope this initial proposal will eventually lead to such established, explicitly phrased common ground.

The current list of principles has been formulated based on initial input from (next to the authors): John Bulles, Inge Lemmens, and Sjir Nijssen. We would like to thank these contributors.

As mentioned in the introduction, we aim to obtain further feedback on the current version of the principles during this year's FBM workshop, with the goal to further develop these principles in a kind of Fact Based Thinking manifesto. Beyond this, we also hope to, together with the FBM community at large, gather compelling evidence (in terms of documented real-world cases) of why Fact Based Thinking has a clear added value (in real world business terms) over other approaches.

References

1. Nijssen, G.M., Halpin, T.A.: Conceptual Schema and Relational Database Design: A Fact Oriented Approach. Prentice Hall, Englewood Cliffs (1989). ISBN 0-13-167263-0
2. Halpin, T.A., Morgan, T.: Information Modeling and Relational Databases. Data Management Systems, 2nd edn. Morgan Kaufman (2008). ISBN 978-0-123-73568-3
3. Zwart, J.P., Engelbart, M., Hoppenbrouwers, S.J.B.A.: Fact Oriented Modeling with FCO-IM: Capturing Business Semantics in Data Models with Fully Communication Oriented Information Modeling. Technics Publications (2015). ISBN 978-1634620864
4. Proper, H.A., Bleeker, A.I., Hoppenbrouwers, S.J.B.A.: Object-role modelling as a domain modelling approach. In: Grundspenkis, J., Kirikova, M. (eds.) Proceedings of the Workshop on Evaluating Modeling Methods for Systems Analysis and Design (EMMSAD 2004), Held in Conjunction with the 16th Conference on Advanced Information Systems 2004 (CAiSE 2004), Faculty of Computer Science and Information Technology, Riga, Latvia, June 2004, vol. 3, pp. 317–328 (2004). ISBN 9-984-97671-8
5. Ogden, C.K., Richards, I.A.: The Meaning of Meaning - A Study of the Influence of Language upon Thought and of the Science of Symbolism. Magdalene College, University of Cambridge, Oxford (1923)
6. ISO/IEC JTC 1/SC 32 Technical Committee on Data management and interchange. Information processing systems - Concepts and Terminology for the Conceptual Schema and the Information Base. Technical report ISO/TR 9007:1987, ISO, 1987
7. Bowkerm, G.C., Star, S.L.: Sorting Things Out, Classification and its Consequences. MIT Press, Cambridge (1999)
8. Spyns, P.: Object role modelling for ontology engineering in the DOGMA framework. In: Meersman, R., Tari, Z., Herrero, P. (eds.) OTM 2005. LNCS, vol. 3762, pp. 710–719. Springer, Heidelberg (2005). https://doi.org/10.1007/11575863_90
9. Brinkkemper, S., Saeki, M., Harmsen, A.F.: Meta-modelling based assembly techniques for situational method engineering. Inf. Syst. 24(3), 209–228 (1999). ISSN 0306-4379
10. Bjeković, M., Proper, H.A., Sottet, J.-S.: Embracing pragmatics. In: Yu, E., Dobbie, G., Jarke, M., Purao, S. (eds.) ER 2014. LNCS, vol. 8824, pp. 431–444. Springer, Cham (2014). https://doi.org/10.1007/978-3-319-12206-9_37
11. Sandkuhl, K., et al.: From expert discipline to common practice: a vision and research agenda for extending the reach of enterprise modeling. Bus. Inf. Syst. Eng. 60(1), 69–80 (2018)

12. Guizzardi, G.: On ontology, ontologies, conceptualizations, modeling languages, and (meta)models. In: Vasilecas, O., Eder, J., Caplinskas, A. (eds.) Databases and Information Systems IV - Selected Papers from the Seventh International Baltic Conference, DB&IS 2006. Frontiers in Artificial Intelligence and Applications, 3–6 July 2006, Vilnius, Lithuania, vol. 155, pp. 18–39. IOS Press (2006). ISBN 978-1-58603-715-4

13. Semantics of Business Vocabulary and Rules (SBVR). Technical report dtc/06–03-02, Object Management Group, Needham, Massachusetts, March 2006

14. Campbell, L.J., Halpin, T.A., Proper, H.A.: Conceptual schemas with abstractions - making flat conceptual schemas more comprehensible. Data Knowl. Eng. **20**(1), 39–85 (1996)

15. ISO/IEC/IEEE. Systems and software engineering - Architecture description is an international standard for architecture descriptions of systems and software. Technical report ISO/IEC 42010, ISO, July 2011

16. Proper, H.A., Hoppenbrouwers, S.J.B.A., Veldhuijzen van Zanten, G.E.: Communication of enterprise architectures. Enterprise Architecture at Work. TEES, 4th edn, pp. 59–72. Springer, Heidelberg (2017). https://doi.org/10.1007/978-3-662-53933-0_4

17. Creasy, N., Proper, H.A.: A generic model for 3-Dimensional conceptual modelling. Data Knowl. Eng. **20**(2), 119–162 (1996)

18. Halpin, T.A.: A logical analysis of information systems: static aspects of the data-oriented perspective. Ph.D. thesis, University of Queensland, Brisbane, Queensland, Australia (1989)

19. Van Bommel, P., ter Hofstede, A.H.M., van der Weide, T.: Semantics and verification of object-role models. Inf. Syst. **16**(5), 471–495 (1991)

20. ter Hofstede, A.H.M., Lippe, E., Frederiks, P.J.M.: Conceptual data modeling from a categorical perspective. Comput. J. **39**(3), 215–231 (1996)

21. ter Hofstede, A.H.M., Proper, H.A., van der Weide, T.: Formal definition of a conceptual language for the description and manipulation of information models. Inf. Syst. **18**(7), 489–523 (1993)

22. Bloesch, A.C., Halpin, T.A.: Conceptual queries using ConQuer-II. In: Embley, D.W., Goldstein, R.C. (eds.) ER 1997. LNCS, vol. 1331, pp. 113–126. Springer, Heidelberg (1997). https://doi.org/10.1007/3-540-63699-4_10

23. Meersman, R.: The RIDL conceptual language. Technical report, International Centre for Information Analysis Services, Control Data Belgium, Inc., Brussels, Belgium (1982)

24. Warmer, J., Kleppe, A.: The Object Constraint Language: Getting Your Models Ready for MDA, 2nd edn. Addison Wesley, Reading (2003). ISBN 0-321-17936-6

25. Moody, D.L.: The "Physics" of notations: toward a scientific basis for constructing visual notations in software engineering. IEEE Trans. Software Eng. **35**(6), 756–779 (2009)

26. Shannon, C.E., Weaver, W.: The Mathematical Theory of Communication. University of Illinois Press, Chicago (1949)

27. Jarrar, M., Meersman, R.: Ontology engineering – the DOGMA approach. In: Dillon, T.S., Chang, E., Meersman, R., Sycara, K. (eds.) Advances in Web Semantics I. LNCS, vol. 4891, pp. 7–34. Springer, Heidelberg (2008). https://doi.org/10.1007/978-3-540-89784-2_2

Using FBM, DMN and BPMN to Analyse and Improve Medical Guidelines

John Bulles[(✉)], Bertil van Beusekom, and Johan Saton

PNA Group, Heerlen, The Netherlands
{john.bulles,bertil.van.beusekom,
johan.saton}@pna-group.com

Abstract. To improve the quality of health care in the Netherlands, medical guidelines are developed. These guidelines describe recommendations for medical specialists based on scientific research, complemented with expertise and experience of medical specialists. Such guidelines are described in texts of sometimes more than 100 pages. A hospital develops its own guidelines based on this national guideline.

In a project at an academic hospital in the Netherlands, such a guideline was analyzed. The analysis covered a conceptual data model, a decision model and process model and all integration between these different models using FBM, DMN and BPMN, methodically orchestrated by cogNIAM.

From this analysis, the local guideline was made more understandable by removing redundant information, replacing ambiguous definitions with unambiguous ones and resolving detected flaws and inconsistencies. The result of the analysis was also used to develop a software prototype that helps medical specialists in following the guidelines and improving them based on user data.

Keywords: Fact Based Modeling (FBM) · Medical guidelines ·
Decision Model and Notation (DMN) ·
Business Process Model and Notation (BPMN) · cogNIAM · Cognitatie

1 Introduction

In the medical health care in the Netherlands, guidelines for medical professionals are developed. Such a guideline is based on scientific research, complemented with the expertise of medical specialists. Such a guideline is not a purpose on its own, it is meant to help in determining which actions should be performed in what order. The goal of this in general is to improve the health care. The guidelines are not compulsory regulations, but they contain explicit evidence-based recommendations.

The guidelines are described for the "average" patient; therefore, actual practice is often more complex. For this reason, it is permitted to deviate from such a guideline. Reasons to deviate should then be described in the health care file of the specific patient.

The guidelines involved often contain a large volume of text. Furthermore, many hospitals use the guideline as a basis to develop their own in-house guidelines. Guidelines sometimes prove to be ineffective as a tool to improve healthcare. They can be difficult to understand because of redundancy of information in the guideline, the

© Springer Nature Switzerland AG 2019
C. Debruyne et al. (Eds.): OTM 2018 Workshops, LNCS 11231, pp. 87–96, 2019.
https://doi.org/10.1007/978-3-030-11683-5_9

use of ambiguous definitions and coverage of possible situations. And of course, because they are currently all text, it is often not possible to easily determine the course of action for a particular situation without reading and understanding a large part of the guideline.

In a project in cooperation with an academic hospital in the Netherlands, such a hospitals guideline was analyzed using Fact Based Modelling (FBM) [6], Business Process Model and Notation (BPMN) [1] and Decision Model and Notation [5]. FBM, BPMN and DMN focus on different aspects of the guidelines. In accordance with the way of thinking of the cogNIAM methodology [3], these different aspects are modelled in coherence and integrated into a singular knowledge model for a specific guideline. The result of the analysis is used to make the hospital's guideline more understandable. As a model will not contain redundant information, it was possible to remove this information from the guideline. For example, multiple conditions were provided to determine which action should be performed, but the result was only dependent on a subset of these conditions (the other conditions did not affect the result of the decision). Also the definitions of terms were improved by removing ambiguities in these definitions.

Another result harvested from the models, is a logical base for a software prototype, which in the future could be used to assist medical specialists in following the guidelines with more predictability and with less time/effort. Further improvements could result from using the prototype (or its production equivalent) and the resulting patient outcomes, as user data from the prototype will be available easily.

The way of working for this project is described in more detail in Sect. 2. Section 3 will explain this way of working further by using an example. The guideline selected for this example is not the local guideline, as this was not allowed due to confidentiality stipulations. Therefore the example is described using the national guideline, which can publically by downloaded at the "Richtlijnendatabase" [8]. Section 4 describes how the analysis was used to generate and use the prototype.

2   Way of Working for Medical Guidelines

The way of working is divided in several steps. Of course, starting point is the medical guideline. Additionally, interviews with medical specialists were performed to challenge and verify the guidelines. So the first step consist of gathering information from documents and interviews. All documents are added to Cognitatie [4], a document based analysis platform, in which annotations are used to collect parts of texts of one or more documents. These specific pieces of text are linked together as a collection of available texts for a specific purpose and can also be classified using a self-defined classification scheme. Relevant concepts are extracted from the text and, where necessary, are related to each other. In this way, all relevant parts of the guideline for a specific purpose are collected, but also a first analysis of the necessary concepts and the definitions in the guideline and other documents is performed.

This result is then analyzed in more detail and formalized into models. The resulting models describe different aspects of the knowledge in the guideline. Procedural information will be used to specify a process model. Definitions are captured in the semantics of an FBM model. The decisions rules which describe on basis of what conditions a specific result or action is given, are specified using DMN. But these rules need input, this input must also be described in the FBM model. And of course the data that is input of the DMN and BPMN model is a coherent set of facts, therefore described in fact types with all necessary constraints to have a consistent set of facts.

So the different models used (FBM, DMN BPMN) describe exactly the kind of information they were tailored for, but also complete integration between these models is part of the knowledge model and overall repository. In cogNIAM this aspect is visualized using the cogNIAM knowledge molecule (Fig. 1).

Fig. 1. CogNIAM molecule

When analyzing the document and specifying the different models and their integration, a lot of questions arise for the analyst. It is often necessary to involve domain experts (various medical staff) to answers these questions. The type of questions will vary from handling ambiguity in used terms, to undocumented (or unknown) results for a combination of conditions in a decision table, which can either lead to a new rule in the model or provide an "exit point" from the model signifying that a scenario is not expressible in formal rules and should be judged by human expertise. To be able to trace every element of the knowledge specification back to its source, all knowledge elements in the different models are linked to the pieces of text on which they are based. Furthermore additional information provided by domain experts is also stored. This will, in the end, provide traceability and verification back to the original document or domain experts. Cognitatie allows for changes in the versions of the documents to be analyzed automatically and the impact on the model is calculated.

Once a version of the knowledge model is logically sufficiently complete, a software prototype is generated from the result. The prototype takes the process model as a starting point and leads the user through the modelled process. If data is involved, this will directly be linked to the data model and semantics. If a process element is a business rule task, this will point to a decision model, which will be executed automatically. The result of such a decision model itself will again be part of the data model as well.

By providing a prototype as soon as possible, fully based on the specifications, domain experts can easily test the knowledge model. Flaws in the prototype will point out flaws in the different models. Such a flaw can be the result of a (human) error when modelling the guideline, or it can point to a flaw in the guideline. This knowledge can thus be used to improve the model and also the guideline.

Summarizing, the way of working consists of three steps, each broken down into smaller steps. The first step is the analysis of the documents, the second step is developing the specifications using different types of models, but fully integrated. The last step is a transformation of the formal model into something that the end user can use (in this case a software prototype and pointers to improve the guideline). Of course, this is an iterative process. Using the prototype will point out improvements for the guidelines and/or models which, since the prototype reads directly from the models, will in turn improve the prototype so it can be directly used to acquire further user feedback. These three steps are displayed in Fig. 2.

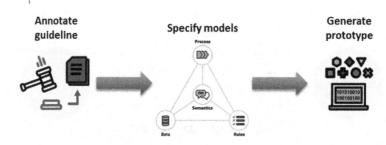

Fig. 2. Three main steps of analyzing the medical guideline

3   Analysing the Medical Guideline for "Perioperative Policy in Treatment with Vitamin K Antagonists"

A guideline which was subject of the project was the antithrombotic policy [9]. One part of this guideline concerns "Perioperative policy in treatment with vitamin K antagonists". In this chapter, the analysis of a small part of this policy is explained for all steps in the way of working.

3.1   Annotating the Texts

The guideline is imported into Cognitatie and annotated to find the different decisions, variables, process steps, etc. The annotation, depending on the chosen classification scheme, can be done by domain experts themselves, by the analysts or combined.

In the guideline, essential parts of the text are annotated. The classification scheme of these annotations is configurable within Cognitatie. In this case, a classification scheme is chosen which holds some (not all) elements of BPMN, DMN and FBM. The text and tables of the guideline must be taken into account as a whole. Because of the textual representation, this is not trivial. Furthermore, in the text references are made to other documents (for example the table for 'thromboembolic risk' refers to another document for the CHA_2DS_2VASc-score), which makes understanding the guideline even more complex. To resolve this, a composite context is defined in Cognitatie, grouping and linking all text across all documents concerning a particular decision. This not only helps during the analysis to ensure that every necessary piece of text is analysed, it also helps with further analysis and impact analysis in the future (Fig. 3).

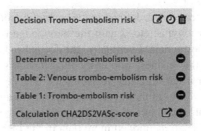

Decision Trombo-embolism risk

Determine trombo-embolism risk

Table 2: Venous trombo-embolism risk

Table 1: Trombo-embolism risk

Calculation CHA2DS2VASc-score

Fig. 3. Composite context

After searching and combining the necessary pieces of text, more detailed analysis is performed on the text. Annotating the decision, its rules, activities, (output and input) variables, etc. points out where in the text what part of the further analysis is defined. Coherence (for example which variables are input or output of a particular decision) is added. Also the entity types to which these variables belong are annotated are connected to the variables. If present in the text, relations between the entity types are defined as well (Fig. 4).

Tabel 1. Trombo-embolie risico

Risico	Jaarlijks risico	Klinische status
Hoog	>10%	- geïsoleerd atriumfibrilleren, zonder klepgebrek, CHA₂DS₂-VASC: 8-9 (zie voor CHA₂DS₂-VASc score: http://eurheartj.oxfordjournals.org/content/33/21/2719.full.pdf) - geïsoleerd atriumfibrilleren met reumatische hartziekte - atriumfibrilleren met MHV of recent (<6 maanden) herseninfarct/TIA ongeacht de CHA₂DS₂-VASC-score

Fig. 4. Annotated text in Cognitatie

3.2   Formalising the Annotations into Formal Models

After annotating the essential pieces of text, the annotations must be formalised into BPMN, DMN and FBM models. This work is performed by the business analyst. The analyst will take the process elements as starting point of his work. All texts, annotations and explanatory notes are taken into account as the analyst defines the process to follow the guideline. Decisions which are not subject to a specialist's opinion are formalised in the process as a business rule task with a gateway; others as a user task with a gateway. A business rule task calls a decision modelled in DMN or a calculation rule (defined in a formal, more mathematical language). In the case of the guidelines, the business rule tasks call a decision. Trying to draw the process in BPMN leads to questions for the domain experts, because the guideline rarely covers all necessary knowledge to draw the process. Also, all activities use and provide data. This data is described in a FBM model, linking each activity to the actual variables of the fact types used in the activity (read or write).

Furthermore, every used term is defined in the semantic model covering definitions, plurals, abbreviations, synonyms, etc. Again the knowledge of the domain experts is needed and secured in the models. Eventually, the formal model is defined.

Subsequently, the in the business rule task called business rule must be modelled. DMN has two levels for describing the decision; the decision requirements diagram (DRD) and the decision logic. On the level of the decision requirements diagram, it is possible to describe what decisions are involved and what their input is (data and/or other decisions). We define all mentioned input data in the FBM model and it is linked as input data. Additionally, reusability and reducing complexity of decision tables will lead to sub-decisions, which will be input to the decision which the analyst wants to define. For the example of the antithrombotic risk analysis, this will lead to the decision requirements diagram, shown below. In this DRD, only a part of the data input elements is displayed (only for 2 of the decisions) (Fig. 5).

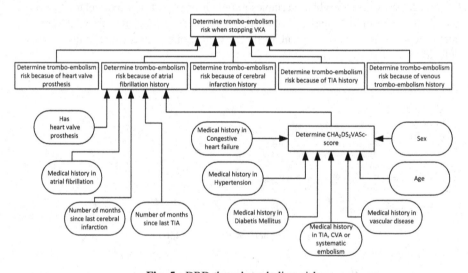

Fig. 5. DRD thromboembolism risk

The decisions in the DRD must be described in detail on the level of the decision logic, using a formal language or a decision table. In this example the decision logic is described in decision tables. A lot of the rules necessary for the decision tables are already annotated in Cognitatie. Figure 6 shows the decision table of the decision "Determine thromboembolism risk because of atrial fibrillation history".

Determine thromboembolism risk because of atrial fibrillation history						
F	History Atrial Fibrillation	CHA$_2$DS$_2$ VASc score	Heart valve prosthesis	Months since last TIA	Months since last cerebral infarction	Thrombo-embolism risk because of AF
1	True	>= 8	-	-	-	High
3	True	-	True	-	-	High
4	True	-	-	<6	-	High
5	True	-	-	-	<6	High
6	True	< 8	-	-	-	Low
7	False	-	-	-	-	Low
8	-	-	-	-	-	Undefined

Fig. 6. Decision table thromboembolism risk because of AF history

As the Business Rule Manifesto [2] states:

"Rules build on facts, and facts build on concepts as expressed by terms."

Therefore all input and output of the decision must be expressed in concepts. In cogNIAM this is handled by having a conceptual data model (FBM-model). Not only are the concepts defined, also all relationships between these concepts are defined as fact types. Furthermore, all data going in and coming out of the process is described in the conceptual data model. This conceptual data model also covers all semantics, such as concept definitions. A part of the conceptual data model for the decision of Fig. 6 is shown in Fig. 7. The FBM model is presented like described in [7].

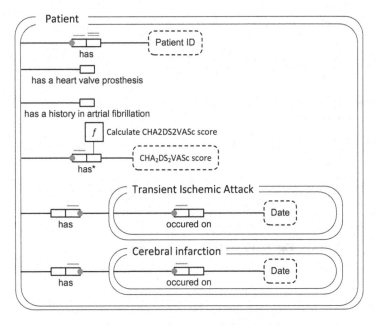

Fig. 7. Part of conceptual data model

Between the conceptual data model and the decision table, boxed expressions define what data input is linked to what element in the data model. These boxed expressions can also contain calculation rules, for example calculating the number of months since the last TIA from the dates in the conceptual data model.

4 Prototyping

After finishing the first version of all the different models (including the integration between them) a prototype is generated. This prototype is used to 'live through' the defined process, using the BPMN-process, DMN-decision and FBM-data model as a logical blueprint. For the decision above this will lead to the following screens in the prototype (Figs. 8 and 9).

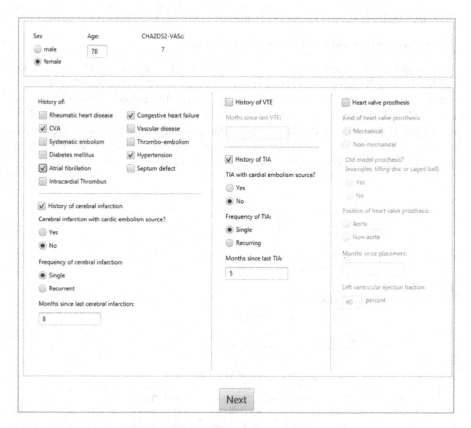

Fig. 8. Example of prototype input screen

Fig. 9. Example of prototype output screen

This will then again lead to new information as the domain expert will see the impact of the models and can test the defined process and rules. Since the prototype utilizes the integrated data model directly, a new version based on a model enhanced according to feedback from the domain experts is easily generated.

5   Summary

Together with medical experts of an academic hospital in the Netherlands, medical guidelines, expressed in documents, are analyzed and defined in process, data and rule models in the standards of BPMN, DMN and FBM.

The guidelines are analyzed in three main steps. First the guideline documents are analyzed. Essential pieces of text are annotated and grouped. Within such a text part, all elements which are needed in one (or more) of the models are annotated and classified. The result of this step is taken as input for defining the conceptual models. A process is modeled in BPMN. All decisions within these processes, which are made on basis of actual facts are described in DMN. And all data structures of the facts used in the process or rule models, including all semantics, are modeled using FBM. Furthermore the integration between these models is defined as well, using the cogNIAM methodology. This leads to a knowledge model, covering all aspects and their integration. The result is a coherent model, without ambiguity in used terms. Also when creating the models, uncovered situations or inconsistency between different parts of a guideline are discovered. In this way, the guideline can be improved.

Finally, a prototype is generated from the created knowledge models, which gives the medical experts more insight in the models created. This helps to iteratively improve the models and from there on the guideline.

The analysis in Cognitatie has another advantage. Changes of the guidelines will be visible in the versions of the documents, pointing out directly where models should be changed. This leads to an efficient and flexible way of handling changes in these documents.

This project proved that using FBM, DMN and BPMN in health care is also a good way of further improving the work done. Of course, the expertise had to come from the domain expert. But the models not only helped to improve the guidelines, it also helped these medical experts in understanding the guidelines better. A more mature piece of model-based software (which in contrast to the prototype meets a pre-defined set of non-functional requirements in addition to the functional requirements) could in the future assist the medical experts in their decisions where and how to follow these guidelines.

References

1. Object Management Group: Business Process Model and Notation (1997). http://www.bpmn. org. Accessed 29 Aug 2018
2. Business Rules Group: Business Rules Manifesto version 2.0 (2003). http://www. businessrulesgroup.org/brmanifesto.htm. Accessed 29 Aug 2018
3. PNA Group: Method (2018). https://www.pna-group.com/en/method/. Accessed 29 Aug 2018
4. PNA Group: Cognitatie (2018). http://www.cognitatie.nl. Accessed 29 Aug 2018
5. Object Management Group: Decision Model and Notation Version 1.2 (2018). http://www. omg.org/spec/DMN/About-DMN/. Accessed 29 Aug 2018
6. Fact Based Modeling: What is Fact Based Modeling (2011). http://www.factbasedmodeling. org. Accessed 29 Aug 2018
7. Lemmens, I.: Integrating modelling disciplines at conceptual semantic level. In: Ciuciu, I., et al. (eds.) OTM 2015. LNCS, vol. 9416, pp. 188–196. Springer, Cham (2015). https://doi. org/10.1007/978-3-319-26138-6_22
8. Richtlijnendatabase: Richtlijnendatabase (2012). https://richtlijnendatabase.nl/en/. Accessed 29 Aug 2018
9. Richtlijnendatabase: Antitrombotisch beleid (Antithrombotic policy) (2016). https:// richtlijnendatabase.nl/richtlijn/antitrombotisch_beleid/antitrombotisch_beleid_-_korte_ beschrijving.html. Accessed 29 Aug 2018

Towards a Complete Metamodel for DEMO CM

Mark A. T. Mulder[✉]

Leusden, Netherlands
mark@mulderrr.nl

Abstract. The Design and Engineering Method for Organisations (DEMO) is the principal methodology in Enterprise Engineering (EE). The Design and Engineering Method for Organisations Specification Language (DEMOSL) states the rules, legends, and metamodel of DEMO. Therefore, any DEMO model must comply with this specification. Moreover, to enable automation of the DEMO model validation, we need a metamodel that can accurately represent DEMO models. In our research we are expanding the DEMOSL to be able to express all DEMO models and rules. This paper reports on the attempt to build this metamodel for four elements of the Construction Model (CM) using mathematical and semantic notation. The findings on the validation done on DEMOSL have been added to the build metamodel. We found the notations to be sufficient to describe and validate the DEMO (CM) models.

1 Introduction

The Design and Engineering Method for Organisations (DEMO) [1] is the principal methodology in Enterprise Engineering [2]. This so-called essential model of an organisation is the integrated whole of four aspect models: the Construction Model (CM), the Action Model (AM), the Process Model (PM) and the Fact Model (FM). Each model is expressed in one or more diagrams and one or more cross-model tables.

The CM is the first and the most comprehensive model to produce when modelling an organisation in DEMO, applying the Organisational Essence Revealing (OER) method. A CM is a model of the construction of an organisation (or rather, of a Scope of Interest), by which is understood the identified transaction kinds and the actor roles that are either executor or initiator of these transaction kinds. The resulting 'network' of transaction kinds and actor roles is always a set of tree structures, which arise from the inherent property that every transaction kind has exactly one elementary actor role as its executor (and vice versa), and that every actor role may be initiator of one or more transaction kinds, or none.

A CM is expressed in an Organisation Construction Diagram (OCD), a Transaction Product Table (TPT) and a Bank Contents Table (BCT). An OCD is a graphical representation of the identified transaction kinds and actor roles, and the links between them. Apart from initiator and executor links, actor roles

© Springer Nature Switzerland AG 2019
C. Debruyne et al. (Eds.): OTM 2018 Workshops, LNCS 11231, pp. 97–106, 2019.
https://doi.org/10.1007/978-3-030-11683-5_10

may also be connected to transaction kinds through information links. They express that the actor role has (reading) access to the history of all transactions of the transaction kind with which it is connected. Therefore, the shape of the transaction kind may also be interpreted as a transaction bank. This paper limits itself to four elements of a CM: Elementary Actor Role (EAR), Composite Actor Role (CAR), Transaction Kind (TK) and Aggregate Transaction Kind (ATK). In the remainder of this paper, we will discuss the DEMO metamodel by first defining the notion of Meta Model. We will subsequently report on our findings on the metamodel for the CM aspect model. We end with conclusions and suggestions for future research.

2   Research Design

This research was conducted using a focus group of professional users of the metamodel. The usage of the DEMO models as well as the requirements for the metamodel were discussed and adapted to the insights collected.

3   Extending DEMOSL

We will use the following definition of a metamodel [3]: "meta-models define sets of valid models, facilitating their transformation, serialization, and exchange." The base of the metamodel is the Design and Engineering Method for Organisations Specification Language (DEMOSL) [4]. This metamodel has been validated [3] and this validation has been taken into account in the metamodel presented in this paper. From this validation paper we know that we have to include eight issues in the metamodel: (a) the Scope of Interest (SoI); (b) interstriction ATK-CAR/SoI; (c) mandatory TK for ATK; (d) interstriction EAR to ATK; (e) CAR to TK relation; (f) TK in CAR relation; (g) CAR hierarchy; (h) mandatory EAR for CAR.

3.1   Extending the Verification Rules

The rules that control the correctness of the model within the meta model can be formulated in mathematical terms of collections. Every entity type in the meta model represents a collection, written bold in the formulas. An instance of an entity type is written in italic. Per entity type we will formulate all relations of the meta model as collections. The base formulas are listed here:

$$
\begin{aligned}
\textbf{construction model} = {}& \textbf{elementary transaction kind} \\
& \cup\ \textbf{elementary actor role} \\
& \cup\ \textbf{composite actor role} \\
& \cup\ \textbf{aggregate transaction kind}
\end{aligned}
\tag{1}
$$

$$
\begin{aligned}
\textbf{actor role} = {}& \textbf{elementary actor role} \\
& \cup\ \textbf{composite actor role}
\end{aligned}
\tag{2}
$$

$$\textbf{elementary actor role} \cap \textbf{composite actor role} = \emptyset \tag{3}$$

$$\textbf{aggregate transaction kind} \cap \textbf{elementary transaction kind} = \emptyset \tag{4}$$

$$\forall x : elementarytransactionkind(x) \iff x \in \textbf{elementary transaction kind} \tag{5}$$

$$\forall x : aggregatetransactionkind(x) \iff x \in \textbf{aggregate transaction kind} \tag{6}$$

$$\forall x : elementaryactorrole(x) \iff x \in \textbf{elementary actor role} \tag{7}$$

$$\forall x : compositeactorrole(x) \iff x \in \textbf{composite actor role} \tag{8}$$

$$\forall x : actorrole(x) \implies elementaryactorrole(x) \lor compositeactorrole(x) \tag{9}$$

$$\forall x : transactionkind(x) \implies elementarytransactionkind(x) \lor aggregatetransactionkind(x) \tag{10}$$

3.2   DEMO Exchange Model

The proposal of a DEMO Exchange model of [5], which is based on DEMO 2 is a good start for the exchange model. It proposes an exchange model for the FM and the CM. The XSD for CM proposes the storage of the id, name, initiator(s), executor, and information link and result type. This information is based on older DEMO specifications and, therefore, lacks important information from the current version.

We will build this XSD structure for every element type in the DEMOSL structure. The whole DEMO model has a name and every component has an internal ID. We will model this name and ID (but we will not mention this in the element explanation).

Guid

The identification of all types and kinds within the exchange model are identified with a Global Unique IDentfier (GUID). A GUID is a 128-bit number used to identify information in computer systems.

Name Conventions

The naming of the elements used in a CM is restricted by rules. One of the rules we will mention in this paper is the transaction kind name. The specification in DEMOSL [4] states that the name is built up of lower case words. This rule can be written in XSD. Note that giving no name is allowed for practical use purposes.

```xml
<xs:simpleType name="TransactionKindName">
  <xs:annotation>
    <xs:documentation>The transaction_kind_name are lower case words.
        </xs:documentation>
  </xs:annotation>
  <xs:restriction base="xs:string">
    <xs:pattern value="[a-z]*([␣][a-z]+)*"/>
  </xs:restriction>
</xs:simpleType>
```

4   Extending DEMOSL for the CM

Different modelling techniques allow for the representation of different properties of the object that is being modelled. Only a combination of those models
will come close to the representation of the whole object. Therefore, for every
component of the meta models we will define

1. Mathematical rules on the collections
    (a) XSD specification for the set
    (b) XSD specification for the item
    (c) XSD specification(s) for the types
    (d) XSD specification for the diagram element
2. Data Model for the item and relations
3. OWL representation.

With this list of models, we think that the representation of the DEMO model is
sufficiently complete to validate the model and exchange information to recreate
the model. We remodelled the meta model according to the findings in [3].

4.1   Transaction Kind

For TK the relation with the CAR was missing in DEMOSL [4]. This relation
has been added in formula 12 *containedinCAR*.

Data Model
The data model in Fig. 1 shows the TransactionSort attribute and the description. The last attribute was added by the focus group to be able to exchange
meta information about the TK.

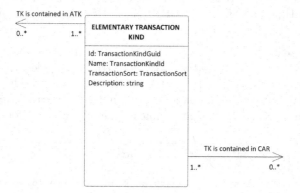

Fig. 1. TK data model

Mathematical Model

The data model relations can be shown in a mathematical way. The relations in the data model denote that a TK can be contained in both an ATK and a CAR. Based on formulas 5, 6, and 8, we can conclude 11 and 12. This last formula solves issue f [3].

$$\forall x, y : TKcontainedinATK(x,y) \implies elementarytransactionkind(x) \land$$
$$aggregatetransactionkind(y) \tag{11}$$

$$\forall x, y : TKcontainedinCAR(x,y) \implies elementarytransactionkind(x) \land$$
$$compositeactorrole(y) \tag{12}$$

When a TK is part of a CAR, the initiator (formula 16) and executor (formula 17) of that TK must also be part of the CAR as in formulas 13 and 14. Only then can we assure that initiation and execution of other transactions are well defined.

$$\forall x, y, p : TKcontainedinCAR(x,y) \land initiator(p,x) \land$$
$$elementaryactorrole(p) \implies EARcontainedinCAR(p,y) \tag{13}$$

$$\forall x, y, p : TKcontainedinCAR(x,y) \land executor(x,p) \land$$
$$elementaryactorrole(p) \implies EARcontainedinCAR(p,y) \tag{14}$$

The example in Fig. 2 shows that CA4, where T2 and T3 are part of CA4, does not comply with formulas 13 and 14 because it is missing the involvement of A1 and A3.

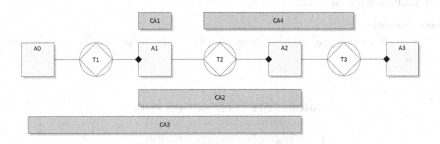

Fig. 2. TK containedinCAR example

Exchange Model

A transaction had the properties of a name, transaction sort, and an identification. We discussed in the focus group to implement the ID of the exchange data as an attribute.

```
<xs:complexType name="TransactionKind">
  <xs:sequence>
    <xs:element name="Identification" type="TransactionKindId"></
        xs:element>
    <xs:element name="Name" type="TransactionKindName"></xs:element>
    <xs:element name="TransactionSort" type="TransactionSort" default
        ="unknown"></xs:element>
  </xs:sequence>
  <xs:attribute name="Id" type="TransactionKindGuid" use="required"/>
</xs:complexType>
```

This exchange rule set described in XSD can sufficiently restrict field content for each TK.

OWL/Turtle Representation

The OWL/Turtle representation [6] allows for defining classes representing the mathematical information. We are building this representation for all entity types, attributes, relations and rules of the data model.

```
:ElementaryTransactionKind a rdfs:Class.
:EtkIdentification a owl:DatatypeProperty;
               rdfs:subClassOf :ElementaryTransactionKind.
:EtkName a owl:DatatypeProperty;
        rdfs:subClassOf :ElementaryTransactionKind.
```

4.2   Aggregate Transaction Kind

The restrictions on the existence of ATK is contained in the TK. ATKs may exist with or without contained TKs.

Data Model

The ATK has the same attributes as the TK, except for the TransactionSort (Fig. 3).

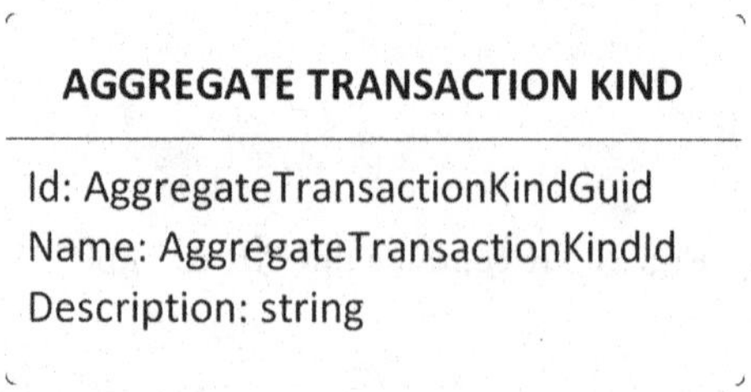

AGGREGATE TRANSACTION KIND

Id: AggregateTransactionKindGuid
Name: AggregateTransactionKindId
Description: string

Fig. 3. DEMOSL ATK metamodel

Mathematical

As can be seen in Fig. 3, no relations are coming from the ATK. Therefore, no collection formulas have been formulated for the ATK.

Exchange Model

In the exchange model the ATK is modelled explicitly. Apart from the TransactionSort element, that is left out, this exchange model is equivalent to the TK exchange model.

4.3   Elementary Actor Role

Data Model

The EAR data-metamodel has five relations to other elements (Fig. 4).

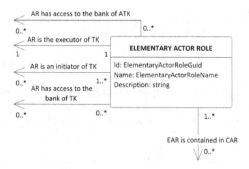

Fig. 4. DEMOSL EAR metamodel

Mathematical

$$\forall x, y : EARcontainedinCAR(x, y) \implies \\ elementaryactorrole(x) \wedge compositeactorrole(y) \tag{15}$$

$$\forall x, y : initiator(x, y) \implies actorrole(x) \wedge elementarytransactionkind(y) \tag{16}$$

$$\forall x, y : executor(x, y) \implies elementarytransactionkind(x) \wedge actorrole(y) \tag{17}$$

$$\forall x, y, z : executor(x, y) \wedge executor(x, z) \wedge \\ elementaryactorrole(y) \wedge elementaryactorrole(z) \implies y = z \tag{18}$$

$$\forall x, y : information(x, y) \implies actorrole(x) \wedge transactionkind(y) \tag{19}$$

Formula 18 makes sure a TK can only be executed by a single EAR.

Formula 19 solves the issues c and d from [3] and the combination of this formula with the inheritance from EAR solves issue b. The inheritance itself solves issue e and h.

The executor of an transaction kind should be an actor role. This can be an elementary actor role or a CAR. When the executor of a TK is an EAR, and this EAR is part of a CAR, the CAR is also an executor of the TK. We use the formulation of CAR and EAR relations, i.e. formula 21. As seen from the execution viewpoint of the transaction kind we get formula 20.

$$\forall x, y, z : executor(x, y) \wedge executor(x, z) \wedge$$
$$elementarytransactionkind(x) \wedge elementaryactorrole(y) \wedge \quad (20)$$
$$compositeactorrole(z) \implies EARcontainedinCAR(z, y)$$

Exchange Model

```
<xs:complexType name="ElementaryActorRole">
  <xs:sequence>
    <xs:element name="Identification" type="ActorRoleId"></xs:element
      >
    <xs:element name="Name" type="ActorRoleName"></xs:element>
  </xs:sequence>
  <xs:attribute name="Id" type="ElementaryActorRoleGuid" use="
      required"/>
</xs:complexType>
```

OWL Representation

```
:executor a [a owl:Restriction ;
            owl:onProperty :executor ;
            owl:onClass :ElementaryTransactionKind ;
            owl:maxQualifiedCardinality "1"^^xsd:int],
            [a owl:Restriction ;
            owl:onProperty :executor ;
            owl:onClass :ElementaryActorRole ;
            owl:maxQualifiedCardinality "1"^^xsd:int],
            owl:ObjectProperty.
```

4.4   Composite Actor Role

Data Model

In the CM, the CAR and the EAR are modelled as separate entity types. By modelling the CAR (Fig. 5) as a specialisation of EAR, the relations of the elementary actor role are also available for the composite actor role. This change allows us to model the composite actor role 'customer' in the pizza case where the customer is the initiator and executor of a TK without any elementary actor roles present.

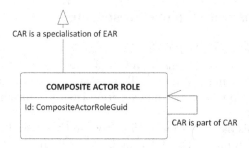

Fig. 5. DEMOSL CAR metamodel

Absent from in the DEMOSL meta model [4], is the SoI itself. We argue that the SoI is equivalent to the CAR When starting a model, the first actor is a composite actor until one is able to retrieve the information to redesign the actor roles into a white box model. The CAR does not vanish. The CAR becomes equal to the SoI as can be seen in Figs. 6 and 7. Therefore the only difference between a SoI and a CAR is its appearance in the diagram.

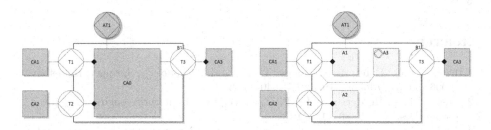

Fig. 6. CM modelling step 1   **Fig. 7.** CM modelling step 2

Mathematical

The *CARispartofCAR* relation describes that the CAR contains another level of CAR. This means that if a CAR is described in more detail, it is connected to the CAR it belongs to.

$$\forall x, y : CARispartofCAR(x,y) \implies compositeactorrole(x) \land$$
$$compositeactorrole(y) \qquad (21)$$
$$\nexists x, y : CARispartofCAR(x,y) \implies CARispartofCAR(y,x)$$

$$\forall x, y, z : executor(x,y) \land executor(x,z) \land$$
$$elementarytransactionkind(x) \land compositeactorrole(y) \land \qquad (22)$$
$$compositeactorrole(z) \implies EARcontainedinCAR(z,y)$$

Exchange Model

The exchange model of the CAR is equivalent to the EAR. The type references have been renamed to match the composite intention.

5 Conclusions and Future Research

Creating a metamodel for DEMO (the CM in particular) is possible from the base DEMOSL created. The omissions found in [3] have been solved using the new data model and mathematical model. The research on OWL is still in progress. We expect it will help us finding the execution rules for automating the mathematical model.

Even though this paper does not explicitly use Fact Based Modelling (FBM) notation, the next topic in DEMO that is going to be meta modelled is the FM. Originally the notation of Object Role Modeling (ORM) has been used in DEMO 2 to express the facts in a graphical way, including the instantiation of the model with examples. The metamodel of the CM is, in fact, modelled using ORM, and simplified using the DEMO 3 notation.

In practice, modelling the CM is done using the same method as the one used for modelling the data. Therefore, part of the research is evaluating the amount of benefit by using FBM methods.

We will further expand this metamodel to cover the whole of DEMO and to be able to exchange all information currently used in DEMO models around the world.

References

1. Dietz, J.L.G.: Enterprise Ontology: Theory and Methodology. Springer, Heidelberg (2006). https://doi.org/10.1007/3-540-33149-2
2. Dietz, J.L.G., Hoogervorst, J.A.P.: The discipline of enterprise engineering. Int. J. Organ. Des. Eng. **3**, 86–114 (2013)
3. Mulder, M.A.T.: Cross channel communication design critical literature review. In: Aveiro, D., Pergl, R., Gouveia, D. (eds.) EEWC 2016. LNBIP, vol. 252, pp. 166–180. Springer, Cham (2016). https://doi.org/10.1007/978-3-319-39567-8_11
4. Dietz, J.L.G., Mulder, M.A.T.: Demo specification language 3.7 (2017)
5. Wang, Y., Albani, A., Barjis, J.: Transformation of DEMO metamodel into XML schema. In: Albani, A., Dietz, J.L.G., Verelst, J. (eds.) EEWC 2011. LNBIP, vol. 79, pp. 46–60. Springer, Heidelberg (2011). https://doi.org/10.1007/978-3-642-21058-7_4
6. Hitzler, P., Krotsch, M., Parsia, B., Rudolph, S.: OWL 2 Web Ontology Language Primer, 2nd edn. (2012). https://www.w3.org/tr/2012/rec-owl2-primer-20121211/

The Lifecycle of a User Transaction in a Hyperledger Fabric Blockchain Network Part 1: Propose and Endorse

Sjir Nijssen[1] and Peter Bollen[2(✉)]

[1] Heerlen, The Netherlands
Sjir.Nijssen@pna-group.com
[2] Maastricht University, Maastricht, The Netherlands
p.bollen@maastrichtuniversity.nl

Abstract. The paper describes the happy and the less happy flows of a user transaction through a Hyperledger Fabric Blockchain Network. The full cycle of a user transaction originates from the Client Application (an actor outside the Hyperledger Ledger Network but inside an organization that is part of a set that runs the Hyperledger Fabric Blockchain Network). In the process of making the Hyperledger Fabric Blockchain network knowledge explicit, essential parts of FBM were applied in cooperation with the developers of the Fabric Blockchain platform. The approach was given the name Visual Vocabulary by the Documentation Working Group of Hyperledger Fabric, a visual vocabulary to represent instances of facts.

1 Introduction

In this paper a high level conceptual overview of the life cycle of an end user transaction is described, from its birth in a client application that is part of an organization that is part of a Hyperledger Fabric Blockchain business network to its eternal "life" in the immutable blockchain.

A step by step description of the development from birth of a business transaction, via various intermediate transitions and states will be described, while providing no single point of failure in the Fabric Blockchain business network; no undetected tempering with recorded knowledge, or immutability of the data and secure communication over the internet. Fabric works only with principals (humans and software agents) that are identified, i.e. have been given a digital Identity by a trusted Certificate Authority. Decision making in a distributed network based on agreed rules (called policies in Fabric) and highly scalable to its final immutable state, the eternal "life" in the blockchain. Hence one could say that for the concept of business transaction, software mankind has found the road towards "immutable immortality". In this article we will explain the first two stages of this transaction life cycle: *Proposing* and *Endorsing*. The conceptual architecture of Fabric is described in [1–4]. Some

---

Sjir Nijssen—Retired from PNA, Heerlen, The Netherlands.

C. Debruyne et al. (Eds.): OTM 2018 Workshops, LNCS 11231, pp. 107–116, 2019.
https://doi.org/10.1007/978-3-030-11683-5_11

blockchain basics are described in [5] and [6]. The unique functionalities of Fabric are described in [7]. The official documentation of the most recent release of Fabric (v1.2, June 2018) is described in [8].

2 Specialization of Nodes in a HyperLedger Fabric Network

The main difference between the permissioned Hyperledger Fabric (HFL) blockchain technology (the largest open source project of the Linux Foundation in history so far) and the extensively publicized technologies underlying crypto-currencies such as Bitcoin, is that Hyperledger Fabric can be used in hospitals, teaching institutions, interactive regulation based government services as the actors are digitally identified by a trusted Certificate Authority, in general in a business environment, and is highly scalable.

It is good for scalability and performance to have the workhorses in Hyperledger Fabric, the nodes, specialized by task. There are three kinds of workshorses, jointly called nodes. A unique characteristic of the HLF architecture is the specialization of the nodes into three related subclasses: *Endorsers*, *Committers* and *Orderers*.

2.1   The Endorsing Peers

The endorsers, a selectable subset of the committing peers, have as task to analyze the transaction proposed by the Client Application, check the signatures and apply if required (hence with an update transaction) by the Client Application, the services of a smart contract. This means a *simulation* of the transaction on the current World State, without modifying the World State. However the endorsers take a copy of all the relevant key-value pairs in the World State and generate the insert and delete statements to be used by the committing peers later in the transaction cycle, assuming the transaction is declared valid. The endorsers can obtain rules, called policies in Fabric, about the domain of the business transaction.

2.2   The Ordering Nodes

Ordering nodes (orderers), sometimes referred to as ordering system, are business domain agnostic. Their job is to guarantee that in a distributed network with many transactions coming in asynchronously and concurrently, from different client applications in different organizations and in different channels, the sequence of transactions submitted is correctly ordered in a block of the HLF blockchain in a specific application channel. In a Fabric network there is exactly one system channel and one or more application channel(s), each having their own blockchain. Hence such a block is primarily composed by the orderers. The orderers are nodes that have no task in common with the endorsing nor committing peers. Therefore no orderer peer can be a committing peer, and thus also no endorsing peer. This is a major design requirement for scalability.

2.3   The Committing Peers

The committing peers receive a proposed block of transactions from the orderer nodes. Each (committing) peer checks that each transaction of the block proposed by the orderers satisfies the endorsement policy, and that no concurrency problem has occurred.

3   The Life Cycle of a User Transaction

In this chapter we will discuss the first steps that together form the first phase of the 'happy path' of a user transaction through a Hyperledger Fabric Network. In the HLF documentation this entire process is divided into 3 phases, the (proposing and) endorsing phase, the ordering phase and the validation-committing phase. These three phases are referred to as Proposal, Packaging and Validation in the Peer topic in the documentation [8], section Chapter Key Concepts, subsection Peers. We will illustrate each state of the user transaction and each subsequent sub transition between principals in the context of the transaction execution time architecture, also known as the conceptual transaction flow, as presented in Fig. 1. Please note how the chain aspect is realized in the blockchain as each block holds a copy of the hash of the payload of the previous block. In this article we will focus on the endorsing phase in the Fabric network(inclusive the proposing sub-phase in the Client application outside the Fabric network but connected via an application channel to the Fabric network).

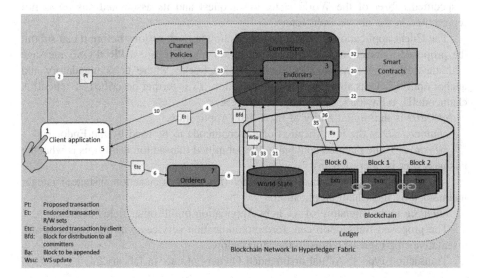

Fig. 1. Conceptual transaction flow architecture

The set Endorsers usually consists of several nodes per organization to neutralize the single point of failure syndrome. The set Committers is a superset of the Endorsers.

3.1   Further Discussion of the Preparation of the Proposed Transaction

The first action (see the finger pointing to 1 in the architecture diagram in Fig. 1) is the preparation by the Client application of a proposed transaction. The client application will very probably have a business user with a digital identity filling in a screen.

The Client application may first ask a committing peer to consult the World State (this consultation is not explicitly presented in the architecture above) and provide those facts to the Client Application such that it can check that the data integrity rules are satisfied, if the proposed transaction would be added to the current World State.

The client application formulates the business transaction and sends the proposed transaction to a selected group of peers, called endorsers. In the latest Fabric version (1.2; June 2018) [8] the client application can use the so called discovery service to find out "dynamically at run time" which are the current endorsers in this application channel, usually operated by more than one organization.

3.2   The Initial Actions by the Client Application Inside Itself

The initial actions by the Client Application is to prepare a proposed transaction of any of the relevant types, before the proposed transaction is submitted to Endorsers of the HLF Network, in a specific application channel. This is a sub activity of the work of the Client application, hence an intra-principal activity, and this sub activity is given the code 1 (see principal Client Application Fig. 1). In this sub activity it is assumed that the Client application will ask a committing peer to provide the Client application with a specified subset of the World state; this request and its associated answer is **not** represented in the above architecture.

The Client application must perform the following sub actions before it can submit the proposed transaction: the Client Application must prepare a PROPOSE message with the following format <PROPOSE, tx, [anchor]>, where tx is mandatory and anchor optional. Tx is abbreviation for transaction. Tx is further described as <clientID, chaincodeID, txPayload, timestamp, clientSig>.

clientID is the digital entity of the Client Application.

chaincodeID is the identification of the chaincode to be used by the Endorsers.

txPayload is the payload containing the submitted transaction itself (this is what the business user is interested in).

timestamp is a monotonically increasing (for every transaction instance) integer maintained by the Client Application.

clientSig is the signature of a Client Application on all other fields of tx.

The proposed transaction can, for communication services with the business representatives, be represented as in the table below:

Transaction type 1: Actual or Intended Owners of cars in fabcarv2

DiID	DateAdmitted	FirstName	NotValidBeforeDate	NotValidAfterDate	Txn-nr
30	2018-01-05	Tomoko	2017-11-30	2022-11-30	1

Fact pattern 1:
The actual or intended car owner with digital id <DiID>, also known as <FirstName> was admitted to the Fabric network on <StartDate>.
The *fact instance* is then for part of transaction 1:
The actual or intended car owner with digital id 30, also known as Tomoko, was admitted to the network on 2018-01-05.

Fact pattern 2:
The certificate of the actual or intended car owner with digital id <DiID> is not valid before <NotValidBeforedate> and not valid after <NotValidAfterDate>.
The *fact instance* is then for the remaining part of transaction 1:
The certificate of the actual or intended car owner with digital id 30 is not valid before 2017-11-30 and not valid after 2022-11-30.

These fact representations of transactions are introduced to have as many non-developer experts as needed in the multidisciplinary decision making about the implementation of a Hyperledger Fabric supported business system. It is assumed that we are at the beginning of populating the ledger, hence the Blockchain on the specific application channel (not the System Channel) is empty as well as the World State.

The Client application will now use its private key to sign the proposed transaction and the Client will encrypt the contents of the proposed transaction (called the payload), to avoid that the contents of the transmission to the endorsers can be seen to non-intended parties. The Client Applications asks an endorsing peer to provide it with the list of endorsing peers that need to be consulted for a given transaction type in a channel, including the associated smart contract. It is recommended that the submitting Client Application addresses a few more than all the endorsers that need to endorse the proposed transaction in order to satisfy the relevant endorsement policy, to avoid the single point of failure syndrome.

The first inter-principal element in the user transaction execution workflow is the transmission of a proposed transaction by the Client Application to the Endorsing peers (see Fig. 2). The Application submits the proposed transaction to every relevant endorser. In a multi-organizational HLF network this in most cases means the agreement of at least one endorser of each organization in the application channel.

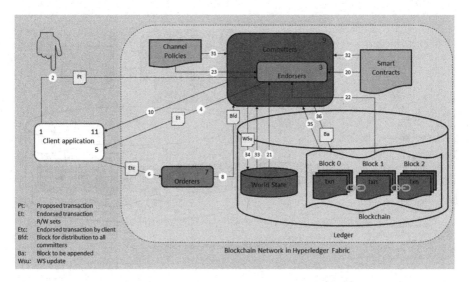

Fig. 2. Conceptual transaction flow architecture

The Client Application is required to indicate to the Endorsers which Smart Contract need to be used. The smart contract is made known by the Client Application to the endorsers by the variable chaincodeID in the message, or proposed transaction. Remember that smart contract is a synonym for application chain code. The Client Application from this moment on in the transaction cycle can only wait for the responses of the Endorsing peers. Of course the Client Application can prepare the next transaction of this type, or the next transaction of another type as this communication is asynchronously. In this case (fabcar, used in the Fabric documentation) an example of a transaction of another type would be the introduction of a new car in the system, or the transfer of ownership of a car, or the change of color of an existing car.

3.3   The Actions by the Endorsers

In this sub section the intra-endorser actions are discussed as a response to a transaction proposed by the Client Application (see Fig. 3). For reasons to avoid single points of failures there are several endorsing nodes, also called endorsing peers. They are collectively called Endorsers in the diagram in Fig. 3. Each endorsing peer independently *simulates* the transaction proposal using a smart contract to generate an individual transaction response, independent of the other endorsing peers. In the Fabric jargon the two terms readset and writeset are used. The readset is the set of key-value pairs that is consulted by the smart contract in the world state and the write set is the set of delete and insert pairs that need to be applied to the world state later by the committing peers.

In the Hyperledger Fabric documentation this type of transaction is described as a message of type PROPOSE.

Each endorser peer checks that the proposed transaction is properly signed by an authorized client application by comparing the clientSig attribute of the tx (this specific

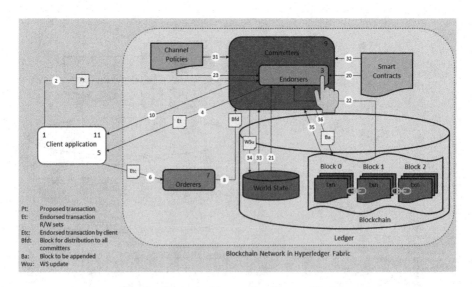

Fig. 3. Conceptual transaction flow architecture

transaction instance) with the knowledge the Client application obtains from the MSP (Membership Service Provider) files.

If the proposed transaction is not properly signed, an Endorser may (!) give in the answer to the Client Application the decision that for this transaction proposal this endorsing peer has given the no-endorsement. The endorser will check that the proposed transaction has not been submitted in the past. This is called replay-attack protection. The endorser checks the required authorization

The endorser checks if this Client application is authorized to perform this type of transaction on this application channel. Hence each endorsing peer ensures that the submitting Client application satisfies the Writers policy of the application channel with respect to this transaction. The endorser uses information flow 23 in the architecture diagram (see Fig. 3). An Endorser will use a Smart contract via information flow 20 to check data integrity rules that are local to an instance of this transaction type (see Fig. 3).

3.3.1   The Endorser Simulates the Transaction

Each addressed Endorser *simulates* the transaction, without performing any actual change to the World State. However the endorser lists the data read from the World State, namely key, attribute, value and version, referred to as readset. This data is later used by the committers in the distributed concurrency control, to check that at commitment time the World State is still the same as it was at simulation time by the endorser. The endorser also produces (in case of an update transaction) a list of inserts and deletes to be applied (later) by the committers to the World State, the writeset.

3.3.2   Prepare the Read Part of the Read-Write Set

An Endorsers records the data from the World State they have used for the simulation and include these data in the read part of the so-called Read-Write set. These data are later in the transaction flow used by the Committing peers for the management of distributed concurrency.

The check to be performed later by the Committers is to find out whether or not the World state has been changed and this can be done by comparing the hash of the involved part of the World State provided by the Endorser and the hash obtained by the Committer of the latest version of the involved part of the World State.

3.3.3   Prepare the Write Part of the Read-Write Set

The Endorser records the data that would have to be added to, and/or deleted from the World State in the Write part of the Read Write set.

We know from the carfabv.2 that color of a car is modifiable. In such a case the key-value pairs look as follows:

Carkey	Color	Version	DateTime
CAR0	Blue	0	2018-01-26-13:00
CAR0	Yellow	1	2018-01-31-15:00
CAR0	Blue	2	2018-02-01-13:00

In fact form:

The car identified by Carkey CARO has the color blue as version 0 since 2018-01-26-13:00.

The car identified by Carkey CARO has the color yellow as version 1 since 2018-01-31-15:00.

The car identified by Carkey CARO has the color blue as version 2 since 2018-02-01-13:00.

These facts are called versioned *key-value pairs* in Hyperledger Fabric. In the key-value pair, the value part may consist of a set of attribute-value pairs.

3.3.4   The Endorsers Pack the Payload, Encrypt It and Sign It

The last task of each Endorser is to attach the Read Write set to the proposed transaction, encrypt it and sign it with its private key. The endorsers first read the World State and the answer in this test scenario is: the World State is empty. If endorsing logic decides to endorse a transaction, it sends

<TRANSACTION-ENDORSED, tid, tran-proposal,epSig>

message to the submitting client(tx.clientID), where:

tran-proposal := (epID,tid,chaincodeID,txContentBlob,readset,writeset),

where

txContentBlob is chaincode/transaction specific information. The intention is to have   txContentBlob   used   as   some   representation   of   tx   (e.g., txContentBlob=tx.txPayload).

epSig is the endorsing peer's signature on tran-proposal

Else, in case the endorsing logic refuses to endorse the transaction, an endorser *may* send a message (TRANSACTION-INVALID, tid, REJECTED) to the submitting client. Notice that an endorser does not change its World state in this step, the updates produced by transaction simulation in the context of endorsement do not affect the World state!

3.3.5   Each Endorsing Peer Sends the Answer to the Proposed Transaction to the Application Client

Each Endorsing peer sends his reaction independent of the other endorsing peers to the proposed transaction, to the submitting Client Application. His reaction contains the original proposed transaction and the Read Write set (in case of an update transaction) and as well the fact that the Endorser has decided to endorse the proposed transaction. (See Fig. 4). When the Client application receives the responses of the endorsers, it collects them until it has obtained sufficient endorsements according to the Endorsing policy (hence knowledge must be obtainable by the Client application from a peer) (see

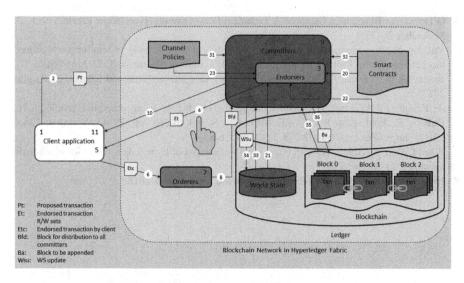

Fig. 4. Conceptual transaction flow architecture

Fig. 4). The submitting client waits until it receives "enough" messages and signatures on (TRANSACTION-ENDORSED, tid, *, *) statements to conclude that the transaction proposal is endorsed. The exact number of "enough" depend on the endorsement policy. If the endorsement policy is satisfied, the transaction has been *endorsed*; note that it is not yet committed. The collection of signed TRANSACTION-ENDORSED messages from endorsing peers which establish that a transaction is endorsed is called an *endorsement* and denoted by endorsement. If the submitting client does not manage to collect an endorsement for a transaction proposal, it abandons this transaction with an option to retry later.

4   Conclusion

In this paper we have analyzed the endorsing stage in the hyperledger fabric user transaction cycle using essential parts of FBM, namely using concrete examples expressed as facts. We have illustrated each step in the endorsement phase of the transaction life cycle with a concrete example of transaction based on the car owner case.

References

1. Androulaki, E., et al.: Hyperledger fabric: a distributed operating system for permissioned blockchains, 30 January 2018
2. The Hyperledger Vision: Hyperledger, Blockchain Technologies for Business (2017)

3. O'Dowd, A.: Blockchain Explored A Technical Deep-Dive on Hyperledger Fabric, vol. 1, 29 November 2017
4. Vukolic, M.: Hyperledger fabric an open source distributed operating system for permissioned blockchains, Swiss Blockchain Summer School, Lausanne, Switzerland, 22 June 2017
5. Brakeville, S., Parepa, B.: Blockchain basics: introduction to distributed ledgers, 21 August 2017
6. de Kruijff, J., Weigand, H.: Understanding the blockchain using enterprise ontology. In: Dubois, E., Pohl, K. (eds.) CAiSE 2017. LNCS, vol. 10253, pp. 29–43. Springer, Cham (2017). https://doi.org/10.1007/978-3-319-59536-8_3
7. Weed Cocco, S., Singh, G.: Top 6 technical advantages of hyperledger fabric for blockchain networks, 21 August 2017
8. Hyperledger-Fabricdocs Documentation, Release master, June 2018

FBM Helps SVB to Improve PGB Service

Jean-Paul Koster[✉] and Roel Baardman

PNA Group, Heerlen, The Netherlands
{jean.paul.koster, roel.baardman}@pna-group.com

Abstract. Processes describe consecutive activities that must be performed by different parties in order to provide products or services. These processes use a common data model from which facts can be requested, inserted to, changed in or deleted from. This in order to realise the requested services or products. The organizational unit DPGB of the Dutch SVB is partly responsible for the execution of the processes that provide the services regarding personal care budgets, i.e. the PGB-domain. The complete PGB-domain is being described, from the data model including all applicable rules and concept definitions, to the processes and the services. These descriptions are done implementation independent, among others by detaching processes from any means of communication (internet, phone, paper) and by detaching from implementation locations within the PGB-domain. A global conceptual model is developed for the complete PGB-domain and divided into local conceptual models depending on the chosen implementation locations, which also provides insight in the communication structure between the chosen implementation locations.

Keywords: Fact-based modelling · Process modelling ·
Global and local conceptual data models

1 Introduction

The organizational unit DPGB of the Dutch SVB is, together with other parties, responsible for the execution and maintenance of the process of the so-called PGB-domain, in order to perform the requested services in a correct and timely manner to the involved stakeholders. One of the challenges faced by the DPGB is that the services regarding the personal care budget are delivered by a large number of processes by different stakeholders that not all have the exact same or common understanding of these processes and the elements they consist of. I.e. the different stakeholders don't have a common understanding of the concepts, fact types, rules and data the processes are based or build upon. The DPGB therefore decided to start using fact-based modelling and more specific the cogNIAM methodology in order to fully describe the complete PGB-domain and by doing so achieve a common understanding between the different stakeholders. The first goal or ambition is to achieve this common understanding within the DPGB itself.

The cogNIAM methodology describes a domain in a complete, consistent and fully integrated way, as is depicted in the so-called "Knowledge molecule" of Fig. 1.

© Springer Nature Switzerland AG 2019
C. Debruyne et al. (Eds.): OTM 2018 Workshops, LNCS 11231, pp. 117–125, 2019.
https://doi.org/10.1007/978-3-030-11683-5_12

Fig. 1. Knowledge molecule.

The knowledge molecule of Fig. 1 indicates that by using the cogNIAM methodology processes, data and rules are described in a fully integrated way with the applicable semantics, i.e. the common understanding placed at the center of all this.

In the following chapter we first introduce fact base modelling as is provided by cogNIAM. In Sect. 3 is discussed how cogNIAM and the use of global and local modelling can help keeping process clearer, i.e. less implementation dependent.

2   Fact-Based Modelling (FBM) – cogNIAM

Fact-based modelling or cogNIAM is a modelling methodology for modelling information at a conceptual level. Conceptual is to be understood as completely independent of any software implementation technology; that is, the concepts used and means of expression do not refer in any way to a possible implementation strategy like e.g. relational, object-oriented or hierarchical. The methodology applies formal modeling based on logic and controlled natural language. The resulting conceptual model captures the semantics of the relevant domain of interest by means of fact types (kind of facts), together with the associated concept definitions – the terms and definitions, the communication patterns as well as the rules applying to these fact types – the system requirements related to the information model.

One of the distinguishing factors of fact-based modeling (compared to other modeling notations) is the fact that validation and testing is integrated in every step of the conceptual modeling process associated to the system requirements production. That is, all intermediate results are validated with the stakeholders before any implementation activity starts. This validation is performed by the use of concrete examples of fact type populations and associated verbalizations in a notation and language a stakeholder is familiar with.

2.1   The Knowledge Triangle

The knowledge triangle is a three-level knowledge framework that over the years has proven to be very productive for developing fact-based conceptual models. It can be considered as an additional stratification of knowledge categories in which logical reasoning is applied. The knowledge triangle is also a visual aid in the development of fact-based conceptual modelling. The knowledge triangle is depicted in Fig. 2.

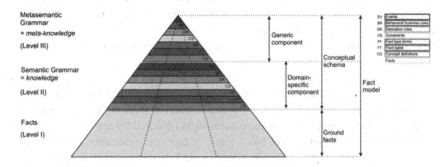

Fig. 2. Knowledge triangle.

Level I: The Ground Facts or Assertions

The assumption of fact-based modelling methodologies is that the most concrete level in any structured knowledge description or business communication consists of ground facts. It is observed that these comprise the vast majority in business, engineering or technical communication.

A ground fact is defined as "a proposition taken to be true by a relevant community" and is expressed as an assertion that either simply predicates over individual objects or simply asserts the existence of an individual object. Examples are: "The healthcare agreement between budget keeper ABC and healthcare specialist 123 started on the 12th of March 2018", "Declaration D212 of budget keeper ABC represents a total value of 234,87 euro" and "Provider Utrecht is a municipality".

Ground facts, expressed by means of sentences, describe factual, planned or imagined situations, in the past, current time or future; they do not prescribe any grammar aspect.

Level II: The Semantic Grammar of the Domain

Level II of the knowledge triangle consists of the domain specific conceptual model. It consists of knowledge categories to which the ground facts of level I must adhere as well as concept definitions to understand the ground facts; it could be said it provides interpretation semantics. In other words, level II specifies the rules that govern the ground facts at level I and defines the concept definitions of the terms used in the facts, so there can be no doubt they could be misunderstood. Moreover, the usage of ground facts is also described at this level. Level II is expressed by means of a series of knowledge categories, namely:

1. *Concept definitions*, which have as function to describe the meaning of every term or group of terms in the ground facts for which it is assumed that the meaning is not fully known to the intended audience and common understanding of the meaning is required. In case the meaning of a term is assumed to be known it is good practice to state this explicitly in order to avoid any confusion.
2. *Fact types*, which provide the functionality to define which kinds of ground facts are considered to be within *scope* of the system, subject or domain of interest. A fact type is a populatable construct, generalizing level I ground facts on the basis of common properties. The boundary (scope) of the system, subject or domain is determined by its set of fact types.
3. *Fact type forms i.e. communication patterns*, whereby there is a distinction between:
   a. *Fact communication patterns*: their function is to act as a communication mechanism to be used as a template to communicate ground facts in a language and using terms the subject matter expert is familiar with. A fact communication pattern is a template whereby the placeholders (denoted by angle brackets can be instantiated by ground level fact values. A fact communication pattern associated with one of the example above would be: *"Declaration <Declaration Id> of budget keeper <Budget keeper Id> represents a total value of <Total value>"*.
   b. *Rule communication patterns*, whose function is to act as communication mechanism for communicating the rules, listed in point 4 below, of the conceptual model. The rule communication pattern associated with the example is: *"[Declaration] of [Budget keeper] represents [Total value]"*. Instantiation might result in the following rule: *"Each [Declaration] of a [Budget keeper] represents exactly one [Total value]"*.

Both types of communication patterns use community-specific terminology.

4. *Constraints*, also known as "integrity rules" or "validation rules", have as function to restrict the set of ground facts and the transitions between the permitted sets of ground facts to those that are considered useful. In other words, integrity rules have the function to restrict populations as well as transitions between populations to useful ones.
5. *Derivation rules*, which are used to derive or calculate new information i.e. ground facts on the basis of existing information. That is, derivation rules describe how to derive new ground facts on the basis of existing ground facts.
6. *Behavioral (business) rules*, which have as function to move ground facts from the domain under consideration into the administration of that domain and vice versa, or to remove ground facts from the administration. In other words, they specify how ground facts are added and/or removed from the system such that the system stays in sync with the communication about the outside world.
7. *Events i.e. event rules*, which specify when to update the set of ground facts by a derivation rule or behavioral rule. That is, an event specifies under which circumstances the set of facts at level I of the knowledge triangle is updated.

The combination of derivation rules, behavioral rules and event rules constitute the process descriptions within the domain specific conceptual model. I.e. they specify when which operations have to be performed by whom, in order to deliver the requested services or products to the relevant stakeholders.

Level III: The Generic Component of the Knowledge Triangle
The third level of the knowledge triangle, the generic component, independent of any specific domain, consists of the knowledge categories to which each conceptual model at level II must adhere. In other words, Level III of the knowledge triangle consists of the generic conceptual model, expressed in the same knowledge categories as any domain-specific conceptual model. Each element in the generic component of the knowledge triangle or the generic conceptual model is independent of any specific part of the domain or system. Interestingly enough, the generic conceptual model is a population of itself.

3   Conceptual Data Model as a Common Basis for Processes

As mentioned in the previous chapter the cogNIAM methodology provides a methodology for modelling at conceptual level, i.e. implementation independent modelling. The cogNIAM methodology furthermore distinguishes between a structural

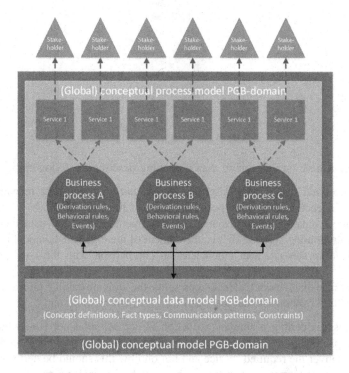

Fig. 3. Conceptual data model as a basis for processes.

and a structuring part in conceptual modelling. The structural part of the methodology specifies all the concepts definitions, fact types, fact type forms and constraints that are of interest to a domain, also called the data (model) perspective. The structuring part of the methodology specifies how and when the different concepts of a domain are used and/or created and by whom, i.e. the derivation rules, behavioral rules and event rules. This is also called the process perspective and is used to specify the processes within a domain. Figure 3 indicates that a (global) conceptual model of domain, for instance the PGB-domain, consist of one common (global) conceptual data model that is the basis for all processes that deliver the different services in that domain. This because all these processes insert, read, update and delete facts described by the common conceptual data model in order to deliver their services.

In data modelling it is common to distinguish the following levels of modelling: conceptual, logical and physical as illustrated by Fig. 4.

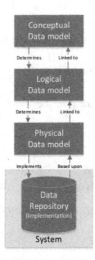

Fig. 4. Levels of modelling.

In general these three levels of data modelling describe the following:

1. The conceptual data model describes the *semantics* of the data relevant to the domain, independently of any possible means of implementation.
2. The logical data model anticipates the implementation of the data model on a specific computing system. That is, the content of the logical data model is adjusted to achieve certain practical efficiencies in comparison with the conceptual data model.
3. The physical data model, which represents the domain taking into account the facilities and restrictions that are part of a given (storage) system.

In process modelling a similar distinction is not common but would have great benefit because the initial focus of process modelling could be on what should be done in order to deliver the required service and not on how this should be performed. Two main issues are of interest in order to establish such similar distinction, being:

1. make use of one common conceptual data model on which the processes are described.
2. detach processes from means of communication.

3.1   Use of One Common Conceptual Data Model

In Fig. 3 it is shown that the PGB-domain makes use of one common conceptual data model i.e. one global conceptual data model, while within the PGB-domain at least the following sub or local domains could be distinguished that could have their own local conceptual data model:

1. The provider domain, where providers provide personal care budgets to people in need of health care, that want to arrange their own health care.
2. The so-called Z-domain, i.e. the health care ('Zorg') domain. This domain describes all arrangements needed in order to support people with a personal care budget that arrange their own health care.
3. The so-called F-domain, i.e. the financial domain. This domain describes all the financial consequences of what is performed in the Z-domain.

Figure 5 shows that the global conceptual data model for the PGB-domain also contains the provider, Z and F domain, i.e. also consists of the concept definitions, fact types, communication patterns and constraints of the conceptual data models for these (local) domains. Figure 5 also indicates that some elements of the global conceptual data model are part of more than one local domain, i.e. these domains overlap.

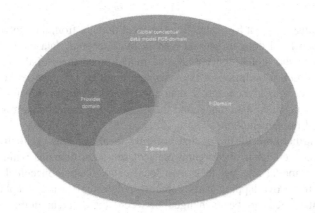

Fig. 5. Global and local conceptual data models.

Making use of one common or global data model of which the different local conceptual data models are part, provides the possibility to develop and describe the different processes on top of this (one) global conceptual and therefore not being concerned about the eventually needed communication at first. This makes the initial development and description of processes less complex and clearer.

Figure 6 illustrates the consequences of abstracting the local conceptual data models from the global conceptual for implementing the local domain in different i.e. separate locations.

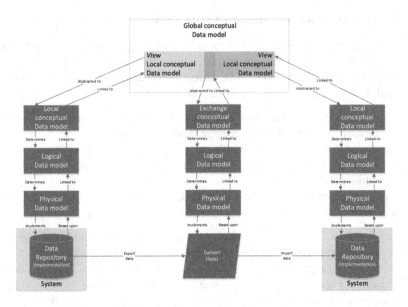

Fig. 6. Abstraction of local domains.

Figure 6 illustrates that by abstracting the local domain from the global conceptual data model each local domain gets its own local conceptual data model, that should remain linked to the global conceptual data model since the global conceptual data model is the central description of the complete domain. I.e. changes are only to be committed to the global conceptual data model and from there persevered to the relevant local conceptual data model and their underlying logical data model, physical data model and implementation.

Figure 6 furthermore illustrates that not only local domains get their own (local) conceptual data model but overlapping parts of the local domains within the global conceptual data model also get their own local or exchange conceptual data model. This because these overlapping parts contain or describe (in a conceptual way) the information that needs to be exchanged between the different domains. I.e. these overlapping parts determine the structure, meaning and rules of messages to be exchanged between the different local or sub domains.

The abstraction of local domains also results in a delta to process descriptions on top of the global conceptual data model, for instance for indicating when messages are to be send and when should be reacted to incoming messages.

3.2 Detaching Processes from Means of Communication

Within the PGB-domain a budget keeper declares the costs of his health care in order to deduct these costs from his health care budget, which is managed by the DPGB, in order to pay his health care professional. The budget keeper has the possibility to submit these declarations on paper or via portal on the internet. In case the healthcare budget of the budget keeper is not sufficient to pay his declaration, he has the opportunity to submit a deposit to his health care budget so that his healthcare professional can be payed despite of his insufficient healthcare budget. The budget keeper can make this deposit directly via the internet (Ideal) or via a separate transition via his bank. I.e. the budget keeper has can choose how he submits his declaration and how he makes a deposit in case he has an insufficient budget, while what he actually does (submitting a declaration or making a deposit) is exactly the same.

Detaching from means of communication or how actions are performed provides means for modelling processes at conceptual level similar to modelling data at conceptual level. This since choosing a means of communication can be considered as an implementation issue and conceptual modelling is considered to be implementation independent. Developing a logical process model and consequently a physical process model would therefore mean adjusting or adding elements to the conceptual process model to provide means for the chosen means of communication.

4 Conclusions

In this paper it is stated that the initial focus of process modelling should be on what is to be done in order to provide a certain service to stakeholder, instead on how it is to be done. I.e. process modelling should be done at conceptual level first without focus on the implementation of the process. This can be realized by making use of one common conceptual data model on which the processes are described and by detaching processes from means of communication. The first makes it possible to abstract from communications between sub or local domains and there implementations, while the second makes it possible to abstract from the implementation of the processes. All this makes it possible to focus on what has to performed in order to realize a service.

References

ECSS: ECSS-E-TM-10-23A: space engineering – space system data Repository, Noordwijk, The Netherlands (2011)

ESA/ESTEC: Fact based modeling unifying system toward implementation solutions for ECSS-E-TM-10-23A, Contract No. 4000107725/13/NL/GLC/al (2013)

Nijssen, G.M.: A framework for discussion in ISO/TC97/SC5/WG3 and comments on 78.04/01 and 78.05/03 (1978)

Lemmens, I., Valera, S., Koster, J.P.: Achieving interoperability at semantic level. In: PV 2013, Ensuring Long-Term Preservation and Adding Value to Scientific and Technical Data (2013)

OMG: OMG Business Process Model and Notation™ Version 2.0

Agile Needs FBM

Jean-Paul Koster[⊠] and Roel Baardman

PNA Group, Heerlen, The Netherlands
{Jean.Paul.Koster,Roel.Baardman}@pna-group.com

Abstract. Although many organisations switch to agile methods for achieving desired changes, reality is that in spite of all efforts certain areas are not organized for agile. In particular changes in organisation and processes are by structure more fit for a waterfall approach. Unless of course this structure is also improved. By default, an organisation maintains an organisation diagram, a process diagram, a data model, and sometimes rules and definitions, without integration. A user story would focus on changing one of these elements. The idea of agile however is that a user story leads to an MVP (Minimal Viable Product), delivered in just 1 sprint of a few weeks. An MVP must be a product that is ready for use, i.e. by software developers and in this case consists of an integrated set of organisational, process, and data models, with the rules and definitions, that precisely match the user story.

Keywords: Fact-based modelling · Agile · Scrum · MVP · User story · Integration · Modelling

1 Introduction

Agile project management [1] emerged in the field of information systems development in the nineties of last century and became a popular method of project management. To date over 30 project management methods are considered to be agile. One of the most used agile methods is agile scrum [2]. In this paper we will concentrate on agile scrum.

Agile scrum comes with a number of artefacts: Organizational (like Program, Tribe, Scrum team, Product Owner, Scrum Master, Team member), Meetings (like Daily stand up, Sprint planning, Retrospective, Demo, Refinement, Brown paper sessions, Storytelling), Goalsetting (like Saga, Epic, Feature, User story, Task) and periods (Program duration, Quarter, Sprint). Not all artefacts are always in use. A program will only be set up for large and complex products to be delivered. In this paper we will concentrate on the artefacts that play a role in every agile scrum approach.

Developing and implementing software is more than just coding new functionalities. It often comes with changes to the user organization, it may affect customers and suppliers, it requires helpdesk to update its knowledge and documentation, and much more. In old school development large documents were written trying to fulfill all the needs for the whole system in sequential runs, like "requirements", "global design", "detailed design", "input and output descriptions", "process model" and "data model". And after the long period of writing these documents were given to the developers for coding. Leading to problems like: "Requirements are not valid any more",

© Springer Nature Switzerland AG 2019
C. Debruyne et al. (Eds.): OTM 2018 Workshops, LNCS 11231, pp. 126–134, 2019.
https://doi.org/10.1007/978-3-030-11683-5_13

"Inconsistence between the documents" or "The authors of the documents have left the organization". Months or years after the project start date the first tangible products are being created and tested.

In agile scrum the approach is to start delivering usable products as soon as possible. So soon as there is a requirement, specific enough, a scrum team can start delivering tangible products that soon can be validated, tested and accepted. However, in the end an organization wants its products to be used in the appropriate way and supported by the helpdesk. To manage that the use of Fact-based modelling is required.

The organizational unit DPGB of the Dutch SVB is, together with other parties, responsible for the execution and maintenance of the process of the so-called PGB-domain in order to perform the requested services in a correct and timely manner to the involved stakeholder. One of the challenges faced by the DPGB is that the services regarding the personal care budget are delivered by a large number of processes by different stakeholders that not all have the exact same or common understanding of these processes and the elements they consist of. I.e. the different stakeholders don't have a real common understanding of the concepts, fact types, rules and data the processes are based or build upon.

The Dutch SVB (Social Security Bank) adopted agile scrum as the sole project management approach. The DPGB therefore decided to start using fact-based modelling and more specific the cogNIAM methodology in order to fully describe the complete PGB-domain and by doing so achieve a common understanding between the different stakeholders.

The cogNIAM methodology describes a domain in a complete, consistent and fully integrated way, as is depicted in the so-called "Knowledge molecule" of Fig. 1.

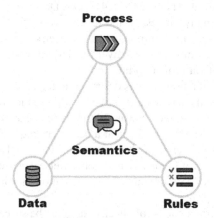

Fig. 1. Knowledge molecule.

The knowledge molecule of Fig. 1 indicates by using the cogNIAM methodology processes, data and rules are described in a fully integrated way with the applicable semantics, i.e. the common understanding placed at the center of all this.

In the following chapter we first introduce the core of agile scrum project management. In Sect. 3 we introduce fact base modelling as in cogNIAM is provided. In Sect. 4 is discussed how cogNIAM improves the results of agile scrum projects in the PGB domain.

2   Agile Scrum

There are many possible implementations of agile scrum, depending on the scale of the project, complexity of the desired products, deadlines, and so on. However, the core of agile scrum is always present. This core consists of user stories, that deliver minimal viable products, executed by the members of a scrum team, led by a scrum master. Finally, it is the product owner (PO) that decides which user stories are accepted to be executed, and who prioritizes the user stories.

For agile scrum to be a success, full understanding of user stories is mandatory. User stories can emerge from many sources. From incidents, problems, requests and changes, to user stories that are part of a larger goal like a feature, epic or even saga. User stories are put on a backlog (to do list), were the PO decides whether a user story is accepted. Rejected user stories will be removed from the backlog. Accepted user stories need to be refined, which means that the requirement in the user story, as well as the acceptance criteria are so clear that a scrum team can start working on it without losing time trying to figure out what should be delivered. Additional information like who the domain experts are or were underlying documents can be found is also required. A well refined user story is called "ready for sprint" and can be prioritized by the PO.

A sprint is a period of time between 1 to 4 weeks. Depending on the type of the user stories a scrum team usually processes, the team chooses the sprint duration. A user story must fit into 1 sprint. If a scrum team pulls a user story into a certain sprint, the team accepts the responsibility to fully deliver the desired product of the user story and meet the acceptance criteria in that sprint.

The desired product of a user story is described in the requirement or description of the user story. It contains the target audience (who will use the product), the description of the product itself in the simplest yet usable form (minimal viable product (MVP)) and what the benefit of the MVP is. Typical a user story requirement will be stated as follows: "As a [budget keeper of a PGB (target audience)] I want to [use 2 phase authentication (MVP)] so that I [am sure that nobody else can use my budget (benefit)]. Further elaboration on the MVP or sources of information may be necessary before the user story is ready for sprint.

The acceptance criteria are a list of checks that must be successfully performed. As each user story requires delivery of a ready to use MVP, it must be validated, tested and finally accepted by the party that inserted the user story.

3   Fact-Based Modelling (FBM) - CogNIAM

Fact-based modelling or cogNIAM is a modelling methodology for modelling information at a conceptual level. Conceptual is to be understood as completely independent
of any software implementation technology; that is, the concepts used and means of
expression do not refer in any way to a possible implementation strategy like e.g.
relational, object-oriented or hierarchical. The methodology applies formal modeling
based on logic and controlled natural language. The resulting conceptual model captures the semantics of the relevant domain of interest by means of fact types (kind of
facts), together with the associated concept definitions – the terms and definitions, the
communication patterns as well as the rules applying to these fact types – the system
requirements related to the information model.

One of the distinguishing factors of fact-based modeling (compared to other
modeling methodologies) is the fact that validation and testing is integrated in every
step of the conceptual modeling process associated to the system requirements production. That is, all intermediate results are validated with the stakeholders before any
implementation activity starts. This validation is performed by the use of concrete
examples of fact type populations and associated verbalizations in a notation and
language the stakeholder is familiar with.

3.1   The Knowledge Triangle

The knowledge triangle is a three-level knowledge framework that over the years has
proven to be very productive for developing fact-based conceptual models. It can be
considered as an additional stratification of knowledge categories in which logical
reasoning is applied. The knowledge triangle is also a visual aid in the development of
fact-based conceptual modelling. The knowledge triangle is depicted in Fig. 2.

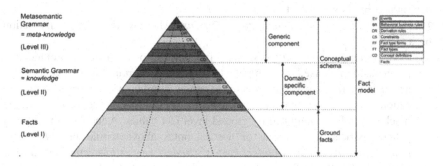

Fig. 2. Knowledge triangle.

Level I: The Ground Facts or Assertions

The assumption of fact-based modelling methodologies is that the most concrete level
in any structured knowledge description or business communication consists of ground
facts. It is observed that these comprise the vast majority in business, engineering or
technical communication.

A ground fact is defined as "a proposition taken to be true by a relevant community" and is expressed as an assertion that either simply predicates over individual objects or simply asserts the existence of an individual object. Examples are: "The healthcare agreement between budget keeper ABC and healthcare specialist 123 started on the 12th of March 2018", "Declaration D212 of budget keeper ABC represents a total value of 234,87 euro" and "Provider Utrecht is a municipality".

Ground facts, expressed by means of sentences, describe factual, planned or imagined situations, in the past, current time or future; they do not prescribe any grammar aspect.

Level II: The Semantic Grammar of the Domain

Level II of the knowledge triangle consists of the domain specific conceptual model. It consists of knowledge categories to which the ground facts of level I must adhere as well as concept definitions to understand the ground facts; it could be said it provides interpretation semantics. In other words, level II specifies the rules that govern the ground facts at level I and defines the concept definitions of the terms used in the facts, so there can be no doubt they could be misunderstood. Moreover, the usage of ground facts is also described at this level. Level II is expressed by means of a series of knowledge categories, namely:

1. *Concept definitions*, which have as function to describe the meaning of every term or group of terms in the ground facts for which it is assumed that the meaning is not fully known to the intended audience and common understanding of the meaning is required. In case the meaning of a term is assumed to be known it is good practice to state this explicitly in order to avoid any confusion.
2. *Fact types*, which provide the functionality to define which kinds of ground facts are considered to be within *scope* of the system, subject or domain of interest. A fact type is a populatable construct, generalizing level I ground facts on the basis of common properties. The boundary (scope) of the system, subject or domain is determined by its set of fact types.
3. *Fact type forms i.e. communication patterns*, whereby there is a distinction between:
   (a) *Fact communication patterns*: their function is to act as a communication mechanism to be used as a template to communicate ground facts in a language and using terms the subject matter expert is familiar with. A fact communication pattern is a template whereby the placeholders (denoted by angle brackets can be instantiated by ground level fact values. A fact communication pattern associated with one of the examples above would be: *"Declaration <Declaration Id> of budget keeper <Budget keeper Id> represents a total value of <Total value>"*.
   (b) *Rule communication patterns*, whose function is to act as communication mechanism for communicating the rules, listed in point 4 below, of the conceptual model. The rule communication pattern associated with the example is: *"[Declaration] of [Budget keeper] represents [Total value]"*. Instantiation might result in the following rule: *"Each [Declaration] of a [Budget keeper] represents exactly one [Total value]"*.

Both types of communication patterns use community-specific terminology.

4. *Constraints*, also known as "integrity rules" or "validation rules", have as function to restrict the set of ground facts and the transitions between the permitted sets of ground facts to those that are considered useful. In other words, integrity rules have the function to restrict populations as well as transitions between populations to useful ones.
5. *Derivation rules*, which are used to derive or calculate new information i.e. ground facts on the basis of existing information. That is, derivation rules describe how to derive new ground facts on the basis of existing ground facts.
6. *Behavioral (business) rules*, which have as function to move ground facts from the domain under consideration into the administration of that domain and vice versa, or to remove ground facts from the administration. In other words, they specify how ground facts are added and/or removed from the system such that the system stays in sync with the communication about the outside world.
7. *Events* i.e. event rules, which specify when to update the set of ground facts by a derivation rule or behavioral rule. That is, an event specifies under which circumstances the set of facts at level I of the knowledge triangle is updated.

The combination of derivation rules, behavioral rules and event rules constitute the process descriptions within the domain specific conceptual model. I.e. they specify when which operations to have to be performed by whom in order to deliver the requested services or products to the relevant stakeholders.

Level III: The Generic Component of the Knowledge Triangle

The third level of the knowledge triangle, the generic component, independent of any specific domain, consists of the knowledge categories to which each conceptual model of level II must adhere. In other words, Level III of the knowledge triangle consists of the generic conceptual model, expressed in the same knowledge categories as any domain-specific conceptual model. Each element in the generic component of the knowledge triangle or the generic conceptual model is independent of any specific part of the domain or system. Interestingly enough, the generic conceptual model is a population of itself.

The cogNIAM methodology furthermore distinguishes between a structural and a structuring part in conceptual modelling. The structural part of the methodology specifies all the concepts definitions, fact types, fact type forms and constraints that are of interest to a domain method, also called the data (model) perspective. The structuring part of the methodology specifies *how* and *when* the different concepts of a domain are used and/or created and by *whom*, i.e. the derivation rules, behavioral rules and event rules. This is also called the process perspective and is used to specify the processes with a domain.

In data modelling it is common to distinguish the following levels of modelling: conceptual, logical and physical as illustrated by Fig. 3.

These three levels of data modelling describe the following:

1. The conceptual data model describes the *semantics* of the data relevant to the domain, independently of any possible means of implementation.
2. The logical data model anticipates the implementation of the data model on a specific computing system. That is, the content of the logical data model is adjusted to achieve certain practical efficiencies in comparison with the conceptual data model.

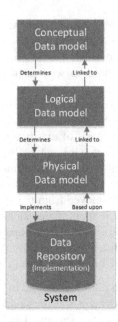

Fig. 3. Levels of modeling.

3. The physical data model, which represents the domain taking into account the facilities and restrictions that are part of a given storage system.

In process modelling a similar distinction is not common but would have great benefit because the initial focus of process modelling could be on *what* should be done in order to deliver the required service and not on *how* this should be performed.

4   How FBM Supports Agile Scrum in the PGB Domain

PGB is a structure by which people who need certain health care can hire health care specialists and have them paid out of their personal health care budget (PGB). Key players are the budget keepers (those who were granted the budget for care they need), health care professionals, the budget suppliers (health insurance companies, health agencies and municipalities) and the SVB, responsible for paying health care professionals out of the personal budgets, financial management and fraud prevention.

The PGB structure is complex, with 4 underlying national health laws, and laws concerning working hours, minimum wages and contracting. The SVB has grown to be the knowledge center for whole PGB domain. There are over 40 software developing companies maintaining systems for budget suppliers and organizations of health care professionals who depend on the SVB for information on changes in laws and regulations, which come frequently.

The SVB has set up one global conceptual data model, integrated with the process model, semantics and rules for the whole PGB-domain. It consists of the complete set of knowledge modules (Fig. 1) through which can be navigated from task to data item, from fact type to rule, from concept definition to source. From each element is recorded why it is recorded (like the Juvenile Care Act) and for which sub domain it is valid. The following sub domains are recognized:

1. The provider domain, where providers provide personal care budgets to people in need of health care that want to arrange their own health care.
2. The so-called Z-domain, i.e. the health care ('Zorg') domain. This domain describes all arrangements needed to support people with a personal care budget that arrange their own health care.
3. The so-called F-domain, i.e. the financial domain. This domain describes all the financial consequences of what is performed in the Z-domain.

Figure 4 shows that the global conceptual data model for the PGB-domain also contains the provider, Z and F domain, i.e. also consists of the concept definitions, fact types, communication patterns and constraints of the conceptual data models for these domains. Figure 4 also indicates that some elements of the global conceptual data model are part of more than one local domain, i.e. these domains overlap.

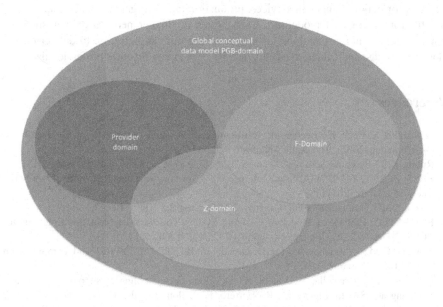

Fig. 4. Global and local conceptual data models.

Making use of one common or global data model of which the different local conceptual data models are part, provides the possibility to develop, describe and integrate the different processes on top of this global conceptual model and therefore not being concerned about the eventually needed communication at first. This makes the initial development and description of processes less complex and clearer.

Each software developer is active in 1 sub domain, although that is a coincidence. They need information concerning their sub domain as well of the interfaces with other sub domains. The interfaces are standardized messages that every system has to support. For these messages the appropriate knowledge molecules are also available.

The SVB delivers the models on a conceptual level (independent of the implementation strategy) as well as the guidelines to convert the data models to the most popular logical levels, being relational and object-oriented.

The software suppliers are responsible for translating the conceptual or logical models into physical models and source code, so that their systems work as required.

The conceptual integrated model is also available for helpdesks from budget providers, health care organizations and the SVB itself to help budget keepers and health care professionals with problems or questions concerning the PGB or using one of portals.

Other parties using the conceptual models are the regulators and communication experts.

5 Conclusions

In this paper we showed that organizations that wish to use agile project management methods for major changes in services, production and or organizational structure, can benefit from fact-based modelling. User stories no longer need to deliver slices of waterfall results like a functional or global design but can be set up to deliver one or more knowledge molecules, ready for use by developers or other professionals.

References

1. Highsmith, J., Beck, K., Beedle, M., van Bennekum, A., et al.: Manifesto for Agile Software Development (2001). The Agile Manifesto authors
2. Rubin, K.S.: Essential Scrum. Addison-Wesley Signature Series (Cohn), Boston (2012)
3. ECSS: ECSS-E-TM-10-23A: Space Engineering – Space system data Repository, Noordwijk, The Netherlands (2011)
4. OMG: OMG Unified Modeling LanguageTM Version 2.5 FTF – Beta 1
5. ESA/ESTEC: Fact based Modeling Unifying System Toward Implementation Solutions for ECSS-E-TM-10-23A, Contract No. 4000107725/13/NL/GLC/al (2013)
6. Nijssen, G.M.: A Framework for Discussion in ISO/TC97/SC5/WG3 and comments on 78.04/01 and 78.05/03 (1978)
7. Lemmens, I., Sgaramella, F., Valera, S.: Development of tooling to support fact-oriented modeling at ESA. In: Meersman, R., Herrero, P., Dillon, T. (eds.) OTM 2009. LNCS, vol. 5872, pp. 714–722. Springer, Heidelberg (2009). https://doi.org/10.1007/978-3-642-05290-3_87

Agile and FBM: A Match Made in Heaven

Inge Lemmens[1]([✉]) and Rob Arntz[2]

[1] PNA, Geerstraat 105, 6411 NP Heerlen, The Netherlands
Inge.lemmens@pna-group.com
[2] i-Refact, Bruistensingel 138, 5232 AC 's Hertogenbosch, The Netherlands
Rob.artnz@i-refact.nl

Abstract. The agile way of working is often abbreviated to the principle: "working software over comprehensive documentation", which is interpreted as "not need for documentation at all". Looking carefully at the Agile manifesto, one also discovers the principle "continuous attention to technical excellence and good design enhances agility". In this paper, we will cover the Agile principles and values mentioned in this manifesto and demonstrate how well fact-based modelling fits these principles and values.

Keywords: Fact-based model · Agile · Agile manifesto

1 Introduction

Agile represents a group of software engineering methodologies which aim to deliver increased productivity, quality and project success rate in software development project when compared to more traditional methodologies. Methodologies that belong to the group are, amongst others, SCRUM [1], XP [2] and Crystal [3].

In [4] the following is stated: "What is new about agile methods is not the practices they use, but their recognition of people as the primary drivers of project success, coupled with an intense focus on effectiveness and manoeuvrability". That is, agile methods are highly people-oriented with focus to adaptivity.

Adaptability is also a key difference between the more traditional methodologies like waterfall and agile methodologies: in an agile methodology, if any major change is required, the work is not "frozen". Instead, the team determines how to handle the changes that occur throughout the project. This in contrast to more traditional methodologies where product requirements are frozen and a predictive approach is taken in terms of planning and deliverables. Traditional methodologies are therefore often referred to as "heavyweight methodologies" as they do not facilitate for change.

1.1 Agile Methods Are People-Oriented

All agile methodologies place emphasis on the social aspects of software development. The people (customers, developers, stakeholders, end users) are considered to be the most important factor for success. In [5] it is stated that the most important implication for managers working in the agile manner is that emphasize is to be given on people factors in a project: amicability, talent, skill and communication.

© Springer Nature Switzerland AG 2019
C. Debruyne et al. (Eds.): OTM 2018 Workshops, LNCS 11231, pp. 135–140, 2019.
https://doi.org/10.1007/978-3-030-11683-5_14

Close collaboration, with customer feedback on a regular and frequent basis is considered essential. As stated in [6]: *"Agile teams cannot exist with occasional communication. They need continuous access to business expertise"*.

1.2   Agile Methods Are Adaptive

Agile teams are not afraid of change: changes are allowed all stages of the project and are considered to be a good thing since changes in requirements means that the team has learned more about what it is required.

The agile methods are thereby more adaptive than predictive, whereby the challenge is not to stop the change but to handle the change in a cost-effectively manner [4]. This has also an effect on the planning strategy used, namely: only detailed plans for the next few weeks, very rough plans for the next few months and extremely crude plans beyond that [7].

According to Fowler [6], being adaptive and people-oriented is the essence of any agile methodology. Adaptive entails not that no plans are made: agile plans a baseline that is used to control change. People-oriented does not mean that there are no processes in place, but means that processes and tools are only needed to enhance the team's effectiveness.

1.3   Fact-Based Modeling

Fact-based modeling is a methodology for modelling the semantics of a subject area. It is a semantically-rich conceptual approach based on logic and controlled natural language. The result of applying the methodology is a fact-based conceptual data model that captures the semantics of the domain by means of fact types, which are attribute-free structures.

Fact-based modelling relies heavily on interaction with the domain experts as the guiding principles of fact-based modelling are the use of concrete examples, as provided by the domain expert, to determine the fact types. Moreover, fact-based modelling relies heavily on communication as the results are expressed in controlled natural language.

A fact-based conceptual model specifies the semantics of the information relevant to the domain: it defines the data of significance to the end-users, including its characteristics, the relationships between the data, the meaning of the data and the rules that apply. It is described implementation-independent and can be the basis for deriving logical and physical data models [8].

Fact-based modeling is a conceptual modelling methodology, meaning that the resulting model is free of any implementation-bias. As described in [9], for correctness, clarity and adaptability, information systems are best specified first at the conceptual level using concepts and language that people can readily understood.

In the remainder of this paper, we will focus on the values and principles of the agile movement and relate these to the fact-based modeling methodology as to demonstrate that fact-based modeling and the Agile movement are a match made in heaven.

2 The Manifesto for Agile Software Development: Its Values

The Agile Manifesto was written in 2001 by 17 independent developers with different backgrounds. Although these developers disagreed on much, they were able to come to an agreement on four values and twelve principles which form the foundation of the Agile movement.

The manifesto for Agile Software Development states the following: *"We are uncovering better ways of developing software by doing it and helping others do it. Through this work we have come to value:*

Individuals and interactions over processes and tools

Working software over comprehensive documentation

Customer collaboration over contract negotiation

Responding to change over following a plan

That is, while there is value in the items on the right, we value the items on the left more" [10].

2.1 The Value: Individual and Interaction over Processes and Tools

The first value entails the recognition of people as the primary drivers for project success. Emphasis is to be placed on teamwork and *communication*. That is, communication is a prerequisite for successful application of an agile method. Hereby, communication is not limited to communication between the developers, but also the communication between the end-users and developers.

Communication is also the central principle for fact-based modeling. In particular, the fact-based modeling methodology adheres to the Helsinki principle [12]: *"Any meaningful exchange of utterances depends upon the prior existence of an agreed set of semantic and syntactic rules. The recipients of the utterances must use only these rules to interpret the received utterances, it is to mean the same as that which was meant by the utterer"*.

In other words, the fact-based modelling methodology relies heavily on communication to achieve its goal.

2.2 The Value: Working Software over Comprehensive Documentation

The second value is based on the idea that agile teams always take the simplest path that is consistent with their goals. The reason for simplicity is so that it is easy to change the design and application on a later date. That is, the developers are urged to keep the code simple and straightforward such that there is no need for extensive documentation. As described in [11]: "the larger the amount of documentation becomes, the more effort is needed to find the required information, and the more effort is needed to keep the information up to date".

Fact-based modeling is a model-driven approach to system development. Model-Based Systems Engineering is defined as: *"the formalized application of modelling to support system requirements, design, analysis, verification and validation activities, beginning in the conceptual design phase and continuing throughout development and later lifecycle phases."* [13]. In [8], it is explained how a conceptual model developed using fact-based model can form the basis for logical and physical models, and illustrated with a concrete example in [15]. In [14], a concrete example of the model-driven approach is given. As demonstrated in that paper, the conceptual model, its underlying structure and the rules associated are the basis for both development of the application repository as well as the definition of the user interface.

A fact-based model is not only the application, it is also at the same time the documentation of the application, since a fact-based model complies to the ISO-100% principle which reads [12]: *"All relevant general static and dynamic aspects, i.e. all rules, laws, etc., of the universe of discourse should be described in the conceptual schema. The information system cannot be held responsible for not meeting those described elsewhere, including in particular those in application programs"*. As such, fact-based modeling aids in taking away the extensive documentation burden.

2.3   The Third Value: Customer Collaboration over Contract Negotiation

Customer collaboration is valued over extensive contract negotiations, meaning that more value is attached to the continuous collaboration of the customer throughout the complete development of the software.

One of the most significant barriers to implementing an agile methodology, however, lies in the inability to establish and maintain close and effective customer collaboration [16]. Even when the relationship begins with the best intentions and the highest expectations on both sides, maintaining the relationship throughout time becomes a challenge. And this challenge becomes even greater if little to no attention is placed on documentation (the second value). Little to no documentation implies relying on memory, which becomes hard as time goes by and things change.

Fact-based modelling aids in establishing and maintaining the customer relationship over time as customer involvement is a prerequisite for the success of the modelling methodology. As depicted in Fig. 1, the fact-based modelling protocol is a stepwise procedure that requires involvement of the customer in most of its steps.

In particular, the customer is involved in step 2 in determining and/or constructing together with the modeler the examples that clarify the knowledge identified in the previous step. In step 3, the examples are validated and complemented by the customer to come to a complete and formally approved set of concrete examples that can be used as a formal starting point for the further development of the model. In step 4, the concrete examples are generalized to the formal fact-based model. This step consists of several smaller tasks, most of which require involvement of the customer.

In conclusion, since the fact-based modeling protocol relies heavily on the involvement of the customer, and the customer's input is required in each step and documented in the model, close collaboration with the customer is achieved easily and does not rely on in-memory knowledge only.

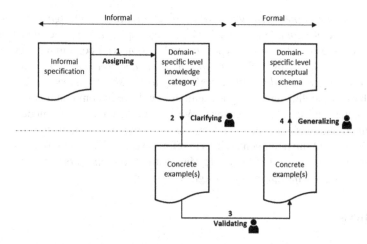

Fig. 1. The fact-based modelling protocol.

2.4 The Fourth Value: Responding to Change over Following a Plan

As described in the introduction, adaptivity is one of the core elements of the agile methodology. As work progresses, the understanding of the problem domain and what is being built changes, and these changes need to be well catered for. As stated in the introduction: responding to change does not mean that no plans are made. Instead, agile plans are constructed as a baseline that is used to control change.

Being able to handle change easily is one of the key feature of fact-based modeling. That is, fact-based modeling is a linear modeling methodology, which means that whether you create the first element of the model of the 100th element, the way of doing is always the same. Moreover, fact-based models are semantically stable, with no design choices that need to be made upfront. With fact types as the building block, there is no need during the process to take into account upfront the possible effect of changes that can take place. This in contrast to other analysis/design methods like e.g. UML, and ERD, where one has to consider upfront whether something must be represented as an attribute or potentially a class (entity) with a relationship.

The other aspect of fact-based modeling that tailors for change, is that fact-based modeling gives true focus as facts that do not belong to the subject area do not hamper the model, as stated through the 100% principle.

3   Conclusions

In this paper, we have demonstrated how fact-based modeling fits the values of the agile methodology. We could have done the same for each one of the 12 principles of the Agile methodology. For example, we could have argued that the early validation principle of fact-based modeling, which consists of validating whether the model is representative and validating whether the model is correct, is part of the protocol step 3 (see Fig. 1.), is an easy and consistent manner to fulfil principle 1 of the agile manifesto which reads *"our highest priority is to satisfy the customer through early and continuous delivery of valuable software"*. Or, for example, that the fact that fact-based modeling focusses on atomic fact types in combination with continuous focus is input for achieving the principle *"deliver working software frequently from a couple of weeks to a couple of months, with a preference to the shorter timescale"*.

Fact-based modeling and the agile methodology have in common that they are both people-oriented and can handle change. We believe that fact-based modeling shows that documenting does not need to be a burden in software development as the model is the application and the documentation. Therefore, we consider fact-based modeling as the fulfilment of principle 9 of the Agile Manifesto: *"Continuous attention to technical excellence and good design enhances agility"*.

References

1. Schwaber, K., Beedle, M.: Agile Software Development with SCRUM, 1st edn. Prentice Hall PTR, Upper Saddle River (2001)
2. Beck, K., Andres, C.: Extreme Programming Explained: Embrace Change. Addison-Wesley Professional, Boston (2004)
3. Cockburn, A.: Agile Software Development. Addison-Wesley Professional, Boston (2001)
4. Highsmith, J., Cockburn, A.: Agile software development: the business of innovation. Computer **34**(9), 120–127 (2001)
5. Cockburn, A., Highsmith, J.: Agile Software development: the people factor. Computer **34**(11), 131–133 (2001)
6. Fowler, M.: The new methodology. https://www.martinfowler.com/articles/newMethodology.html. Accessed 25 July 2018
7. Highsmith, J.: Adaptive Software Development: A Collaborative Approach to Managing Complex Systems. Dorset House Publishing, New York (2000)
8. Lemmens, I., Sgaramella, F., Valera, S.: Development of tooling to support fact-oriented modeling at ESA. In: Meersman, R., Herrero, P., Dillon, T. (eds.) OTM 2009. LNCS, vol. 5872, pp. 714–722. Springer, Heidelberg (2009). https://doi.org/10.1007/978-3-642-05290-3_87
9. Halpin, T.: Object-role modeling (ORM/NIAM). In: Bernus, P., Mertins, K., Schmidt, G. (eds.) Handbook on Architectures of Information System, pp. 81–101. Springer, Berlin (1998). https://doi.org/10.1007/978-3-662-03526-9_4
10. Homepage manifesto for agile software development. http://agilemanifesto.org/. Accessed 24 July 2018
11. Wendorff, P.: An essential distinction of agile software development processes based on systems thinking in software engineering management. In: Third International Conference on eXtreme Programming and Agile Processes in Software Engineering (2002)
12. Van Griethuysen, J.: Information processing systems – concepts and terminology for the conceptual schema and the information base. Technical report ISO TR9007 (1987)
13. INCOSE: Systems Engineering Vision 2020 (incose-tp-2004-004-02), INCOSE (2007)
14. Lemmens, I., Koster, J.P.: The rule configurator: a tool to execute a model and play with the rules. In: Debruyne, C., Ciuciu, J., Panetto, H., et al. (eds.) OTM 2016 Workshops. LNCS, pp. 155–163. Springer, Heidelberg (2016). https://doi.org/10.1007/978-3-319-55961-2_15
15. Lemmens, I., van de Laar, B., Saton, J., Bulles, J.: How to fulfil regulatory requirements consistently: a semantic-based approach. In: Debruyne, C., et al. (eds.) OTM 2017. LNCS, vol. 10697, pp. 202–211. Springer, Cham (2018). https://doi.org/10.1007/978-3-319-73805-5_21
16. Paulk, M.C.: Agile methodologies and process disciplines. Crosstalk: J. Defense Softw. Eng., **15**(10) (2002)

The Role of a Fact-Based Model for Defining Data Quality

Inge Lemmens[1][(✉)], Lars Ritzen[2], Olivier Vijgen[2], Koen Souren[2],
and Calvin Slangen[2]

[1] PNA, Geerstraat 105, 6411 NP Heerlen, The Netherlands
Inge.Lemmens@pna-group.com
[2] Loyalis, Oude Lindestraat 70, 6411 EJ Heerlen, The Netherlands
{Lars.Ritzen,Olivier.Vijgen,Koen.Souren,
Calvin.Slangen}@loyalis.nl

Abstract. Increasing expectations of customers, the need for operational efficiency and an increasing amount of regulations to fulfill forces organizations to create true value out of their data. Creating this true value can only be achieved if the data is of the correct quality. Ensuring correct quality requires not only insights in the rules that apply to the data, but also entails ensuring that the correct meaning is associated with the data. In this paper we demonstrate how a fact-based model serves as the basis for implementing a data quality program at Loyalis.

Keywords: Fact-based model · Data quality · DMBok · cogNIAM

1 Introduction

More and more organizations establish data science programs with the aim to create new insights which might result in new products and competitive advances. At the same time, organizations start to realize that, in order to create true value out of data, the data must be of the correct quality since poor data can damage an organization's reputation, and have a negative impact on customer satisfaction [1].

The need for data of high quality is also underwritten by regulators. In their "Guidance Solvency II data quality management by insurers" [2], the DNB (DeNederlandscheBank), explains its expectations with respect to data quality and provides guidelines to achieve the required level of data quality.

High quality of data is also important to provide the correct service to customers, in a professional and progressive manner. Moreover, high quality of data is important to fulfil the customers' increasing demands about the correctness, availability and privacy of their data.

High quality of data also aids in achieving a higher performance, in ensuring better, data driven decision making and aids in faster development of IT systems.

In other words, external as well as internal drivers require organizations to create value out of their data which in turn requires their data to be of high quality.

C. Debruyne et al. (Eds.): OTM 2018 Workshops, LNCS 11231, pp. 141–149, 2019.
https://doi.org/10.1007/978-3-030-11683-5_15

1.1   The Essence of Data Quality

But what does it mean exactly, data quality? As described in [1] the term data quality has a dual usage as it refers both to the process used to measure or improve the quality of data as well as to the characteristics associated with high quality of data, whereby data is of high quality is defined as "*the degree in which the data meets the expectations and needs of data consumers*" [1]. Data quality then is an indication that specifies how well the data fits its intended use.

Knowing whether data meets the expectations and needs of data consumers implies understanding these expectations and needs. In this paper, we will explain the approach taking by Loyalis on implementing a data quality program within the organization. In this approach, the Semantic Loyalis Information Model (SLIM) is the cornerstone for implementing the program.

1.2   Loyalis' Motivation for Data Management

Loyalis is an insurance company which offers income insurance solutions for employers and employees. With approximately 450,000 insured employees working at approximately 10,000 employers, Loyalis has a stable group of customers. As an insurance organization, Loyalis has to comply to, amongst others, the Solvency II regulation. The Solvency II regulation includes data requirements which focus on ensuring that data used in the calculations for the reporting of Solvency II are of the correct quality.

Increasing customer satisfaction, fulfilling regulatory requirements as well as the strategy to become a data-driven organization, are the reasons for Loyalis to activate the data management program.

1.3   Structure of the Paper

In this paper, we will first introduce Loyalis' ambition level with respect to data quality. To achieve this ambition, 4 components of data quality and the associated dimensions that are of relevance for Loyalis are introduced.

Identifying the components and dimensions is one thing, to identify the rules and requirements that need to be fulfilled is the second part. This is achieved through the development of the SLIM, which will be explained in Sect. 3. Section 4 then describes the process that is put in place to enhance data quality. Conclusions and way forward for Loyalis are described in Sect. 5.

2   Components of Data Quality and Their Dimensions

Data quality programs typically focus on data quality dimensions that apply to data values (the concrete data that is stored and maintained in systems). Typically, data quality dimensions like accuracy, usability, timeliness, … are associated with these data values, [1, 3, 4]. In [5], it is recognized that data quality not only entail the quality of the concrete data values, but also the quality of the data model and the associated representation. At Loyalis, we followed this approach and considered data quality to be a function consisting of 4 components, namely:

1. the *data values*: the data as it is stored and maintained in the system,
2. the *data representation*: the representation of the data in documents, interfaces, websites,...,
3. the *data architecture*: the coordination of the data and associated activities throughout the organization,
4. the *data model*: the conceptual and logical representation of the data, which is required for effective communication between data suppliers and data consumers.

For each of these components, several dimensions can be identified.

2.1   The Data Quality Dimensions of Concrete Data Values

As explained in the previous section, data quality is most of the time associated with the quality of the data values, as stored and maintained within the systems. Typically, the approach of the DAMA is followed, which defines a list of data quality dimensions about which there is a general agreement [1].

At Loyalis, we consider the following 6 data quality dimensions for the data values:

1. *Accuracy*: the extent to which the data is a correct representation of reality.
2. *Validity*: the extent to which the data falls within the expected range.
3. *Completeness*: the extent to which the required data is available.
4. *Consistency*: the extent to which several representation of the same are alike, and no contradictions appear in the data.
5. *Coherency*: the extent to which the data is not only consistent but also a coherent whole.
6. *Usability*: the extent to which the data fits its definition, is relevant and can be used in the required situation (Fig. 1).

Fig. 1. Data quality dimensions for data values.

2.2   The Data Quality Dimensions of Data Representation

When data values are correct but are represented incorrectly to the consumers (and customers in particular), the quality of the data suffers. Therefore, the following data quality dimensions are taken into considerations for data representation:

1. *Completeness:* the extent to which the represented data is a complete picture.
2. *Clarity:* the extent to which the data can be understood by the stakeholders and corresponds to its definition.
3. *Unambiguity:* the extent to which the data is defined such that only one interpretation is possible.
4. *Relevancy:* the extent to which the data is relevant for the situation at hand.

2.3   The Data Quality Dimensions Related to Data Architecture

Data architecture is responsible for providing an overview of the data needed within the organization, its availability and the systems in which the data is stored and maintained. Moreover, data architecture is also about the data flows within the organization.

For data architecture, the following data quality dimensions are identified:

1. *Availability:* the extent to which the data is available to the user when he needs the data.
2. *Traceability:* the extent to which the data can be followed throughout the organization (the extent to which the data flows are described).
3. *Compliancy:* the extent to which the data is consistent with the norms and standards.
4. *Up-to-date:* the extent to which the data is a representation of the current state (without lag/delay).
5. *Integrated:* the extent to which the data from different sources can be integrated to one whole.

Note that, data architecture is also responsible for the identification of the golden sources. Identification of these is of relevance to data quality as golden source aid in containing possible sources of data quality problems.

2.4   The Data Quality Dimensions Related to Data Model

A data model prescribes the structure of the data and, depending on which representation is used, the rules to which the data must apply. Data models themselves also have to comply to certain data quality dimensions, namely:

1. *Completeness*: the extent to which the required data can be captured in the structure of the model.
2. *Conceptually correct*: the extent to which the model structures and regulates the required data.
3. *Syntactically correct*: the extent to which the model is developed according to the modelling paradigm used.
4. *Coherent*: the extent to which the model represents a whole.

5. *Clear*: the extent to which the model is understandable for all stakeholders involved.

To achieve data quality, the different components have to be investigated to ensure that the quality of the data, and by derivation the quality of the products and services of the organization are is correct.

3 A Consumer-Driven Approach to Determine DQ Rules

The concept "fit for use" is introduced in [8] to define the quality of a services and products. and is widely applied in data quality literature as a measure for data quality [6, 9, 10].

As explained in Sect. 1.1, the quality of data is the degree in which the data meets the expectations and needs of data consumers [6, 7]. This means that, in order to measure the quality of data, one needs to ensure that the needs and expectations of the data consumers are well understood. In [11], it is argued that most studies identify multiple dimensions of data quality, but none of them empirically collect data quality attributes from data consumers. In other words, none of them take the viewpoint of the data consumer (the business user) to determine the rules the data must conform to.

3.1 The Semantic Loyalis Information Model

To get the required insight in the needs and expectations of data consumers, Loyalis has chosen to create a *semantic information model*, called SLIM. SLIM aims to be the trusted source of information for the business concepts, the associated terms and definitions as well as the relationships between the concepts and the rules that apply to these business concepts and relations.

The SLIM is a fully integrated model, developed using the cogNIAM methodology, covering the process, information and rules perspective on the data. That is, the SLIM consists of the following knowledge categories:

1. *Concept definitions*, which have as function to describe the meaning of every business concept or group of business concept in such a manner that no confusion can exist about the meaning of the business concept.
2. *Fact types*, which have as function to define the relationships between the business concepts, and provide the functionality to define which data is in scope for Loyalis. Fact types are expressed using natural language sentences.
3. *Rules*, where we distinguish between:
   a. *Constraints*, which are the rules to which the data must comply, and
   b. *Derivation rules*, which are used to derive or calculate new data on the basis of existing data.
4. *Process descriptions*, which specify which activities are performed by the different actors and which data is needed to perform the activities.
5. *Work instructions*, which specify how the activities are to be executed.

3.2 Development of the SLIM

The SLIM is developed using the cogNIAM protocol. This means that a stepwise procedure is used to develop the SLIM. Concretely, we start by collecting all the relevant documentation. Through using the cogNIAM protocol, we create a first version of the SLIM, which is validated by the business user. In most cases, the first validation is done with the business users responsible for the definition of the data under consideration. Based on this validation, the model is updated and refined, after which a second validation takes place. The second validation is not only done with the business user responsible for the definition of the data, but focusses on validation by the business users that consume the data. Only after all parties have agreed, the model is published (Fig. 2).

Fig. 2. The model cycle.

4 The Data Quality Process

As we consider data quality to be determined largely by the end users (the consumers of the data), the data quality process relies heavily on the SLIM. In the following figure, the overall process is depicted (Fig. 3).

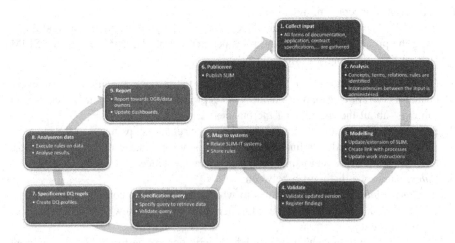

Fig. 3. The overall process.

The process starts with a data user to stipulate its data requirements. These data requirements can be the need for new data, or can take the form of a "finding" in case the data at hand does not fulfil the requirements.

In both cases, the data modellers start with gathering and analysing the available documentation to identify the business terms, relations and rules. This documentation can be product specifications, the website, manuals,…

In case there are inconsistencies between the documentation, ambiguity might arise or the documentation is not clear or usable in the situation at hand (e.g. out-of-date), they will register their findings. These findings are presented to the data owners (the persons responsible for the data) or the data governance board, who will determine whether actions to improve the quality of the data representation have to be taken.

Once the documentation is filtered, the modeller starts developing the model, together with the business user (as described in Sect. 3.2). This results in an update or extension of the SLIM, which is validated by the different stakeholders. Moreover, the link with the process descriptions and the work instructions are updated and validated by operations to ensure that they reflect the current way of working.

Once the model is completed updated and validated, the rules identified in the SLIM are given to the data stewards, who are responsible for executing the rules on the data to check the compliance of the data to the user requirement. In order to be able to do so, the mapping of the SLIM concepts and relations to the IT systems has to be take place. That is, for the data stewards to be able to check the data against the identified rules, they have to identify in the used systems which column(s) of which table(s) correspond to the concepts and relations of the SLIM.

The rules are then translated into SQL queries that are to be applied. These SQL queries are validated by the system owners, after which the data is uploaded and checked against the rules.

Once the rules are executed on the data, the result is analysed. If the data is not of the required quality (i.e., the number of erroneous records is high), a root cause analysis is performed, whereby the data flows are inspected on data manipulation. Where possible, data improvement actions are identified and transferred to the DevOps teams that are responsible for the system enhancements.

The results of the process are reported towards the Data Governance Board, and the DQ dashboard is updated to reflect the changes.

4.1   Matching the Data Quality Dimensions in the Data Quality Process

One of the most important functions of the SLIM is that it regulates the communication between the stakeholders by clearly defining the concepts and ensuring that an unambiguous interpretation can be achieved. By achieving this, the data quality dimensions *accuracy* and *usability* of the data values, *clarity*, *unambiguity* and *relevancy* of esc.

The SLIM serves as a spider in the web. It is the single source of definition for the business concepts, their relationships and rules. The concepts of the SLIM are mapped to the logical models of the different applications, whereby the mapping is maintained within the model, ensuring for the dimensions of *traceability* of data architecture.

In some cases, the SLIM is the source for development of logical and physical data models. That is, the logical and physical data models are derived from the conceptual model, as described in [12]. As the SLIM is developed and validated using the cogNIAM methodology, the *completeness, conceptual correctness, syntactical correctness, coherence* and *clarity* of the data model can be guaranteed.

Since the SLIM also contains the process descriptions and associated work instructions, for each concept it is clear what it is used for, where it is presented and how it is presented. That is, the dimension *usability* of data values, *relevancy* of data representation and *availability* of data architecture can be checked against these descriptions.

Compliancy, up-to-date of data architecture, coherence and completeness of both the data as well as the model, are checked during the data quality process, when doing the analysis of the documentation as well as during the root cause analysis.

5   Conclusions and Future Work

The term "fit for use" is in data quality literature used to refer to the quality of data. That is, data is of high quality if it is fit for use, i.e. if it fulfils the needs and requirements for data consumers. We stated that, for data to be of high quality (fit for use), it is not sufficient to look only at the data values, but it is necessary to take into account the representation of data, the data model to which the data complies, as well as the data architecture component. For each of these components, Loyalis identified several data quality dimensions that are the focus for the first two years.

To identify the stakeholders needs and requirements, Loyalis has chosen for a business user-oriented approach by developing the Semantic Loyalis Information Model (SLIM). The SLIM is developed using the cogNIAM methodology and as well the development of the SLIM as the SLIM itself is used to verify the data against the dimensions identified.

Future development involve amongst others further development of the SLIM, the development of a data warehouse on the basis of the SLIM, and improvement activities both on the data as well as on the representation of the data. The latter entails amongst others rationalization of the terminology used on the website, in product specification and contracts with the customer.

References

1. DAMA International: DAMA-DMBOK: Data Management Body of Knowledge, 2nd edn. Technics Publications, Denville (2017)
2. De NederlandscheBank: Guidance Solvency II data management. http://www.toezicht.dnb.nl/binaries/50-236703.pdf
3. English, L.: Information Quality Applied: Best Practices for Improving Business Information, Processes, and Systems. Wiley Publishing, Hoboken (2009)
4. DAMA UK Working Group: The Six Primary Dimensions for Data Quality Assessment – Defining Data Quality Dimensions (2013)

5. Redman, T.: Data Quality: The Field Guide. Digital Press, Boston (2001)
6. Wang, R.Y.: A product perspective on total data quality management. Commun. ACM **41** (2), 58–65 (1998)
7. Orr, K.: Data quality and systems theory. Commun. ACM **41**(2), 66–71 (1998)
8. Juran, J.M.: Juran on Planning for Quality. The Free Press, New York (1988)
9. Deming, E.W.: Out of the Crisis. Center for Advanced Engineering Study, MIT, Cambridge (1986)
10. Dobyns, L., Crawford-Mason, C.: Quality or Else: The Revolution in World Business. Houghton Mifflin, Boston (1991)
11. Wang, R.Y., Strong, D.M.: Beyond accuracy: what data quality means to data consumers. J. Manag. Inf. Syst. **12**(4), 5–33 (1996)
12. Lemmens, I., Sgaramella, F., Valera, S.: Development of tooling to support fact-oriented modeling at ESA. In: Meersman, R., Herrero, P., Dillon, T. (eds.) OTM 2009. LNCS, vol. 5872, pp. 714–722. Springer, Heidelberg (2009). https://doi.org/10.1007/978-3-642-05290-3_87

The Lifecycle of a User Transaction in a Hyperledger Fabric Blockchain Network Part 2: Order and Validate

Sjir Nijssen[1] and Peter Bollen[2(✉)]

[1] Heerlen, The Netherlands
Sjir.Nijssen@pna-group.com
[2] Maastricht University, Maastricht, The Netherlands
p.bollen@maastrichtuniversity.nl

Abstract. The paper describes the second part of the happy path of a user transaction through a Hyperledger Fabric Blockchain Network. The full cycle of a user transaction originates from the Client Application (an actor outside the Hyperledger Ledger Network but inside an organization that is part of a set of organizations that jointly run the Hyperledger Fabric Blockchain Network). In the process of making the Hyperledger Fabric Blockchain network knowledge explicit, essential parts of FBM were applied in cooperation with the developers of the Fabric Blockchain platform.

1 Introduction

In this paper the second part of a high level conceptual overview of the life cycle of an end user transaction is described, from its birth in a client application that is part of an organization that is part of a Hyperledger Fabric Blockchain business network to its eternal "life" in the immutable blockchain. In [1] the first stage in the transaction life cycle was explained: *proposing* and *endorsing*.

In this article we will explain the second and third stage of this transaction life cycle: *Ordering* and *Validating*. In [1] the endorsing stage was discussed. The endorsing strategy (a part of the channel strategies) is important for the final outcome of the endorsing stage and hence the transition to the next stage in the transaction life cycle. In a distributed decision making process like Fabric an endorsement policy prescribes how many and which kind of actors need to endorse a transaction proposal.

The architecture of Fabric and design decisions are described in [2–5]. Reference [6] has some general information about permissioned blockchains, while [7] has the focus on the unique aspects of Fabric.

How useful the endorsement policies are will depend on the application, on the desired resilience of the solution against failures or misbehavior of endorsers, and on various other properties. Examples of these endorsing policies are given in Appendix A.

S. Nijssen—Retired from PNA, the Netherlands.

C. Debruyne et al. (Eds.): OTM 2018 Workshops, LNCS 11231, pp. 150–158, 2019.
https://doi.org/10.1007/978-3-030-11683-5_16

In Sects. 2 and 3 we will address the ordering and validating stages respectively. In Sect. 4 we will finally conclude that the transaction process will lead to an updated Ledger that consists of a new world state (in case of a valid transaction) and the updated blockchain (irrespective of transaction is classified as valid or not valid).

2   The Life Cycle of a User Transaction Part 2: The Ordering Phase

In this chapter we will discuss the next steps that together complete the 'happy path' of a user transaction through a Hyperledger Fabric (HLF) Network. In the HLF documentation this entire process is divided into 3 phases, the (proposing and) endorsing phase, the ordering phase and the validation-committing phase. In this section we will illustrate the 2nd main phase in the happy path of a Fabric user transaction life cycle by continuing from the 1st main stage: endorsing and the possible results of this stage to the description of the 2nd stage in the transaction life cycle: ordering.

2.1   The Possible Outcomes of the Endorsing Transaction Stage

In this section we will show what happens when the outcome of the endorsing stage is either *sufficient, not sufficient* or *inconsistent*.

2.1.1   With Sufficient Endorsements

As soon as the Client application has decided it has obtained a sufficient number of endorsements from the endorsing peers for a given submitted transaction instance, it sends the transaction message (= proposed transaction by client application, the Read-write sets and the signatures of the Endorsing peers) to the Orderers, of course properly signed and *encrypted.*

2.1.2   Not Sufficient Endorsements After a Set Time

When the Client application comes to the conclusion that there are not a sufficient number of endorsements, the Client application will decide to stop this proposed transaction as it will anyway be later rejected by the Committers, would it be sent to the orderers and from there packaged into a block to the Committers.

2.1.3   Client Application Detects That There Are Inconsistent Transaction Responses

If the client application detects that not all endorsed responses are consistent, it may decide to stop the transaction workflow early. Should the client application in such a situation nevertheless decide to forward the inconsistent set of responses to the ordering service, the transaction will be declared invalid during the committing process.

2.2   The Client Application Sends the Responses of the Endorsers to the Orderers

The next step in the business transaction flow is to have the Client Application send the answers by the Endorsing peers to the ordering service (see Fig. 1).

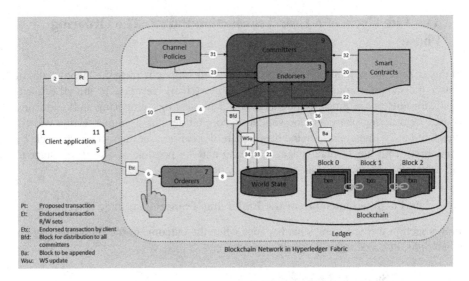

Fig. 1. Conceptual transaction flow architecture

2.3   The Orderers Prepare a Block to Be Included in the Block Chain

The next step in the transaction flow is to have the orderers prepare a package of transactions, called proposed block (see Fig. 2).

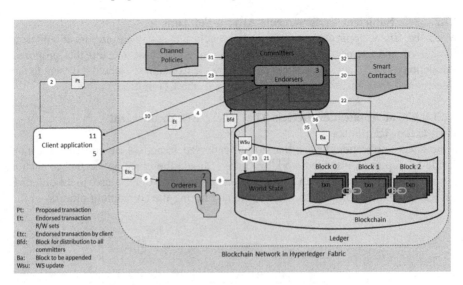

Fig. 2. Conceptual transaction flow architecture

The ordering peers receive transactions from all channels and from potentially *different* Client Applications. The ordering service brings the transactions in a strict order. Please recall that each channel in the Hyperledger Fabric business network has its own blockchain and its own World State, for privacy reasons. Different channels may use different ordering strategies.

When the new block that was in the process of being formed by the orderers, has reached the desired block size, or the endorsing process of the new block has reached the time limit, (and those two parameters can be different in different channels), the orderers have to submit the newly formed block to the Committers (see Fig. 3).

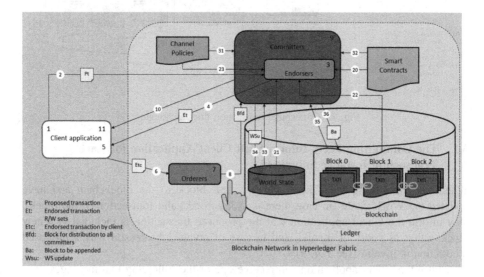

Fig. 3. Conceptual transaction flow architecture

3   The Life Cycle of a User Transaction Part 3: The Validating Phase

In this section we will illustrate the 3rd main stage in the happy path of the Fabric user transaction life cycle by continuing from the 2nd stage: ordering to the description of the 3rd stage in the transaction life cycle: validating and committing.

The committing peers receive the proposed block from the orderers (see Fig. 4). Each committer checks that each transaction in a proposed block satisfies the associated endorsement policy, using information flow 31. If not, the transaction will be marked as invalid, yet will be left in the block, but it has no effect on the World State.

Each committer uses the Read set of a proposed transaction to check that that Read set used by the endorsing peers in the simulation (during the endorsing phase) is still the same as now is available in the World set. If not the same, the transaction will be marked as invalid by the committer as invalid in the block, and has no effect on the World State.

The committers append the proposed block to the blockchain and update the World State for all the valid transactions in the block.

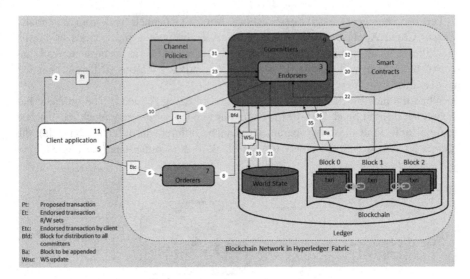

Fig. 4. Conceptual transaction flow architecture

3.1 The Committing Peers Inform Each Client Application for Each Transaction Instance Submitted

When the committing peers have added a new block to the blockchain and have updated the World State (in case there is at least one valid transaction in the block), they inform the Client application that the proposed transaction is included in a new block, either as valid, or invalid, and in case of invalid, the reason why a proposed transaction is invalid (see Fig. 5).

Hence the Client application can receive one of the following two messages.

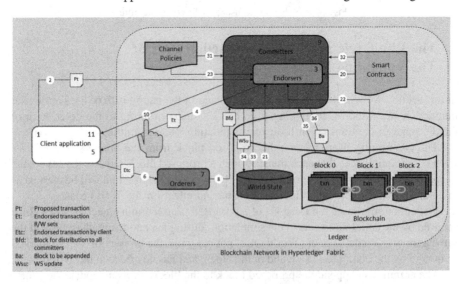

Fig. 5. Conceptual transaction flow architecture

3.1.1   Transaction Is Accepted as Valid and Is Now Part of the Immutable Blockchain, with Effect on the World State

The committers inform each Client application that has submitted a transaction to the Fabric Network that the transaction is now part of the blockchain, that it is a valid transaction and that the World State has been updated accordingly, in case the transaction satisfies all rules.

3.1.2   Transaction Is Not Accepted, Hence Declared Invalid, But Part of the Immutable Blockchain, Without Effect on the World State

The second option is that the committers inform the submitting Client application that the transaction has been declared invalid, nevertheless included with the label invalid in the Block Chain and that this proposed transaction has had no influence on the World State.

The final step in the workflow of a business transaction is the processing by the Client application of the response of the Committers (see Fig. 6).

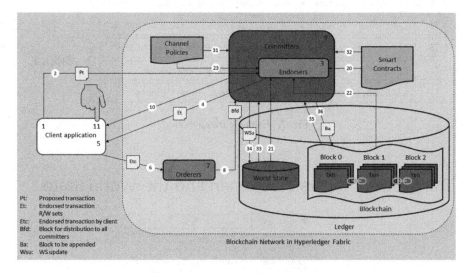

Fig. 6. Conceptual transaction flow architecture

4   Transactions and the Ledger

In this paper we have analyzed the ordering and validation-committing stage in the Hyperledger Fabric user transaction cycle using essential parts of FBM, namely consistently using concrete examples expressed as facts. We have illustrated each step in the endorsement phase of the transaction life cycle with a concrete example of a transaction based on the car owner case (called Fabcar with Fabric documentation). In this paper and [1] we have explained the separate stage and sub-stages in the HLF transaction life cycle leading ultimately to an update of the channel block chain and the world state (the last update only when there is at least one valid transaction in the block, see Fig. 7).

The transactions

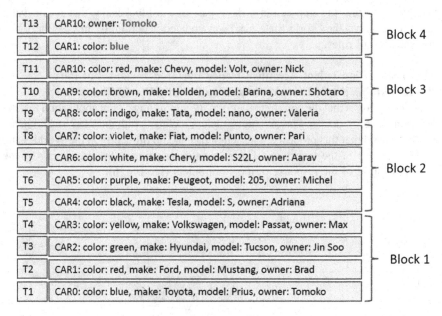

T13	CAR10: owner: Tomoko

Block 4

| T12 | CAR1: color: blue |

| T11 | CAR10: color: red, make: Chevy, model: Volt, owner: Nick |

Block 3

| T10 | CAR9: color: brown, make: Holden, model: Barina, owner: Shotaro |

| T9 | CAR8: color: indigo, make: Tata, model: nano, owner: Valeria |

| T8 | CAR7: color: violet, make: Fiat, model: Punto, owner: Pari |

Block 2

| T7 | CAR6: color: white, make: Chery, model: S22L, owner: Aarav |

| T6 | CAR5: color: purple, make: Peugeot, model: 205, owner: Michel |

| T5 | CAR4: color: black, make: Tesla, model: S, owner: Adriana |

| T4 | CAR3: color: yellow, make: Volkswagen, model: Passat, owner: Max |

Block 1

| T3 | CAR2: color: green, make: Hyundai, model: Tucson, owner: Jin Soo |

| T2 | CAR1: color: red, make: Ford, model: Mustang, owner: Brad |

| T1 | CAR0: color: blue, make: Toyota, model: Prius, owner: Tomoko |

Fig. 7. Example transactions

Transactions in the blockchain and the World State

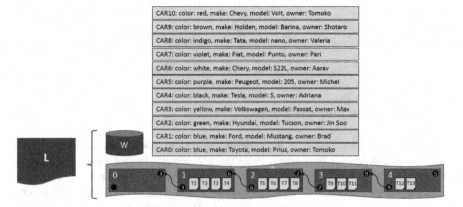

Fig. 8. Ledger = World State + Blockchain

5   Conclusion

By going through all stages of the Fabric user transaction cycle we have developed a deeper understanding of the main elements in HyperLedger Fabric and one of the main take-aways of this article and [1] lies in the observation that we can define a Ledger in this context now as the union of the World State and the immutable block-chain (see Fig. 8).

Appendix A

Example endorsement policies (Source: Fabric Docs 1.2, Architecture Reference, Sub Section Endorsement Policies, Sub Section Example Endorsement Policies) [8].

Suppose the endorsement policy specifies the endorser set E = {Alice, Bob, Charlie, Dave, Eve, Frank, George}. Some example policies:

- A valid signature on the same tran-proposal from all members of E. [Please remember that tran-proposal means endorsement; hence is common language: all endorsers from set E have to endorse.]
- A valid signature from any single member of E[on a tran-proposal].
- Valid signatures on the same tran-proposal from endorsing peers according to the condition (Alice OR Bob) AND (any two of: Charlie, Dave, Eve, Frank, George).
- Valid signatures on the same tran-proposal by any 5 out of the 7 endorsers. (More generally, for chaincode with $n > 3f$ endorsers, id signatures by any $2f + 1$ out of the n endorsers, or by any group of *more* than $(n + f)/2$ endorsers.)
- Suppose there is an assignment of "stake" or "weights" to the endorsers, like
  - like {Alice = 49, Bob = 15, Charlie = 15, Dave = 10, Eve = 7, Frank = 3, George = 1}, where the total stake is 100: The policy requires valid signatures from a set that has a majority of the stake (i.e., a group with combined stake strictly more than 50), such as {Alice, X} with any X different from George, or {everyone together except Alice}. And so on.
  - The assignment of stake in the previous example condition could be static (fixed in the metadata of the chaincode) or dynamic (e.g., dependent on the state of the chaincode and be modified during the execution).
  - Valid signatures from (Alice OR Bob) on tran-proposal1 and valid signatures from (any two of: Charlie, Dave, Eve, Frank, George) on tran-proposal2, where tran-proposal1 and tran-proposal2 differ only in their endorsing peers and state updates.

References

1. Nijssen, S., Bollen, P.: The lifecycle of a user transaction in a Hyperledger Fabric Blockchain Network part 1: Propose and Endorse 2018 (forthcoming)
2. Androulaki, E., et al.: Hyperledger Fabric: A Distributed Operating System for Permissioned Blockchains, 30 January 2018

3. The Hyperledger Vision: Hyperledger, Blockchain Technologies for Business (2017)
4. O'Dowd, A., Blockchain Explored A Technical Deep-Dive on Hyperledger Fabric v1, 29 November 2017
5. Vukolic, M.: Hyperledger Fabric an open source distributed operating system for permissioned blockchains. Swiss Blockchain Summer School, Lausanne, Switserland, 22 June 2017
6. Brakeville, S., Parepa, B: Blockchain basics: Introduction to distributed ledgers, 21 August 2017
7. Weed Cocco, S., Singh, G.: Top 6 technical advantages of Hyperledger Fabric for blockchain networks, 21 August 2017
8. Hyperledger-Fabricdocs Documentation, Release master, Key Concepts, sub section Peers, June 2018

Scale Your Information Modeling Effort Using the Power of the Crowd

Jan Mark Pleijsant[(✉)]

ABN AMRO, Amsterdam, The Netherlands
jan.mark.pleijsant@nl.abnamro.com

Abstract. Data is increasingly important for companies to get insights, allowing to better serve their customers and to generate new business opportunities. The increase of data with all its hidden potential is so large, that to keep up in understanding that data, we need to scale up by involving the power of the (business) crowd. This starts with knowing what the data is and how it relates to other data. Renowned methods like Fact Based Modeling (FBM) require the participation of specialists, and take time before business people can benefit from this data knowledge. A new approach allows the business to do *self-service modeling* to quickly capture and share relevant knowledge about the data. This approach uses a checklist with questions, guiding the development of an *informal model*. Self-service modeling enables a crowd of people to describe their knowledge about data, scaling up the use of data and its hidden potential.

Keywords: Data semantics · Data/information modeling · Informal models · Business vocabularies · Self-service modeling · Crowd sourcing

1 Introduction

As we all know, data is in the spotlights of many organizations. Data gives unprecedented insights in customer behavior, optimization of processes, cancer research, and drives many new innovations like Blockchain and Artificial Intelligence (AI).

Some analysts predict an enormous rise in business benefit and state that companies that are successful in innovation with data are the ones that have enabled their staff to work with it [1]. The immense volume of data seems only manageable by an immense crowd of humans, potentially with assistance from AI technologies.

Looking at organizations like banks, data often resides in the realms of IT. For years business people worked with data. Even in the old days when bankers registered transactions with quill pens, they were managing and using data. However with the introduction of IT, data became something of IT, with the business following the implementation. With the focus on applications and processes, data was merely a byproduct of these. Not anymore. The value of data is nowadays widely recognized. And business people begin to feel ownership again. An essential aspect of this ownership is knowing what the data is all about. This encompasses both defining data where it is stored, and defining the 'data need'. Surprisingly many data sources do not provide clear meaning and structure understandable for a wide audience.

© Springer Nature Switzerland AG 2019
C. Debruyne et al. (Eds.): OTM 2018 Workshops, LNCS 11231, pp. 159–170, 2019.
https://doi.org/10.1007/978-3-030-11683-5_17

How can we enable business people (anyone who wants to get value from data) to get grip on the data again? How can we get grip on the ever growing amount of data? How can we scale up the efforts to describe data, while there is a limited number of Fact Based Modeling (FBM) or other information modeling specialists around the world? Can we engage business people to help describing the data themselves, and letting information modeling specialists focus on the complex aspects of data for which only they have the knowledge and experience?

2   Information Modeling Is Key

What is a 'customer', what is a 'product'? What do we mean by 'name' of the customer: the family name (e.g. Van Gogh), the full name (e.g. Vincent Van Gogh), or the official name as it is on a passport (e.g. Vincent Willem Van Gogh)? And what is the 'name' when the customer is an organization: the name as it is officially registered by (e.g. Anonymous Beer Company Ltd.) or the everyday name as people will use it (e.g. ABC)? This is for the business to determine.

Data modeling in all its varieties is since long an important tool to design and describe knowledge about data. Often as starting point for development of an application intended to capture and manage data. However, these data models are typically targeted at IT engineers, and used as *technical drawings* guiding them to develop and implement the application. And all too often these models are too complex to be comprehended by normal business people who have not been trained in the technical syntax of such engineering models. A data model is intended to communicate meaning and structure for people with and without specific modeling skills [2].

In my work, I recognize the necessity for business people to understand the structure and meaning, and moreover that they determine both. Often, the business recognizes the importance of meaning, as in many reports, documents, policies, and websites they include business glossaries: terms and definitions.

While a glossary is useful, it lacks a key aspect: structure of how the terms relate to each other. Moreover, the glossaries are often scattered around organizations and not easily to find. As such they are not widely used by business people themselves and also not by IT as starting point for application development.

In the world of Fact Based Modeling it is not a surprise that the structure is just as important as the meaning. Therefore, we need to guide the business somehow, so that their efforts on creating glossaries can be directed towards developing coherent, semantically relevant information models.

Can the business use Fact Based Modeling methods like CogNIAM, ORM 2, FCO-IM [3]? Yes and no. Yes, these are very relevant for them and have better focus on the meaning of the terms than logical data modeling methods like Entity-Relationship modeling or UML, which specifically focus on application development. No, as these methods still require specific syntax for specialists and engineers rather than making it simple for non-IT people. These methods are often just as complex as UML and other standards like OWL[1] for the semantic web [2].

3   Informal Model and Formal Model

In many situations it is of tremendous help when the business defines their own terms to describe data, the context of these terms (structure) and its definitions (meaning). The formal modeling methods guide that, and add specifications relevant for rules and for 'model-based systems engineering' [4].

While that remains important, in my opinion the formal specifications extend the first step to just know what the business means by the terms they use and how it relates to other terms to understand the context. It all starts with the meaning and structure of the terms used by the business, before we can go into the specific details of the rules.

Therefore, we make distinction[2] between *informal models* and *formal models*. A *formal model* is a (semantic) information model that is developed using a method such as FBM, to design structure, meaning and specifications for rules using a strict syntax. An *informal model* is a (semantic) information model that consists of terms, relations, and definitions for a certain scope, allowing a business domain expert the freedom to express his/her knowledge in its own natural language.

As mentioned in the introduction of this paper, the immense growth in data and our wish to engage business people to describe their data and their 'data need', implies that these people should be able to make (semantic) information models themselves. Formal models require expertise and precision, while informal models provide a lower threshold for business people to step in and work with that. And if they succeed, the development of formal models can benefit from a kick start, as the foundation is provided by the informal model.

3.1   Modeling for the Crowd

There is more data than people. And there are more people than modeling specialists. Consequently, it would speed up the capturing of knowledge about all this data when people, without the modeling skills, are able to make informal models. However, even for informal models, we have experienced that some basic skills are needed, next to domain expertise. Without basic modeling skills, people may choose the short way of making definitions for terms, without thinking in a coherent structure of relations between terms. Informal models can then end up as traditional glossaries or as models

---

[1] UML: Unified Modeling Language. OWL: Web Ontology Language.

[2] Please note that the distinction between formal and informal models may be subjective as some may argue that FBM is not as formal as some other methods. In this paper, I consider FBM a formal modeling method.

whereby relations lack consistency or whereby the most relevant relations have been overlooked.

Modeling specialists typically ask business domain experts questions challenging them to reveal the hidden knowledge and capture that in the model. Without those specialists, the domain expert lacks guidance on how to model. But what if we can provide that guidance so that the crowd is engaged to apply self-service modeling resulting in a proper and relevant informal model that facilitates understanding and communicating about data? (Fig. 1).

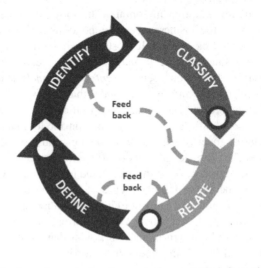

Fig. 1. The four phases in development of a semantic information model.

In our earlier work [6], we introduced an approach to make a model:

1. Identify the term.
2. Classify (determine the hierarchy of) the term.
3. Relate the term to other terms.
4. Define the term.

The new crowd modeling approach extends phase 2 and 3 with questions that people can use as checklist and guidance to understand and capture the relevant context in their informal model.

3.2   Informal Modeling Methods

The *self-service modeling method* does not include a specific modeling language and syntax, as formal models require. The informal model offers a low threshold for people, so they can focus on the meaning, context and understand-ability of their model. Informal models can be created by using the likes of Concept Mapping [2, 5] or simply by drawing a model on a piece of paper or whiteboard: *whiteboard modeling*. These methods offer a wide range of possibilities and freedom. It is easy to make something useful, and just as easy to make something less useful. Experiences with Concept Mapping in education of children, however, show some great results in helping children to understand the subject they were modeling [5].

We introduced a similar approach in our organization, to describe the data and data need for various business domains in the company. This has led to an increase of shared data knowledge in a relatively short time.

4   A Guide to Information Modeling for the Crowd

In the literature, many references are made to some standard relations [7–9]. The following Table 1 lists some of the most recognized standard relations.

Table 1. Some of the most recognized standard relations.

Relation	Example	Relation type
Is a (is a kind of/is a subtype of)	A chair *is a* piece of furniture	Hierarchical relation
Is a part of	A seat *is a part of* a chair	Part-whole relation
Consists of	A chair *consists of* a seat	Part-whole relation
Contains a	A bottle *contains* wine	Part-whole relation
Is in	Wine is in a bottle	Part-whole relation
Has a	A chair *has a* seating height	Attributive relation
Is same as	Customer is same as Client	Synonym relation

For each of these relations, you can ask a specific question. But information modeling is more than just this limited set of standard relations. In fact, we follow the FBM principle of using relations in natural language, to capture the true meaning in the model. Therefore, the method allows many different verbalizations.

4.1   Terms: Entity Types and Value Types

For application development it is common use to develop a conceptual data model, a logical data model, and a physical data model [10]. Although conceptual data models are intended to facilitate communication at business level, in many cases these models are bypassed to go directly to application specific logical data models. The conceptual data model is implementation independent, and describes the concrete and abstract objects in the world that are relevant for the scope: *entities*, such as 'person', 'customer', 'loan'. The technology independent logical data model targets at a specific application, adding field lengths and primary keys, and adds details that describe the entity: *attributes*, the placeholders for data values, the numbers and letters themselves. For example, the entity 'person' may have the attributes 'name', 'date of birth', 'address', and so on. The physical data model further specifies the logical data model for a given technical implementation.

Sometimes, discussions arise about whether a term represents an entity or an attribute. For example the term 'address' is ambiguous. You can argue that it is an attribute, the placeholder for a text like 'First Street 10, 1234AB Amsterdam, the Netherlands'. However, you may also argue that an 'address' is a place, a location and therefore an entity, with attributes like 'street name', 'postal code', etc. To avoid these discussions, the informal model should be *attribute agnostic* as much as possible, meaning that we essentially don't make distinction between entities and attributes, and just talk about *terms*.

The informal model intends to facilitate discussion and common understanding. This implies that the informal model contains terms for both entities and attributes (or in FBM terminology *entity types* and *value types*), as both are equally important and relevant to business people. And by just having *terms* in the model, users can concentrate on the meaning instead of on entity versus attribute. That distinction becomes only relevant in the logical data model or other formal model.

4.2   Self-service Modeling

The idea of information modeling for the crowd comes with a set of questions you can apply to any term, both entity type and value type. These questions are grouped along four dimensions:

- Hierarchical dimension (generalization in super-type and specialization in subtypes, typically covering the 'is a' relations)
- Whole-part dimension (typically covering the 'is part of' relations)
- Attributive dimension (object and its characteristics, typically covering the 'has a' relations)
- Associative dimension (other semantic relations).

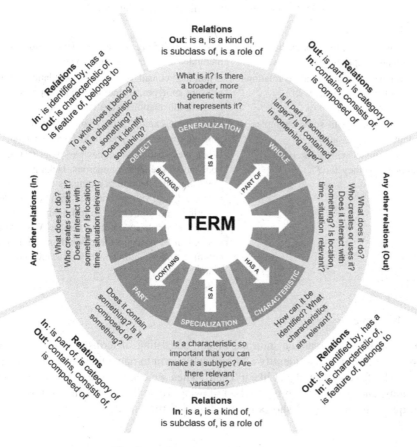

Fig. 2. Self-service modeling template.

The resulting template with per dimension questions and associated relations is shown in Fig. 2 above.

The template does not attempt to be collectively exhaustive. When, as next step, Fact Based Modeling is applied to develop a formal model, more tailor made questions can be asked to reveal all important detailed specifications. But when you consider these standard questions as self-service guidance, in most cases, with willing and knowledgeable people, they can help to make and use own relevant informal models to make knowledge about data explicit and available.

When applying the template with questions to your case, please use examples to validate your answers. And use contra-examples to invalidate and fine-tune your model where needed. Apply these questions to all terms in your model, and for each question ask yourself whether to include the term, that resulted from the answer, in the model or not. Remember that each term should be relevant for the given *universe of discourse* (the scope). The following Table 2 contains questions to test your informal model.

Table 2. Questions for testing your informal model.

Question	Explanation
Are the relations unique for each term or do they also apply to other terms?	Can you rightfully move the relations up in the hierarchy to the term's super-type?
If a term has subtypes, do all its relations apply to the subtypes as well?	If not, then consider moving those relations to the relevant subtypes. Remember that subtypes inherent all relations from its super-type
Test your model with some examples. Do they pass?	When these examples pass your test with a positive result, then your model seems sound
Test your model with some contra-examples. Do they fail?	When these contra-examples pass your test, then your model seems too generous, lacking precision. Use the contra-examples to fine-tune the model until you are satisfied with your model. Note that you don't need to test against every possible example and contra-example. When your model can be used for clear communication and common understanding with your stakeholders, you can stop

4.3   Example

When you want to create an informal model, consisting of terms, relations and definitions, the first step is to identify a 'thing' and a term to name that thing. As example, let's think of a concrete object like a 'chair'. Then we can try to answer the following questions, and see what it brings. The following Table 3 contains the proposed standard questions, and Fig. 3 shows the resulting informal model.

Table 3. Questions for developing an informal model

Question	Explanation	Example
Hierarchical dimension		
What is a it?	Is there a broader, more generic term that represents it? This question is the first important step in understanding what it actually is. It is the 'kick-off word' [11]	Chair is a piece of furniture
Can you distinct variations so that you can make subtypes?	Are there more specific variations with narrow meaning that are relevant to consider?	Office chair is a chair Lounge chair is a chair
Is a characteristic so important that you can make it a subtype?	You may consider to promote a characteristic to a subtype	Swivel chair is a chair

(*continued*)

Table 3. (*continued*)

Question	Explanation	Example
Whole-part dimension		
Is it composed of something? What?	This question helps to think of it, and to discover if it is relevant to know what it consists of	Chair consists of a seat
		Chair consists of a back
		Chair consists of a stand
Does it contain something? What?	Is there something that you can put into it that is relevant for your informal model?	For a chair this question may not be relevant, but for a container, it may be relevant that it can contain a package, or freight
Does it belong to a larger group? Of what?	This question helps you to think about the larger picture. It could be that the group of which it is a member, has its own characteristics and relations	Chair is part of a set
		Chair is a member of a set
Attributive dimension		
Is there a moment in the lifecycle that is relevant?	You can think of a start date, end date, maturity date, settlement date, birthdate, event date	Chair was made at production date
How can it be identified?	This question helps to make it concrete	Chair is identified by serial number
What characteristics are relevant?	How would you describe it to someone on the phone?	Chair has a height
		Chair has a color
		Chair has a style
		Chair has a price
Associative dimension		
What does it do? What function or role does it fulfil?	This is often the main reason for including the term in your model	Person can sit on a chair
Who creates or uses it?	It may be relevant to identify an actor that interacts with it	Chair was designed by a designer
Does it interact with something?	This is to identify relevant relations to other objects	Chair stands on the floor
Is there a location that is relevant?	This is typically dependent on the universe of discourse, your scope, whether this is a relevant question	Chair is in a room
Is it derived or calculated from something?	This question helps to think of it, and to discover if it is relevant to know if it is composed of some other characteristics	Price is derived from cost price
		Price is derived from sales margin

(*continued*)

Table 3. (*continued*)

Question	Explanation	Example
Who determined the value of it, when, where, why, how?	These questions may be relevant for the model, but not always. Make sure to only include in the model what is relevant to your scope	Sales manager determines price Price is determined using market analysis
Should it be consistent with some other term in the model?	Some characteristics interact with other characteristics. This relation can be relevant to make explicit in the model, as it can be the basis for business rules such as data quality rules	Price is aligned with sales status

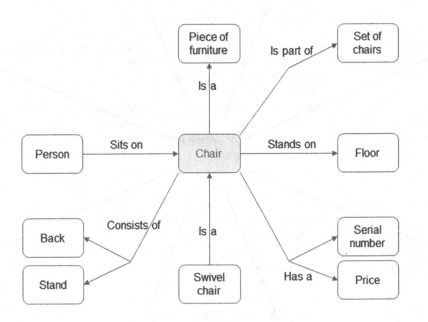

Fig. 3. Applying the self-service modeling template to the term 'chair'.

4.4   Guidance on Direction of Relations

While in a formal model the relations can be bi-directional with matching verbalizations, the informal model simply uses one-directional relations. For the direction we apply two basic principles:

1. From the 'most important' term to the 'less important' term. E.g. 'Person has a name', 'Person sits on a chair'. In a visualization of the model, these 'most important' terms will stand out, as many relations 'flow out' of them. Which term is more important than the other, relies on subjective judgement.
2. Use natural language as much as possible to express the relation. Use the verbalization that feels most natural, as others should be able to instantly understand what you mean.

5   Conclusions and Future Work

We believe that empowering the crowd to work with data is essential for organizations to become the new leaders in turning data into value. To enable them, a checklist with standard questions gives guidance for self-service modeling.

An informal model will help people to understand and use data more quickly and easily, while their involvement deepens their knowledge and engagement. An informal model will *not* replace a formal model like FBM models, as the higher detailing and specification in the formal model is still required for (e.g.) business rules. When the crowd lays the foundation of coherent terms, relations and definitions, the modeling specialists can fine-tune, extend and take up the real challenges where modeling precision is key.

We will continue our experiments with crowd modeling and adjust and extend the approach where possible and useful.

References

1. Marr, B.: Data Strategy. Kogan Page Limited, London (2017)
2. Frisendal, T.: Graph Data Modeling for NoSQL and SQL, 1st edn. Technics Publications, Basking Ridge (2016)
3. Fact Based Modeling. http://www.factbasedmodeling.org/. Accessed 01 Aug 2018
4. SEBoK. Guide to Systems Engineering Body of Knowledge. http://www.sebokwiki.org. Accessed 01 Aug 2018
5. Novak, J.D., Cañas, A.J.: The Theory Underlying Concept Maps and How to Construct Them. Florida Institute for Human and Machine Cognition (IHMC) (2006)
6. Lemmens, I., Pleijsant, J.M., Arntz, R.: Using fact-based modelling to develop a common language. In: Ciuciu, I., et al. (eds.) OTM 2015. LNCS, vol. 9416, pp. 197–205. Springer, Cham (2015). https://doi.org/10.1007/978-3-319-26138-6_23
7. Is-a. https://en.wikipedia.org/wiki/Is-a. Accessed 01 Aug 2018
8. W3C OWL Web Ontology Language Reference. https://www.w3.org/TR/owl-ref/. Accessed 01 Aug 2018

9. van Renssen, A.: Semantic Information Modelling Methodology. Gellish.net, Zoetermeer, The Netherlands (2015)
10. DAMA-DMBOK: Data Management Body of Knowledge, 2nd edn. Technics Publications, Basking Ridge (2017)
11. Ross, R.G.: How To Define Business Terms In Plain English: A Primer. Business Rule Solutions, LLC (www.BRSolutions.com) (2017)

Industry Case Studies Program 2018 (ICSP) 2018

ICSP 2018 PC Co-chairs' Message

Cloud computing, service-oriented architecture, business process modelling, enterprise architecture, enterprise integration, semantic interoperability—what is an enterprise systems administrator to do with the constant stream of industry hype surrounding him, constantly bathing him with (apparently) new ideas and new "technologies"? It is nearly impossible, and the academic literature does not help solving the problem, with hyped "technologies" catching on in the academic world just as easily as the industrial world. The most unfortunate thing is that these technologies are actually useful, and the press hype only hides that value. What the enterprise information manager really cares about is integrated, interoperable infrastructures, industrial IoT, that support interoperable information systems, so he can deliver valuable information to management in time to make correct decisions about the use and delivery of enterprise resources, whether those are raw materials for manufacturing, people to carry out key business processes, or the management of shipping choices for correct delivery to customers.

The OTM conference series have established itself as a major international forum for exchanging ideas and results on scientific research for practitioners in fields such as computer supported cooperative work, middleware, Internet/Web data management, electronic commerce, workflow management, knowledge flow, agent technologies and software architectures, Cyber Physical Systems and IoT, to name a few. The recent popularity and interest in service-oriented architectures & domains require capabilities for on-demand composition of services. These emerging technologies represent a significant need for highly interoperable systems.

As a part of OnTheMove 2018, the Industry Case Studies Program on "Industry Applications and Standard initiatives for Cooperative Information Systems - The evolving role of Cyber Physical Systems in Industry 4.0 implementation", supported by OMG, IIC (Industrial Internet Consortium), IFAC TC 5.3 "Enterprise Integration and Networking" and the SIG INTEROP Grande-Région, emphasized Research/Industry cooperation on these future trends. The focus of the program is on a discussion of ideas where research areas address interoperable information systems and infrastructure. Five short papers have been presented, focusing on industry leaders, standardization initiatives, European and international projects consortiums and discussing how projects within their organizations addressed software, systems and architecture interoperability. Each paper has been reviewed by an international Programme Committee composed of representatives of Academia, Industry and Standardisation initiatives. We thank them for their dedication and interest.

We hope that you find this industry-focused part of the program valuable as feedback from industry practitioners, and we thank the authors for the time and effort taken to contribute to the program.

September 2018

Hervé Panetto
Wided Geédria
Gash Bhullar

RDA Europe and Industry

Fabrizio Gagliardi[(✉)] and Amalia Hafner

Barcelona Supercomputing Center, Jordi Girona 29, 08034 Barcelona, Spain
fgagliar@bsc.es

Abstract. The Research Data Alliance (RDA) Europe Industry Advisory Board (RDA IAB) was created in the context of RDA-EU3, a Coordination and Support Action (CSA) funded by the European Commission to support in Europe the global mission of the RDA initiative. The RDA IAB, besides other actions, conducted a series of interviews with private sector representatives. The interviews focused in four areas: the role of data in the companies' activity, the recurring problems that the companies encounter in this scenario, the initiatives to solve these recurring problems, and the opportunities for academia and industry to collaborate in their mutual benefit. The conclusions of this survey are reported and explained.

Keywords: Data industry · Business models · Standards

1 Research Data Alliance

The Research Data Alliance (RDA) [1] is an international member-based organisation focused on the development of infrastructure and community activities to reduce the social and technical barriers to data sharing and re-use. And to promote the acceleration of data driven innovation and discovery worldwide.

RDA Europe [3], the European plug-in to the Research Data Alliance (RDA), ensures that European political, research, industrial and digital infrastructure stakeholders are aware of, engaged with and actively involved in the global RDA activities. Launched in September 2015, RDA Europe 3 was mandated to ensure that European research, industrial, e-infrastructure and policy stakeholders were all aware of its achievements, engaged with and actively involved in the global RDA activities and advance the use of its results. European domain scientists and data scientists were involved in and drove a series of working and interest groups, generating first results of RDA and fostered adoption and dissemination of RDA outputs [2].

2 The RDA Europe Industry Advisory Board

The overall majority of RDA members (both individual and organizational) come from the academic field and public research institutions. Representation of the private sector, though slowly growing, is still quite low.

Industry engagement is an important priority: sharing data between researchers and innovators with the aim to tackle the big challenges of society is in the core of RDA's

C. Debruyne et al. (Eds.): OTM 2018 Workshops, LNCS 11231, pp. 173–177, 2019.
https://doi.org/10.1007/978-3-030-11683-5_18

vision. RDA, as a community-based initiative, aims to become a common ground in which academia and industry can collaborate.

RDA-EU3 was a Coordination and Support Action (CSA) whose aim was to promote the RDA mission in Europe and support a stronger participation of Europeans in RDA. For the long-term sustainability of RDA in Europe and worldwide, industrial uptake of RDA output is essential.

In this context, the Industry Advisory Board (IAB) [4] was created as an entity of RDA-EU3.

Fabrizio Gagliardi, from the Barcelona Supercomputing Center, chaired the Board. The members had been chosen to represent a mix of industrial IT solutions providers, major data consumers and SMEs, which base their business models on large scientific data repositories. The members contributed by critically reviewing the outputs that RDA had produced, by performing a gap analysis of the services and the activities that RDA was carrying out, which should be relevant for industry, and made suggestions for the long term sustainability of RDA. Full list of the members is available on the RDA web site.

3   The Interviews

Thanks to the contacts established with several RDA Working Groups and Interest Groups (Use Cases Group, BioSharing Registry WG, Scholix WG, Weather, Climate and Air Quality IG, BioDiversity Data Integration IG, Publishing Data Workflows WG, Data Citation WG, Data Fabric IG, Big Data IG), the RDA Industry Advisory Board was able to contact a number of private sector representatives and some of them eventually became members of the RDA Europe IAB.

Among the IAB activities, we conducted seven interviews to private sector representatives, who offered their valuable insights regarding the data landscape in Europe. We interviewed representatives of IBM, Predictia, Terradue, EDP Renováveis, Engineering SPA, Rasdaman and Springer Nature.

Moreover, considering that RDA Europe will continue to organize activities addressed to the private sector in the region with the ongoing RDA-EU4 CSA, our aim was to pave the road to offering interesting and useful activities for data-intensive companies. For that reason, with RDA Europe's future activities in mind, we tried to get an overview from the private sector's perspective, in order to understand the needs and expectations of the Industry and the way in which RDA could address their demands.

The interviews focused on four areas: the role of data in the companies' activity, the recurring problems that the companies encounter in this scenario, the initiatives that aim to solve these recurring problems, and the opportunities for academia and industry to collaborate in their mutual benefit.

3.1   A Subsection Sample Data and Business Models

With the interviews we conducted, we tried to cover three different types of companies, regarding their relationship with data:

- Companies that own the data they produce themselves;
- Companies that offer technologies and services to work on external data;
- Companies that offer consultancy services and expertise.

Most of the companies we interviewed are working with external data sources, both from their own clients' repositories and/or from public repositories. For some of the interviewees, open data (especially scientific data) is a very important resource: on the one hand, it can be used to do experiments and tests and, on the other, it can even be considered as a "business driver". Some companies derive their own business models from open data and, while doing so, foster collaboration between different stakeholders, beyond their specific business.

Our interviewees stressed the fact that "it is of utmost importance to continuously be aware of (and extend) the state of the art". Therefore, participation in collaborative initiatives with academia is key.

Even though most of the interviewees make use of public data sources under open data licenses, one of them pointed to the fact that usage restrictions are usually applied to this kind of data in some cases (open access for non-commercial use only, for instance). He added, "These are interesting cases because it means very often that the data provider is also 'open' to discuss terms and conditions for a commercial use".

3.2   Recurring Problems and Bottlenecks

A recurring bottleneck is the skills gap, and finding suitable skilled staff tends to be a problem for the companies that participated in this survey. Moreover, it was stressed that leadership teams and other workers (such as editors in the Publishing industry) should be aware of data-related terminology, methods and tools.

Data traceability is a very relevant requirement for the data-services community, especially for those who work with several data sources, both public and private. Traceability is linked to data authenticity and security, which are identified as main concerns for some companies' customers. Quality assurance and quality control should be easier to use and less expensive, according to some interviewees and "efforts are still needed on the technology providers side to help in this goal".

Compliance with privacy rules (GDPR was specifically mentioned by most of our interviewees) is considered as a potential challenge for industry.

The usage of different types of data sources is usually linked to an important issue: standards. The adjustment to specific standards is sometimes identified as a customers' demand and, therefore, being aware of the market's demand for specific standards is of utmost importance for the private sector.

While the interviewees recognized that there is usually sufficient documentation and metadata available to enable meaningful sharing and reuse, "a plethora of local conventions often impede exploitation". Some interviewees explained that some regions tend to offer more open datasets than others, and therefore the standards implemented differ. In addition, since standards are continually evolving, it is necessary to consider that "technology and the software implementations sometimes follow these evolutions with disparate timeframes". For these reasons, the interviewees claim that standards should be ideally global and stable.

3.3   Solving Problems Through Collaboration. What Could RDA Do?

Active participation in relevant standardization bodies is an approach followed by several companies for fostering the application of standards. Besides implementing standards, some interviewees have collaborated as editors of such open standards.

Moreover, some of them have taken active roles in community-based organizations such as RDA, in order to promote data sharing and data reuse.

Regarding RDA outputs, some of the companies that participated in this survey have implemented some RDA recommendations and outputs [2]. It was pointed out that general principles, guidelines and proofs of concept have been much easier to implement than technical outputs. In this line, it was stressed that, for outputs to be easily implemented, they must be maintained for the longer term, and funded accordingly.

Another positive outcome of collaborating with others is the fact that, people working together better understand limits and constraints when reusing data. These experiences can, therefore, encourage standardization efforts and avoid "reinventing the wheel" by in-house ad-hoc developments.

4   Conclusions

The interviewees see RDA as a forum in which computer science and data experts can work together with the public and private sectors and foster collaboration. For that reason, they encourage RDA to advertise its outputs and organize activities in which academics and industry representatives can get together and find opportunities to collaborate in their mutual benefit. OTM is a potential good venue for this.

They also suggested that some pilot test cases on the use of the RDA outputs in their companies could have been very useful, if RDA-EU had identified the necessary resources to support this exercise.

In summary we can conclude that large commercial companies still manage data mostly in separate and compartmented 'silos'. IT industry in general is not very interested in standards and common solutions for data sharing, since they see in promoting their own formats and procedures a way to keep their customer base captive. There is therefore a role here for regulatory authorities to break this situation and promote interoperability, standard adoption, and best practices for the common good.

References

1. Research Data Alliance (RDA): https://www.rd-alliance.org/
2. A complete list of outputs and recommendations: https://rd-alliance.org/recommendations-outputs/adoption-recommendations
3. RDA Europe: https://www.rd-alliance.org/rda-europe
4. RDA-EU3 IAB: https://www.rd-alliance.org/groups/rda-europe-industry-advisory-board

Self-optimization in Quality Assurance with Cyber-Physical Systems

Roland Jochem[(✉)]

Technical University Berlin, Pascalstr. 8-9, 10587 Berlin, Germany
roland.jochem@tu-berlin.de

Abstract. The paper outlines the history and further development of our demonstrator, draws the connection between classical and future production and shows novel approaches from process data to self-optimization with focus on product quality. A focus will be laid on data analysis and the steps from process data to knowledge of the product quality. Furthermore, an assistance system named QS-Services is presented to support the user in understanding process data for quality assurance in industry 4.0.

Keywords: Quality assurance · Smart micro factory · Cyber-physical system

1 Introduction

The increasing amount of sensor data generated in production systems together with the ever-growing interconnectedness of all systems result in new opportunities for quality assurance. Process data can be accurately monitored, analyzed and connected to assess product quality already during the production process. While being announced as a theoretical concept, the practical transition of Industry 4.0 to autonomous flexible production plants with complete data exchange between all components is now in full swing. But the technical changes provide far more opportunities than just modernizing the classical schemes, it opens the door to a whole range of digitally assisted new ways to rethink production. Quality, time and money are essential factors to ensure the competitiveness of businesses. In order to maintain the top position of German industry among the industrialized countries, a work group being instituted by the German government announced the fourth industrial revolution in 2013 [1]. The aim is to increase the rate of innovation, therefore enhancing the development of new processes, technologies and business models. Today, Industry 4.0 is one of the decisive drivers of numerous developments in Germany and beyond [2–4].

With the digitalization and networking of production systems, the amount of data available for quality assurance and quality management increased immensely. Assistance systems offer the possibility of intuitive and efficient control of production processes through acquiring, analyzing and evaluating data in real time. In the long term, a fully networked processes chain together with an integrated management system will optimize production machines in real time [5].

Industrial production is highly automated today, there are correspondent sensor data available for each regulation. Furthermore the interconnectedness of machines is

C. Debruyne et al. (Eds.): OTM 2018 Workshops, LNCS 11231, pp. 178–183, 2019.
https://doi.org/10.1007/978-3-030-11683-5_19

growing more and more, more and more data are generated, which are available at central places.

Instead of using the data only for the maintenance of the production they could also be viewed out of the perspective of quality assurance. Through real-time observation, information about the quality of a product can be generated and assessed already during the production process. This will actively be lead back into the process, because a qualitatively high result will be achieved with the regulation of the process parameters. Learning algorithms are installed, which adapt the process flow automatically to an ideal result. At the same time deviations are identified early and waste and downtime are minimized. Alongside long-run analysis and pattern recognition give evidence about the machine's condition, downtimes can be avoided through intervention in time.

Since the 1980s the catapult has been established as standard learning instrument for the acquisition of the Design of Experiments (DoE) methods and got worldwide fame. Because of the broad acknowledgement and acceptance even of decision-makers, the catapult is extremely well suited for the implementation of the new approach of Quality in the Industry 4.0 and to accompany and support the change of industry.

2 Smart Micro Factory as Enabling Infrastructure for Digital Quality Assurance

To study the changes and opportunities of Industry 4.0, a completely autonomous production plant has been built on a lab scale. The small micro factory (SMF) incorporates all aspects of Industry 4.0 as a demonstrator and creates the opportunity to test and study new concepts in a safe environment as well as providing the platform for teaching concepts (Fig. 1).

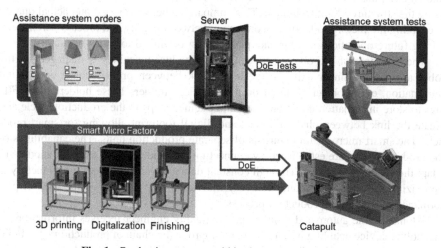

Fig. 1. Production process within the smart micro factory

The experimental setup to produce valid and reliable answers while also optimize the cost to benefit ratio by the so-called design of experiments method. To teach this, the catapult experiment is well established. In our lab setup, the classical catapult, where the experimenter tries to throw an object a given distance by manually varying force, angle and length of the catapult arm, has been transferred into the fully automated cyber-physical system "catapult 4.0". An app guides the user through the necessary steps and monitors his progress, while the experiments are performed automatically. A camera system systems tracks the trajectory of thrown objects and the flight stability is analyzed. The landing position is accurately measured by a rotating laser scanner and the object is picked up and placed back into the catapult by a five axes industrial robot arm mounted on a linear axis.

Around the setup of this experiment, a modular and autonomously working manufacturing plant has been constructed to produce the object that is thrown. It consists of 3D printers, a 3D scanner and a tumble finisher. As with the experiment design parameters, an app guides the customer through the process of designing an object and helps deciding on its quality in terms of accuracy versus production time. The small micro factory handles the individual production process autonomously. During the entire time, all process parameters are accurately tracked and quality of the outcome is being assessed.

For instance, layer height is a dominant factor for product quality in the 3D printing process, the first step in our production line. If sensors detect an error, it is possible to analyze the cause and effect in real-time using the help of statistical algorithms. In the future, all sensor data will be analyzed and cross-referenced with known data patterns. Should patterns occur, that indicate deviations from the target quality, the smart factory can adapt the production process and either correct the edges by including the tumble finisher in the production process or reprint the part. If data analysis does not result in a known case, the surface quality of the produced object is measured in the 3D scanner using the structured light technique. This comparison between target and actual quality is enabling the factory to learn the connection between quality and process parameters, during future operations similar data patterns can be linked to states of quality.

The transport of the object between the individual machines is managed by the robot arm on the linear axis. To create the link between printed object and digital information, every object is stored on a work piece holder. These holders use RFID tags to store information about previous and planned steps in the production cycle and create the link between physical object and digital footprint allowing for smart products. The smart micro factory consists of separate production units. The capabilities of the production line are established by connecting the modules with a central module to adapt the production orders. Through constant data analysis, the smart micro factory is optimizing the quality outcome of every individual step as well as the overall performance of the entire production process.

Alongside the automated production, the quality engineer receives information on his mobile device enabling him to react and improve the chain of production or to build the basis of communication to relevant persons. Quality dashboards demonstrate the links between process data and predicted outcome. While being a project in itself to demonstrate the next steps in the future of production, the smart micro factory has become the basis for other projects and collaborations that build on its opportunities, as well as training courses in an industry 4.0 environment.

A focus will be laid on data analysis and the steps from process data to knowledge of the product quality. Furthermore, practical implications and future projects are being presented. Upon completion, participants will be able to describe novel approaches to quality assurance in industry 4.0.

3 QS-Services Supporting Digital Quality Assurance Tasks

Accordingly, an assistance system named QS-Services has been developed to support the user in understanding process data. Following the Define-Measure-Analyze-Improve-Control Methodology [6], the application guides the user through the individual steps. By asking more and more specific question, the user interactively characterizes a problem in the define phase. Adding additional parameters, such as tolerance limits have a positive influence on the algorithms and enable more specific recommendations.

During the development of QS-Services, experimental tests were conducted to determine and correlate significant influencing factors on product quality. In the measure phase the user is assisted in defining relevant sensors and tracking sufficient process data. Statistical algorithms as well as methods for quality improvement form the basis of the analyze phase in QS-Services. To improve the production process, a detailed report is containing in-depth analysis of previously entered issues and recommendations to solve identified problems in future production cycles. By this, the responsible quality engineer or machine operator is enabled to adjust the process settings at an early stage and actively influences quality in a positive way.

It is to be emphasized that the results of the implementation of measures in QS-Services are documented and stored for further usage, forming the control phase. Therefore, a control loop is implemented, that enables the system to learn continuously and thus derive targeted preventive measures even more precisely.

QS-Services provides a framework to identify causes and derive measures in a transparent way, even without in-depth knowledge in the field of statistical data evaluation. In particular, the analysis of data correlations with regard to product quality is a major challenge. To be able to make statements about the product quality, laboratory tests have been conducted and methods developed in order to derive statements about interaction of process parameters. QS-Services differentiates between the analysis of individual parameters and parameters in correlation to find solutions within increasingly complex production environments (Fig. 2).

Due to the findings of QS-Services, it is possibly to intervene directly in the production process. Complaint and error management costs are lowered, and organizations are enabled to further increase their competitiveness through introducing tar-

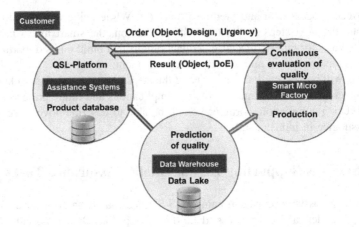

Fig. 2. QS-Services provided by an assistance system in the QSL-Platform

geted preventive measures to eliminate errors. The assistance system describes a first step towards predictive quality [7].

In a sample implementation the assistance system has been integrated in an Industry 4.0 production environment. The Quality Science Lab (QSL) [8] is a production system consisting of independent cyber-physical units. An off-the-shelf 3D printer with additional sensors and data processing units has been equipped as a key technology in industry 4.0. Prints of low quality are identified and process parameters are analyzed with the help of QS-Services. Further implementations with industry partners are in preparation.

4 Summary and Outlook

A small micro factory has been built, that incorporates all aspects of Industry 4.0 as a demonstrator and creates the opportunity to test and study new concepts in a safe environment as well as providing the platform for teaching concepts. Based on the current research, QS-Services provides a framework to be further developed and to encompass ever more complex scenarios. With the implementation of further technologies and their continuous improvement, the reliable prediction of product quality is possible. With the realization of industry 4.0 in a comprehensively networked, digitalized production environment this will give quality engineers the opportunity to intervene and adapt process parameters already during production process. Through monitoring and analyzing process parameters, negative outcomes can be avoided and customer requirements can be fulfilled.

Presently QS-Services focuses on statistical methods, in next steps machine learning technologies will be implemented. Comparison of this classical and modern approaches will lead to insights about applying data science techniques like cluster analysis and neuronal networks in a production environment.

References

1. Adolph, A., et al.: Deutsche Normungs-Roadmap: Industrie 4.0, Version 2, DIN e. V, p. 8, Berlin (2015)
2. Kagermann, H., Wahlster, W., Helbig, J.: Deutschlands Zukunft als Produktionsstandort sichern: Umsetzungsempfehlungen für das Zukunftsprojekt Industrie 4.0. In: Abschlussbericht des Arbeitskreises Industrie 4.0, acatech – Deutsche Akademie der Technikwissenschaften e.V, p. 1, München (2013)
3. Bauernhansl, T., et al.: Industrie 4.0 in Produktion, Automatisierung und Logistik, p. 9. Springer, Wiesbaden (2014)
4. Roth, A.: Einführung und Umsetzung von Industrie 4.0, pp. 3–6. Springer, Heidelberg (2016)
5. Kiem, R.: Qualität 4.0: QM, MES und CAQ in digitalen Geschäftsprozessen der Industrie 4.0, pp. 5–6. Carl Hanser Verlag GmbH & Co. KG, München (2016)
6. Jochem, R., Herklotz, H., Geers, D., Giebel, M.: Six Sigma leicht gemacht: Ein Lehrbuch mit Musterprojekt für den Praxiserfolg, p. 24. Symposion Publishing, Düsseldorf (2015)
7. Hagerty, J.: Planning Guide for Data and Analytics, Gartner Inc., p. 13, Stamford (2016)
8. Seiffert, K., et al.: Traditionelles neu gedacht: Das Katapult als Lernzeug für die Qualität in der Industrie 4.0. In: Refflinghaus, R., Jochem, R., Kassler: Schriftenreihe Qualitätsmanagement, pp. 43–59. Fachgebiet Qualitäts- und Prozessmanagement an der Universität Kassel, Band 6, Kassel (2016)

Modeling Sensor Networks for Predictive Maintenance

Jan Zenisek[1,2]([envelope]), Josef Wolfartsberger[1], Christoph Sievi[1],
and Michael Affenzeller[1,2]

[1] Institute for Smart Production, University of Applied Sciences Upper Austria,
Campus Hagenberg, Softwarepark 11, 4232 Hagenberg, Austria
`jan.zenisek@fh-hagenberg.at`
[2] Institute for Formal Models and Verification, Johannes Kepler University Linz,
Altenberger Straße 69, 4040 Linz, Austria

Abstract. Predictive Maintenance is one of the most intensively investigated topics in the current Industry 4.0 movement. It aims at scheduling maintenance actions based on industrial production plants' past and current condition and therefore incorporates other trending technological developments such as the Internet of Things, Cyber-Physical Systems or Big Data Analytics. In this short paper we motivate the employment of machine learning algorithms to detect changing behavior as indication for the necessity of maintenance on a microscopic level and describe how cyber-physical environments benefit from this approach.

Keywords: Predictive maintenance · Machine learning · Digital twin

1 Introduction

Predictive Maintenance (PdM) plays an essential role in the current Industry 4.0 movement, since it is considered to increase the productivity of today's tightly synchronized manufacturing businesses, where minor unforeseen machinery breakdowns can quickly lead to huge monetary losses. However, the topic is still in its infancy. Working real-world implementations of PdM are rare, although the enabling technologies and methods already exist (cf. Internet of Things (IoT), Cyber-Physical Systems (CPS), Big Data Analytics) and production industry is committed to invest in this area. Collecting data from sensors and checking empirically set thresholds are common auxiliary features of manufacturing execution systems on modern production plants, but they rather enable to react to already present malfunctions, than to predict upcoming ones. Thus, the majority of recent work in the PdM area concentrates on analyzing the monitoring data of entire machine fleets with sophisticated algorithms to find error indicating patterns in real-time and trigger maintenance operations proactively [4]. As the eventual goal of PdM the exact estimation of a production plant's remaining useful lifetime is frequently mentioned. However, data sets which allow

C. Debruyne et al. (Eds.): OTM 2018 Workshops, LNCS 11231, pp. 184–188, 2019.
https://doi.org/10.1007/978-3-030-11683-5_20

to make such ambitious predictions are difficult to produce, starting with carrying out a large number of *Run-to-Failure* experiments [5]. In the research project *Smart Factory Lab, EFRE/IWB 2014–2020* we have lately achieved promising results by employing a microscopic machine learning approach, which is in the spotlight of this short paper.

2   Condition Monitoring Approach

In Fig. 1 our approach of creating a Digital Twin for modern industrial plants is outlined and the following sections elaborate on its two phases: *modeling* (offline) and *evaluation* (online). Initially, the production system is modeled for all known normal and erroneous states based on sensor data collected in a supervised phase with machine learning algorithms. Subsequently, these models are evaluated on the data stream in order to check if the system is behaving normal, drifting from its original concept, or already in a known erroneous condition.

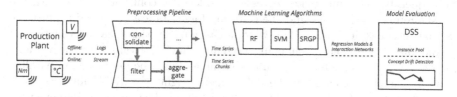

Fig. 1. From raw sensor data to concept drift detection in a decision support system.

2.1   Machine Learning

The success of machine learning algorithms heavily depends on the quality of the data they are working with. Hence, one's attention should first be directed to correct data recording and proper preprocessing. For the offline modeling phase, usually large sets of recorded data from different plants are prepared under supervision, which have been labeled as representitive for a particular system state by domain experts. In a subsequential step a pipeline of rules is developed (e.g. to filter outliers, aggregate features etc.), which all data, offline or online, must pass to ease the successive modeling process.

Following recent work on Condition Monitoring and PdM we employ prominent machine learning methods, such as Random Forests (RF), Support Vector Machines (SVM) or Genetic Programming based Symbolic Regression (SRGP) to train time series regression models for different system states [2,6]. More specifically, we propose to train ensembles of models, one for each physical sensor by using the others' past values as input vectors. Based on these sensor models variable interaction networks are generated by using the most influencial variables for each sensor. Therefore, the impact of each variable used in the developed models is calculated by alternately deactivating them from the model's input vector and reevaluating it (cf. [3] for more details). Exemplary regression models and a variable interaction network with sample weighting for the sensors x_4 and x_n are illustrated in Fig. 2.

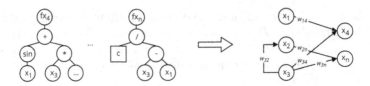

Fig. 2. Building variable interaction networks based on regression models.

2.2 Model Evaluation

In the second phase the developed models and networks are evaluated with the aim to detect drifts off from normal system behavior before reaching erroneous states and hence, to determine a reasonable point for maintenance. Therefore, the online data stream may be transferred from the plant to the analysis environment e.g. via the *MQTT* protocol in order to pass the built preprocessor pipeline. Subsequently, the time series regression models are continuously fed with the latest preprocessed values and the resulting forecasts are evaluated against the factual sensor series in a sliding window fashion. By this means an increasing prediction error indicates changing system behavior. Evaluating the variable interaction networks follows a similar routine and may be performed in parallel. However, herein a change in the determined weight of variable impacts holds accountable for drift detection. The outlined methodology has been implemented as a plugin for the open source framework HeuristicLab[1].

3   Real-World Challenges and Applications

Continuous monitoring of system conditions results in high volume of time series data, which poses challenges for hardware and software in CPS environments. While sensor and storage equipment is getting cheaper, networking possibilities in production halls are still quite limited and thus, centralized analytical services might not always be feasible. Even if networking is no issue for a particular case, the repeatedly targeted large scale monitoring approaches on fleets of production plants tend to turn into opaque data graveyards. Macroscopic data analysis still might lead to some general statements, e.g. vague trends for wear and tear, but unlikely to deeper insights, such as particular failure root causes.

The presented approach contributes to mitigate some of the stated real-world problems. For instance, since the focus of the resulting machine learned sensor models and networks is quite constrained, they can be evaluated even on microcontrollers within milliseconds and hence, enable reducing network traffic as they may replace single physical sensors, which are entirely describable by others. Following this, the entire drift detection routine may be implemented directly on the plant controller. This way a plant itself aggregates raw sensor data to a single performance indicator and thus, acts more intelligent, as frequently demanded

---

[1] https://dev.heuristiclab.com.

[4] and causes less networking traffic. Furthermore, the microscopic modeling approach might help to gain deeper insights for domain experts, especially when *White-Box-Modeling* approaches (e.g. Symbolic Regression) are employed [1].

We tested our approach on a set of challenging synthetic time series, as well as on data from real-world applications with promising results, which will be part of upcoming work due to the limited space in this paper. However, for more details the reader is referred to recent work, where we performed experiments with similar approaches [1, 3, 6].

4   Conclusion and Outlook

In this work we presented an approach for identifying malfunctioning industrial plants. Therefore, regression models and variable interaction networks are used to evaluate a continuous data stream, identify deviations from normal behavior and enable triggering maintenance actions proactively. For quantitative analysis of the performed experiments and case studies the reader is referred to the referenced and upcoming work. As a promising next step to enhance the described approach we consider to investigate how closer integration of modeling and evaluation phase may lead towards online- and self-learning machinery.

Acknowledgments. The work described in this paper was done within the project "Smart Factory Lab" which is funded by the European Fund for Regional Development (EFRE) and the country of Upper Austria as part of the program "Investing in Growth and Jobs 2014–2020".

References

1. Affenzeller, M., Winkler, S., Wagner, S., Beham, A.: Genetic Algorithms and Genetic Programming: Modern Concepts and Practical Applications. CRC Press, Boca Raton (2009)
2. Ahmed, N.K., Atiya, A.F., Gayar, N.E., El-Shishiny, H.: An empirical comparison of machine learning models for time series forecasting. Econ. Rev. **29**(5–6), 594–621 (2010)
3. Kronberger, G., Fink, S., Kommenda, M., Affenzeller, M.: Macro-economic time series modeling and interaction networks. In: Di Chio, C., et al. (eds.) EvoApplications 2011. LNCS, vol. 6625, pp. 101–110. Springer, Heidelberg (2011). https://doi.org/10.1007/978-3-642-20520-0_11
4. Lee, J., Kao, H.A., Yang, S.: Service innovation and smart analytics for industry 4.0 and big data environment. Proc. Cirp **16**, 3–8 (2014)

5. Saxena, A., Goebel, K., Simon, D., Eklund, N.: Damage propagation modeling for aircraft engine run-to-failure simulation. In: International Conference on Prognostics and Health Management, pp. 1–9. IEEE (2008)
6. Zenisek, J., et al.: Sliding window symbolic regression for predictive maintenance using model ensembles. In: Moreno-Díaz, R., Pichler, F., Quesada-Arencibia, A. (eds.) EUROCAST 2017. LNCS, vol. 10671, pp. 481–488. Springer, Cham (2018). https://doi.org/10.1007/978-3-319-74718-7_58

Framework for Collaborative Software Testing Efforts Between Cross-Functional Teams Aiming at High Quality End Product

Prabal Mahanta[1(✉)] and Georg Bischoff[2]

[1] SAP Labs India Pvt Ltd., Bangalore 560076, Karnataka, India
p.mahanta@sap.com
[2] SAP SE, Dietmar-Hopp-Allee 16, 69190 Walldorf, Germany
georg.bischoff@sap.com

Abstract. Currently software testing has become critical, expensive (time and cost), effort intensive activity. There are times when software development teams keep the testing activities until a feature development completion which impacts the delivery and quality. To overcome certain friction in quality, there are methods like automation which are applied to various phases of development but often the regression element is skipped. The paper stresses on key elements like automation, quality metrics, feedback and collaboration between cross units in case of diverse team sets in a large organization. The paper tries to present a framework where collaboration, standardization of software testing approach at each level of development becomes critical for successful and high-quality software delivery.

Keywords: Collaboration · Coaching · Automation · Testing ·
Software development · Quality

1 Introduction

Testing automation is an integral part of software development. With the increase in size of the project in terms of systems, modules, features, the complexity increases leading to requirement of testing being intensive for the initial delivery of the software. The notion of software testing calls large team collaboration due to the criticality of product quality. The requirement of collaboration also presents the DevOps way of development in teams distributed across the geography [1].

If we consider agile products, the differently located teams come together to provide a solution to a specific problem or a customer requirement. Most often test and quality are the processes which are often ignored until the base functionality of the product is ready. This seldom leads to hotfix-based development activities during acceptance stages. Most often we ignore the importance of having a quality landscape dedicated to testing before migration to production to cease issues reported by development teams [2].

Using this short paper, we would like to touch upon the challenges, approaches to formulate-execute-manage tests and the methods that can leverage better collaboration

© Springer Nature Switzerland AG 2019
C. Debruyne et al. (Eds.): OTM 2018 Workshops, LNCS 11231, pp. 189–195, 2019.
https://doi.org/10.1007/978-3-030-11683-5_21

and more insightful hands-on practice sharing between the teams. We also touch upon the concept of line of application testing and context aware testing which also forms an integral part of any application since we currently also have to consider user accessibility and consistency [3, 4].

2 Outlook and Approach Towards Quality

As many of the on-premise solutions are moving to the cloud, the development practices are evolving in terms of approaching and delivering a solution. The perception of quality is mandatory to be realized in the solution design phase where parameters like scale and resilience be considered. Moving on to the development, the pre-requisites for any solution should be met before the code setup is started. The quality of code and effort of developers' variance must be observed to make sure that the developers are not suffering a burn out and effective code are being delivered for high quality product. The approach described is difficult to follow up in practice due to the existing cultural notions in teams.

The key elements that requires a rethinking and confirmation before any feature development is the user experience consistency, functional correctness and accordingly developers and quality should design their tests cases and make sure that they include the tests for execution in the continuous delivery and integration pipelines [5]. To further investigate in detail the test paradigms that we need to take into consideration:

a. Design of Test Suites – For any product, designing of test suites are a critical phase and it encourages a team to define their quality factor which can serve as a baseline for future releases
    i. Coverage – Code coverage.
    ii. Exploration – Exploratory test cases should cover tests which may come across during manual tests apart from the cases covered in automation.
    iii. Security – Security tests cases should be covered in adherence to domain requirements and also data privacy should be taken care of.
    iv. Performance – Performance tests cases should also cover future scalability cases.
    v. Automation – Segregated Unit and E2E test cases.
    vi. Evaluation – Corrective actions based on the failures or modifications.
    vii. Reporting – Segregated reports should be designed for users since it matters for developers to have granular details and for management it is critical to have overview.
    viii. Management – Proper management of test cases.
    ix. Tools and Frameworks – Choice of tools and frameworks should be in accordance with the use cases, requirement and expertise in the team.
    x. Prioritization – Tests should be prioritized during the design phase and tests should be written with boundary conditions before the development starts.

b. Context Aware – The application test case definition also requires the process of identification of contextual information, and characterize context-aware application behavior on the basis of -
   i. User Context
   ii. Time Context
   iii. Computing Context
   iv. Location
   v. Orientation

c. Selection of Tests – Test case selections should be based as per the feature delivery prioritization. This criteria can be also accomplished using the greedy prioritization algorithm.

d. Execution of Tests – Testing should be made mandatory for Continuous Integration process.

e. Functionality based Product line Tests so that adherence to delivery KPIs are met by the development.

The above listed parameters or paradigms are comprising of the real-world challenge for achieving any quality product. Often when executing a product we rarely look into the aspects that can make the product quality go higher. The reason that sometimes during our product development lifecycle we overlook the quality factors is due to the lack of coordination, product focus and skills among the teams.

Testing a product begins with testing the design of the mock-ups, workflows, user experience guidelines, test suites, architecture, infrastructure and overall management of the test cases which should not be limited only to the functional requirements of the product but extend it to the non-functional requirements [6].

In any organization, testing activities are often allocated to cross functional units and the developers are involved when the design thinking phase completes along with starting of the development of the required features. By this point, often the design shortcomings are masked with additional development requirements. Now there is a need of streamlining the shortcomings be it design, architectures, features using a methodological and also a collaborative way of supporting the product development phases [7] (Fig. 1).

The ownership mindset in development teams needs to build in order streamline the complete process and testing aspects. Also quality criteria should not only be owned by development but by cross functional collaborating teams [8] as this helps in exploring quality parameters. This is a critical paradigm which is required from the perspective of a cloud based development aspect. Since cloud development also advocates that the delivery cycles be shorter, it is often harder to trigger this aspect to adopt to the complete lifecycle based on context aware mechanisms. Here we can adopt or implement a framework for developing the attitude towards productive quality. To overcome the challenge of mindset and to realize the potential of quality we all need to understand and be disciplined in following practices and practices that govern an agile project and believe in "Quality is in the code" [9].

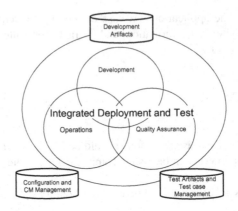

Fig. 1. Towards a "Quality is in the code" mindset

3 Perspectives

In the course of development to delivery, there are various challenges that can be overcome by guided hands. This aim can be achieved by building an active community and a consortium which provides a platform for collaboration and knowledge sharing. There are various challenges in building up of community, nurturing it and also thriving it setting up successful deliveries which is accepted by the development units and also cross unit collaborations.

Teams often overrule priority of designing tests and extend the same to delivery of functionality of the product. Decisions like these are very harmful in the long running product practices leading to lack of quality. The aspect that we can check is to have an anonymous external crowd sourced platform that leads to better decisions, collaborations for feature feedbacks and bug detection. The decision key stakeholders here are defined but the voting for a decision should be made anonymous since in cases of exception there is no personal issues that come up during the overall process [10].

Companies can also form expert teams which can perform the cross-collaboration bridge for various aspects of product development leading to increase of the developer efficiency. These teams should nurture the intellectual property of the product, bring out the use cases with hands-on experience and increase the productive outcomes to build up a quality product [11].

Another aspect is crowd testing, or a more open approach can be beta testing, which can be made applicable at the early stages of development where these tasks can be carried out with partners to perform Non-Functional, Exploratory, Assurance and Performance aspects of testing. Overall the implementation forms a quality gate before releases. Here the key driving force should be relevant users performing such operations globally for a line of product mostly being the functional experts.

4   Retrospective

Many products also require a thorough implementation of the features for a specific device and hence our traditional approach to determine the key elements for testing is not effective and here we need to focus in device based test suites. Similarly for machine learning and artificial intelligence based applications, it is critical to test the context awareness from time and space perspective [12] but not only limited to series analysis using the time series analysis method. Likewise for an upcoming technology for e.g. blockchain, new paradigms should be determined to finding the unknowns and then basing the test suites on the lines of the unknowns to better the product and understand the adoption of the process that is required [13].

Determining the critical elements for delivery of a successful product quality aspects are –

a. Extension of Testing in design and user experience
b. Proper Mapping of customer requirements
c. Reporting granularity of Tests
d. Infrastructure based Tests
e. Tests for resilience.

The need of automation also resonates with above key elements and hence it becomes the only means where the overall costs can be minimized or kept in check for overflowing feature development scenarios. Automation and Continuous delivery are critical for success of any product since it enables outreach of product features to the customers in a short period of time [15] (Fig. 2).

Interoperability, infrastructure and resilience are key to any agile development projects. Hence there is a need to synchronise the continuous integration which has become disruptive in the development and this also recognizes the need to identify the tool which can support, adapt and scale based on projects. In doing so, we also evolve

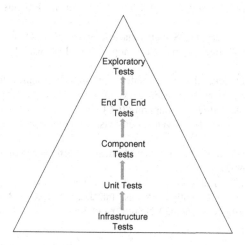

Fig. 2. Extension proposal of the typical test pyramid [14]

our practices internally as well externally from a team perspective if we adopt the notion of crowd sourcing, beta testing within an organization [1].

5   Conclusion

Test automation approach differs from product to product as per the quality requirements. The higher the degree of test automation, the higher the increase of quality of any industry product and same applies not only to a software testing organization but a manufacturing organization also. If the planning and design of the test suites along with inclusion of the test strategy earlier in the planning stage of the product development yields a better ROI. The thought of going beyond and exploring the unknowns for upcoming technologies and also considering the testing of the environment with equal importance is the key to a consistent and a high quality customer product.

References

1. Leicht, N., Blohm, I., Leimeister, J.M.: Leveraging the power of the crowd for software testing. IEEE Softw. **34**(2), 62–69 (2017). https://doi.org/10.1109/MS.2017.37
2. Buffardi, K., Robb, C., Rahn, D.: Tech startups: realistic software engineering projects with interdisciplinary collaboration. J. Comput. Sci. Coll. **32**(4), 93–98 (2017)
3. Abrahamsson, P., et al.: Agile software development methods: review and analysis. arXiv preprint arXiv:1709.08439 (2017)
4. Grechanik, M., Xie, Q., Fu, C.: Creating GUI testing tools using accessibility technologies. In: International Conference on Software Testing, Verification and Validation Workshops, ICSTW 2009. IEEE (2009)
5. Zhao, Y., et al.: The impact of continuous integration on other software development practices: a large-scale empirical study. In: Proceedings of the 32nd IEEE/ACM International Conference on Automated Software Engineering. IEEE Press (2017)
6. Davis, F.D., Venkatesh, V.: Toward preprototype user acceptance testing of new information systems: implications for software project management. IEEE Trans. Eng. Manag. **51**(1), 31–46 (2004)
7. Bell, J., Sheth, S., Kaiser, G.: Secret ninja testing with HALO software engineering. In: Proceedings of the 4th International Workshop on Social Software Engineering. ACM, New York (2011)
8. Banzai, T., et al.: D-cloud: design of a software testing environment for reliable distributed systems using cloud computing technology. In: Conference on 10th IEEE/ACM International Cluster, Cloud and Grid Computing (CCGrid). IEEE (2010)
9. Lauesen, S., Younessi, H.: Is software quality visible in the code. IEEE Softw. **15**(4), 69–73 (1998)
10. Thomas, K.W.: Conflict and conflict management: reflections and update. J. Organ. Behav. **13**(3), 265–274 (1992)
11. Fiore, S.M., Salas, E.: Team cognition and expert teams: developing insights from cross– disciplinary analysis of exceptional teams. Int. J. Sport Exerc. Psychol. **4**(4), 369–375 (2006). https://doi.org/10.1016/0022-2836(81)90087-5

12. Burrell, J., et al.: Context-aware computing: a test case. In: Borriello, G., Holmquist, L.E. (eds.) UbiComp 2002. LNCS, vol. 2498, pp. 1–15. Springer, Heidelberg (2002). https://doi.org/10.1007/3-540-45809-3_1
13. Garousi, V., et al.: What industry wants from academia in software testing?: hearing practitioners' opinions. In: Proceedings of the 21st International Conference on Evaluation and Assessment in Software Engineering. ACM (2017)
14. Fowler, M.: Testpyramid, May 2012. https://martinfowler.com/bliki/TestPyramid.html. Accessed 04 May 2017
15. Hansen, P., Hacks, S.: Continuous delivery for enterprise architecture maintenance. Full-scale Software Engineering/The Art of Software Testing 56 (2017)

CONSENSORS: A Neural Network Framework for Sensor Data Analysis

Burkhard Hoppenstedt[(✉)], Rüdiger Pryss, Klaus Kammerer,
and Manfred Reichert

Institute of Databases and Information Systems, Ulm University, Ulm, Germany
burkhard.hoppenstedt@uni-ulm.de

Abstract. Machine breakdowns in industrial plants cause production delays and financial damage. In the era of cyber-physical systems, machines are equipped with a variety of sensors to monitor their status. For example, changes to sensor values might indicate an abnormal behavior and, in some cases, detected anomalies can be even used to predict machine breakdowns. This procedure is called predictive maintenance, which pursues the goal to increase machine productivity by reducing down times. Thereby, anomalies can be either detected by training data models based on historic data or by implementing a self-learning approach. In this work, the use of neural networks for detecting anomalies is evaluated. In the considered scenarios, anomaly detection is based on temperature data from a press of a machine manufacturer. Based on this, a framework was developed for different types of neural networks as well as a high-order linear regression approach. We use the proposed neural networks for restoring missing sensor values and to improve overall anomaly detection. An evaluation of the used techniques revealed that the high-order linear regression and an autoencoder constitute best practices for data recovery. Moreover, deep neural networks, especially convolutional neural networks, provide the best results with respect to overall anomaly detection.

Keywords: Anomaly detection · Sensor data recovery

1 Introduction

In modern industrial plants, a rising number of sensors offers advanced opportunities for automatically detecting machine faults. In this context, machine-learning methods have proven to be beneficial [1]. Although first models related to neural networks were already introduced in the 1940s [2], their usage in an industrial context only increased significantly during the last years. Thereby, data storage capabilities constitute an important factor for the development of neural networks as large training data sets usually enhance the overall outcome.

© Springer Nature Switzerland AG 2019
C. Debruyne et al. (Eds.): OTM 2018 Workshops, LNCS 11231, pp. 196–200, 2019.
https://doi.org/10.1007/978-3-030-11683-5_22

Furthermore, the developments in the field of deep learning enable a better readability of neural networks. This improvement is achieved by abstracting information into hierarchically ordered layers. In this work, we apply neural networks techniques to an industrial data set, provided by an automotive press company. More precisely, the data set contains temperature sensor data from three engines in a press and the difference between engine temperatures is used to represent anomalies (cf. Fig. 1, left). These data have been collected over a year of operation before a machine breakdown occurred. With the help of machine learning techniques, we tackle two use cases: First, we aim to recognize anomalies. Second, we try to recover lost (i.e., missing) sensor data. Regarding the first use case, the results can be utilized in advanced information systems for the provision of alerts and condition monitoring. Following the idea that anomalies occur more frequently before a breakdown, they can be used as input for predictive maintenance. Concerning the second use case, data recovery is useful to improve overall data quality and, therefore, enhance data analytics approaches.

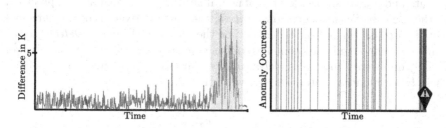

Fig. 1. Extract from measured sensor data (left) and increasing occurrences of anomalies before a breakdown (right)

2   Data Set and Evaluation

The data set stems from a machine manufacturer and consists of values from a press line with six presses. It was recorded over a period of one year, using a sampling rate of one measurement per minute. At the end of this year, a breakdown of one press occurred (cf. Fig. 1, right part). To apply methods of *supervised learning*, the data points are labeled. Thereby, a single data point was marked as anomaly if any of the three engine temperature differences was greater than 5 Kelvin (K). Then, a data section of 120 data points (i.e., each with three temperature values) was used as the input for the neural networks. Note that this corresponds to a 2-h measurement. Furthermore, an input is labeled as anomaly when it contains at least 105 single data points that are regarded as an anomaly. Using this approach, we train the neural network to recognize *anomaly patterns*. Hereby, we recognize exceeded temperature thresholds as well as the time series structure. Next, the data set is split up into training and test data. As the anomalies are underrepresented in the whole data set (cf. Table 1), test

Table 1. Distribution of the data set

ID	Data label	Data set size	Percentage of parent
1	All data	524162	
2	Normal data	518095	98.8% of 1
3	Anomaly data	6067	1.2% of 1
4	Training data normal	512915	99.0% of 2
5	Training data anomaly	4854	80.0% of 3
6	Test data normal	5180	1.0% of 2
7	Test data anomaly	1213	20.0% of 3

data is randomly generated by 1% normal input data and 20% of the anomaly input data.

The proposed framework hierarchy is shown in Fig. 3. It is optimized for sensor data and includes various types of neural networks. To calculate the precision for the use case *Sensor Value Restoration*, the mean derivation of the expected value is used as evaluation criterion. For the use case *Anomaly Detection*, the number of unrecognized anomalies (*false negative*) as well as the number of wrongly discovered anomalies (*false positives*) are used to calculate the F_1-score. These two evaluation criteria are shown in Fig. 2.

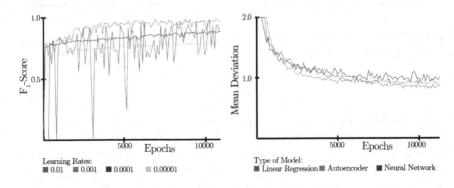

Fig. 2. F_1-scores (left) and mean deviation (right)

In Fig. 3, the most promising results of the framework are shown. The *autoencoder* (AE) performed well for recovering sensor data, but its variants *denoising-autoencoder* (DAE) and *compression-autoencoder* (CAE) achieve a low F_1-score. In contrast, a *fully connected neural network* (FCNN) performed better for anomaly detection than sensor value recovery. Note that the order of the best linear regression (LR) was four. Finally, *convolutional neural networks* are promising for anomaly detection.

3   Summary and Outlook

The presented framework performs well on the shown data set. It restores missing temperature values with an average deviation of less than 1 K and recognizes anomaly patterns reliably. Overall, the main advantages of the framework are as follows: First, due to the hierarchical class structure, it is possible to switch between performance and reliability. High-level networks (e.g., the autoencoder) need more computation time, but achieve better results. Second, the framework is designed for sensor data and allows to select a time window to be evaluated. However, the neural networks need high computation power and, for supervised learning, a pre-labeled data set is required. In future work, *recurrent neural networks* [3] may provide further improvements, as they include previous decisions into a classification. Other approaches dealing with the application of neural networks for sensor data exist. For example, [4] discusses an application of neural networks in a motor system, where vibration signatures are analyzed with the help of neural network agents. Next, [5] reached F_1-scores up to 0.987, using linear autoencoders to detect anomalies in labeled audio databases. However, to our best knowledge, the presented framework combined with data of a press manufacture illustrate new insights.

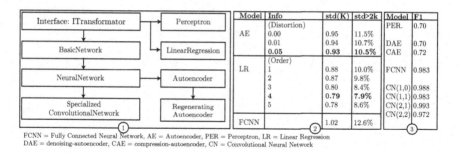

FCNN = Fully Connected Neural Network, AE = Autoencoder, PER = Perceptron, LR = Linear Regression
DAE = denoising-autoencoder, CAE = compression-autoencoder, CN = Convolutional Neural Network

Fig. 3. Framework (1), recovery results (2) and anomaly detection results (3)

Altogether, neural networks are able to adapt to production changes by adjusting their weights. Moreover, they are robust to irrelevant noise, as they are trained to discover only relevant sensor patterns. Therefore, the application of neural networks is promising in the fields of sensor data recovery and anomaly detection.

References

1. Zhao, R., et al.: Deep learning and its applications to machine health monitoring: a survey. arXiv:1612.07640 (2016)
2. Schmidhuber, J.: Deep learning in neural networks: an overview. Neural Netw. **61**, 85–117 (2015)

3. Gugulothu, N., et al.: Predicting remaining useful life using time series embeddings based on recurrent neural networks. arXiv:1709.01073 (2017)
4. Li, B., et al.: Neural-network-based motor rolling bearing fault diagnosis. IEEE Trans. Ind. Electron. **47**, 1060–1069 (2000)
5. Marchi, E., Vesperini, F., Squartini, S., Schuller, B.: Deep recurrent neural network-based autoencoders for acoustic novelty detection. Comput. Intell. Neurosci. **2017**, 14 p. (2017). Article ID 4694860

Flexibility and Interoperability of Production Processes Units

Georg Weichhart[(✉)]

PROFACTOR Gmbh, Steyr, Austria
georg.weichhart@profactor.at

Abstract. In this short paper, we briefly reflect on the project LOISI (Logistics Optimization In Steel Industry), and the use of multiple enterprise models to support the analysis and management of resilience of production processes. We identify one shortcoming in the project with respect to planning of process routes. Based on reflection on the industrial case, research ideas based on process units and (enterprise) interoperability are briefly outlined.

Keywords: Process interoperability · Enterprise interoperability · Enterprise modelling

1 Introduction

The Austrian research project LOISI (LOGISTICS OPTIMIZATION IN STEEL INDUSTRY) has started in October 2016, running till September 2019. The overall goal of LOISI is to support the analysis and design of resilient production processes in the steel manufacturing industry.

A general trend in the steel industry in Europa, and other high wage countries, is to focus on high quality steel production. A lot of research and developments are undertaken to improve the metallurgical quality of the steel casting process. However, to be able to reach the desired high quality steel, logistical process aspects are also of importance. An important function in the context of logistics, is the cooling process of steel. Different temperatures and cooling times for steel influence the quality. Certain missed quality parameters, can be compensated by allowing the steel to cool down more slowly. In other quality related situations, manual re-work of the surface, can improve the steel bloom's quality. Depending on the result of the casting process, different processes and logistical routes are used to reach the desired quality of the steel products.

Given the increased demand for high quality steel, a regular change of the initially planned processes and routes is expected. More high quality products, increase the volatility of the production system and triggers the need for measures, supporting and increasing the resilience of the system.

This industrial case study paper is structured as follows. We briefly describe the current work in the LOISI project, and propose an extension based on the idea of interoperable process units.

© Springer Nature Switzerland AG 2019
C. Debruyne et al. (Eds.): OTM 2018 Workshops, LNCS 11231, pp. 201–204, 2019.
https://doi.org/10.1007/978-3-030-11683-5_23

2   Industrial Models

The enterprise has been identified as a complex adaptive system [2]. To capture the complexity of the system in a single model is not possible. It is required to use multiple models. Different decision makers have different requirements and have their own world view captured in models of their domain [3]. In LOISI multiple enterprise models are used to support the identification of short-time events and long-term trends that disturb the production system.

Examples for short-time events that disturb the *standard* production process are, breakdowns of sub-systems, like transport vehicles, and missing spaces for cooling, due to unexpected additional cooling requirements by other product orders.

Examples for long term trends disturbing the production, are an increase in demand for high quality steel which implies tighter corridors for acceptable steel quality parameters and, longer cooling phases for steel to reach the desired quality.

Both types of disturbances will occur in the future more often and have negative impact on the production system's performance. However, it can not be predicted to what extend different possible scenarios will emerge.

To improve the situation of decision makers, and support process management, three different models are developed in LOISI.

- A performance measurement system is developed to make the effect of disturbances visible to the decision makers.
- A scheduling system optimizes the use of alternative processes and logistical routes to improve the resilience.
- A simulation system allows to model different configurations of the production system and the effect of the use of process alternatives in different scenarios.

The modelling process happening within the project, supports learning of participants and knowledge exchange between participants [1]. The three models share a single point of view. The major difference is the goal of the model as indicated in the list above.

The overall strategy to increase resilience in this project, is to elaborate different processes and routes which are then chosen after the result of the casting process of steel blooms is known. Such alternative process routes for steel blooms become necessary in situations when a steel bloom is re-classified to a lower quality steel. That implies the need to produce replacement steel blooms with the initially desired high quality. Next to these and similar reasons, also breakdowns of production sub-systems are a major factor that trigger the need for alternative processes and routes. For example the steel needs to be transported with different vehicles, needing a different duration.

The simulation environment allows to design scenarios with e.g. different probability of breakdowns and different customer order mixes with different demand for quality. The performance measurement system makes the need for different process routes visible, and allows to measure the impact of different strategies for selecting certain routes as a counter-measure.

However, in the current project the alternative process routes are fixed. This limits the solution space. In the following we elaborate on extending the project to support the dynamic planing of steel bloom process routes through the production system.

3   Process Units for Dynamic Production Process Planning

Above we have discussed the current conceptual approach in an applied research project. Based on observed limitations we discuss an extended research project with a larger solution space.

By dividing production processes into smaller units, it is possible to react to many parameters on the spot. Such process units, allow to place the planning process between a pure rules based approach (very dynamic but no stability) and a pure process based approach as described above. Chaining of multiple units to form larger processes is supported. By building an environment that supports the formation of interoperable processes, using the process units, negative impacts of the complexity will be reduced.

The underlying idea is similar to replacing business processes with business rules, but is placed somewhere between both approaches. Task sequences which need to be fixed (e.g. due to physical requirements) may be modelled as single unit.

First an abstract process of different stages the physical product (steel bloom in this case) follows needs to be modelled. However, in exceptional situations, these stages may be very different. The process units describing the same stage may also be very heterogeneous. Second, it is necessary to specify input and output properties and conditions used to support the automated chaining.

For the formation, a set of alternative process units for each stage need to be identified. Then it is necessary to decide which unit to choose. The choice will be dependent on the impact the choice has on the product, and general system states.

Different process units have to be specified for different transport means. Process units have to be specified for quality related function steps (e.g. cooling) depending on the place where the step takes place. A process unit might have different result in different places. Different process units might also have different impacts on the place where these are executed. For example process units are associated with different costs.

Open to further research are issues related to the description of process unit interfaces. In particular when keeping the initial requirement of generating resilient processes loosely coupled systems are desired [3]. Interface concern general services related to process planing, chaining, execution, and monitoring. There will also be domain specific interfaces related to connecting process units so these can be chained in a (domain-specific) useful manner. Next to the interface descriptions, services need to be identified that trigger and execute the planning and chaining. Here some logic-based domain-specific language is desirable to be able to encode the applicability of a process unit in certain situations and to react to events and disturbances [2].

Reasoning environments, and accompanying logic languages, need to be evaluated to support the modelling of such units and also the validation of the results by experts. A simple PROLOG-like mechanism is not sufficient, as that allows only single chains without process specifications of parallel etc. A more expressive language is needed, capable of being extended to meet the vocabulary and logic of the domain experts encoding the system.

4   Upcoming Challenges

In the LOISI project we improve the resilience of the system by supporting different production processes and logistic routes for steel products. The complexity and dynamics of the production system is made manageable for decision makers by using an optimization model, a performance measurement system (numerical model), and a simulation model. Based on observations made in the industrial case, we have identified potential for further research.

We have identified process units as a means for making the production more agile, while allowing to specify physical properties and constraints along processes. The mechanism needs to be more elaborated than simple chaining mechanism like offered by PROLOG. Units form larger processes by following an abstract description of stages a steel bloom has to go through. Some stages requires parallelism or XOR like conditions.

Acknowledgement. The research described in this paper has been funded by the Governments of Upper Austria, Styria and the SFG: FFG Project "Logistics Optimisation in Steel Industry (LOISI)" Contract nr.: 855325.

References

1. Oppl, S.: Supporting the collaborative construction of a shared understanding about work with a guided conceptual modeling technique. Group Decis. Negot. 26(2), 247–283 (2017). https://doi.org/10.1007/s10726-016-9485-7
2. Weichhart, G., Guédria, W., Naudet, Y.: Supporting interoperability in complex adaptive enterprise systems: a domain specific language approach. Data Knowl. Eng. 105, 90–106 (2016). https://doi.org/10.1016/j.datak.2016.04.001
3. Weichhart, G., Stary, C., Vernadat, F.: Enterprise modelling for interoperable and knowledge-based enterprises. Int. J. Prod. Res. 56(8), 2818–2840 (2018). https://doi.org/10.1080/00207543.2017.1406673

International Workshop on Methods, Evaluation, Tools and Applications for the Creation and Consumption of Structured Data for the e-Society (META4eS) 2018

META4eS 2018 PC Co-chairs' Message

The future eSociety, addressed with our workshop, is an e-inclusive society based on the extensive use of digital technologies at all levels of interaction between its members. It is a society that evolves based on knowledge and that empowers individuals by creating virtual communities that benefit from social inclusion, access to information, enhanced interaction, participation and freedom of expression, among other.

In this context, the role of the ICT in the way people and organizations exchange information and interact in the social cyberspace is crucial. Large amounts of structured data – Big Data and Linked (Open) Data – are being generated, published and shared on the Web and a growing number of services and applications emerge from it. These initiatives take into account methods for the creation, storage and consumption of increasing amounts of structured data and tools that make possible their application by end-users to real-life situations, as well as their evaluation. The final aim is to lower the barrier between end-users and information and communication technologies via a number of techniques stemming from the fields of semantic knowledge processing, multilingual information, information visualization, privacy and trust, etc.

To discuss, demonstrate and share best practices, ideas and results, the 6th International IFIP Workshop on Methods, Evaluation, Tools and Applications for the Creation and Consumption of Structured Data for the eSociety (Meta4eS 2018), an event supported by IFIP TC 12 WG 12.7, BYTE Big Data Community (BBDC) and Data Licenses Clearance Center (DALICC) project, with a special focus on cross-disciplinary communities and applications associated with Big Data and their impact on the eSociety, brings together researchers, professionals and experts interested to present original research results in this area.

We are happy to announce that, for its seventh edition, the workshop raised interest and good participation in the research community. After a thorough review process, with each submission refereed by at least three members of the workshop Program Committee, we accepted 3 full papers and 3 short papers and one poster paper covering topics such as ontology engineering, natural language processing, sentiment analysis, multimodal search, storytelling, unsupervised automatic keyphrase extraction, evaluation, cross-language information retrieval, query translation disambiguation, text mining, social semantics, decision making, data management and applied to the fields of software quality, air quality monitoring, smart city, cryptocurrency investment, open archives, multimedia cultural content, multilingual resources and media.

We thank the Program Committee members for their time and effort in ensuring the quality during the review process, as well as all the authors and the workshop attendees for the original ideas and the inspiring discussions. We also thank the OTM 2018 Organizing Committee members for their continuous support. We are confident that Meta4eS will bring an important contribution towards the future eSociety.

October 2018

Ioana Ciuciu
Anna Fensel

A NLP Approach to Software Quality Models Evaluation

Simona Motogna$^{(\boxtimes)}$, Dana Lupsa, and Ioana Ciuciu

Computer Science Department, Babes-Bolyai University, 1, M. Kogalniceanu,
Cluj-Napoca, Romania
{motogna,dana,ioana.ciuciu}@cs.ubbcluj.ro

Abstract. This paper aims to analyze and identify the variations and similarities between models/standards in the software quality domain. The approach combines analysis at several levels, starting with a naive comparison done by the software quality expert, going through several NLP specific similarities measures. The final goal is to be able to rapidly identify solutions to make a software compliant with new standard. The focus of the current study is on the lexical analysis of software quality models based on natural language processing.

Keywords: Software quality · NLP · Similarity between words

1 Introduction

Software quality is an important aspect of software development and it represents an efficient method to differentiate applications and to evaluate the development process.

We can mention at least three main ways in which software quality may be proved useful:

Firstly, Considering the plaetoria of applications existing on the market, how to choose in which to invest, in order to be sure that it will comply to different standards. Software quality can offer uniform measurements to compare different applications. Secondly, the applications that are developed today are more and more complex, with several versions being developed over considerable amount of time, and the software development process can become difficult to manage. Software quality measures can indicate changes between versions that might generate such unmanageable situations. Complying to software quality standards makes this process more controllable. Lastly, from a software company perspective, a label of software quality compliance can be a way to gain trust and attract more clients.

A software quality model represents a set of factors that completely characterize a software system. They capture both external aspects (such as usability, efficiency, reliability a.s.o.) and internal aspects (such as maintainability, reusability, testability a.s.o.).

C. Debruyne et al. (Eds.): OTM 2018 Workshops, LNCS 11231, pp. 207–217, 2019.
https://doi.org/10.1007/978-3-030-11683-5_24

Since the first software quality model introduced by McCall [12], several other proposals have been issued and the lasts of them have been standardized. McCall model defined 11 factors, which form the basis for following models. Some factors, like maintainability and reliability, have been present in all models, while other factors appeared in later models. Such an example is security, which is understandable to be promoted as an important characteristic of software systems, due to the spred of web and mobile applications. An overview of software quality models and their corresponding factors is presented in Table 1.

Table 1. Software quality models

SQ model	Factors
McCall	Correctness, Reliability, Efficiency, Integrity, Usability, Maintainability, Testability, Flexibility, Portability, Reusability, Interoperability
Boehm	Portability, As in Utility - containing Reliability, Efficiency, Human Engineering Maintainability - including Testability, Understandability, Flexibility
FURPS	Functionality (F), Usability (U), Reliability (R), Performance (P) and Support (S)
ISO 9126	Functionality, Reliability, Usability, Efficiency, Maintainability, Portability
ISO 25010	Functional Suitability, Performance Efficiency, Compatibility, Usability, Reliability, Security, Maintainability, Portability

The study of those models lead us to the following remarks:

- The domain of software quality uses several concepts and terms with different definitions and meaning;
- The domain of software quality is very variable: even software quality (SQ) standard models change in time, and terms differ from one issue to another. For example, in ISO 25010 [9], issued in 2011, the term "appropriateness" replaced "suitability" from ISO 9126 [1], issued in 2001.

The research question addressed in this study is to investigate a method to compare software quality models, by identifying changes in models, as well as identifying new introduced factors or removed ones. Our approach is from a Natural Language Processing (NLP) perspective, and for computational purposes, we used Natural Language Toolkit (NLTK) [3]. The two models that we studied are ISO9126 [1] and ISO25010 [9].

The rest of the paper is organized as follows: next section presents a comparison based of observations between the two SQ models. Section 3 introduces the similarity measures applied for the two SQ models, and compares the models based on these computations. In the end, we discuss some related work, present the conclusions and describe our future ideas for this study.

2   Naive Comparision of ISO9216 and ISO25010

Introduced in 1991, ISO9126 [1] represented the standard for software evaluation, addressing quality model, external, internal, and quality in use metrics. The software quality model, known as ISO9126-1, proposed a set of six characteristics, each further divided into subcharacteristics: functionality, reliability, usability, efficiency, maintainability and portability.

ISO25010 [9] replaced, in 2011, ISO9126, and is the current standard used for software products. The standard proposes eight characteristics, further divided into subcharacteristics, that complete describe the standards that a software product should comply.

A simple comparison between the two models identified the following similarities, respectively differences:

Firstly, four characteristics have been preserved between the two versions, namely: Reliability, Usability, Maintainability, Portability. However, if we look at the subcharacteristics corresponding to them, we notice that none of the ISO9126 characteristics remained the same. For example, Reliability may be considered the characteristic with the minimum change, as shown in Table 2, since only Availability has been added as a subcharacteristic. Availability is defined as "degree to which a system, product or component is operational and accessible when required for use", which is justified by the fact that component based development as increase significantly in the last years.

Table 2. Reliability in ISO9126 and ISO25010

ISO9126	ISO25010
Maturity	Maturity
	Availability
Fault tolerance	Fault tolerance
Recoverability	Recoverability

Another aspect worth noticing is that some modifications are not very clear since the newly introduced term is very similar to the one existing in ISO9126, which make it difficult to realize the distinction. Such examples are: Changebility replaced Modifiability as subcharacteristics of Maintainability, respectively Resource behavior replaced by Resource utilization in Efficiency.

Two of the characteristics have been renamed with small differences, namely: Functionality - Functional suitability, respectively Efficiency - Performance efficiency.

Two new characteristics have been added to ISO25010, Compatibility and Security. A closer look to their definition will show that even in this case there are some similarities with the previous model: Compatibility is formed of Coexistence and Interoperability, the later being present also in ISO9126, as a subcharacteristic of Functionality. Security was defined in ISO9126 also as a subcharacteristic of Functionality, so in this case we can say that security has been promoted to a more significant importance, which is quite obvious considering the type of applications developed today (web, mobile, component based).

3   A NLP Based Approach to Software Quality Models Comparison

In the context of having many software quality models, many of them having a lot in common, but many of them reorganizing factors and sub-factors, to have a tool to automatically emphasize changes can be extremely useful for software projects that are already known as meeting some quality standards.

Having two software quality models, our approach in finding their similarities is based on text similarity computations. Given a model and its description, the aim is to find how different a new model is and which items matches the previous one.

The approach presented in this work is based on the information provided by a software quality model. The problem we address is to match the categories of a second model to those in the first model. It is based on similarity computation at a word level (Sect. 3.1) and similarity computation based on lexical similarity (Sect. 3.2).

3.1   Set-Based Similarity

Phrases can be seen as set of words. One method to compute the similarity between phrases is based on common words and does not take into account the meaning behind words. The intuition says the more common words two texts share, the more similar they are.

From common similarity measures that can be used with sets [4,7,17] we use: overlap, Jaccard and Dice.

If A and B are sets, then **overlap** is computed as cardinal of the intersection over the minimum cardinal of the two sets, that is:

$$overlap(A, B) = \frac{card(A \cap B)}{min(card(A), card(B))} \tag{1}$$

Dice similarity measure is computed as twice the cardinal of the intersection over the sum of the cardinals of the two sets:

$$Dice(A, B) = \frac{2 \times card(A \cap B)}{card(A) + card(B)} \tag{2}$$

Jaccard similarity measure is computed as the cardinal of the intersection over the cardinal of the union of the two sets:

$$Jaccard(A, B) = \frac{card(A \cap B)}{card(A \cup B)} \tag{3}$$

3.2   Lexical Similarity

Many methods to compute small text similarity are based on word-to-word similarity. The two main approaches for computing word-to-word similarity and relatedness are corpus-based measures and knowledge-based measures [14]. The first uses corpora to discover semantic information based on the idea [8] that words used in the similar contexts will also be semantically similar. These methods use distributional information such as co-occurrence frequencies or statistical measures of association. Among these methods, word embedding techniques such as word2vec [15] are very popular.

Knowledge-based approaches uses linguistic resources, such as semantic networks to extract lexical information. They were shown that provide high correlation scores with the goldstandard in [2] in an evaluation exercise on Semantic Textual Similarity on SemEval 2012.

There are recent studies [13,18] that combine both the information from a corpus-based vector space representation with semantic information extracted from an ontology. They report the same or higher correlation with human judgments as reported by some different word embedding approaches.

In this work we chose to use a knowledge based approach as the first approach to our problem. We also have the intention for the future to further extend our work by using word embedded techniques and then extending the study by combining semantic similarity and corpus-based vector space representation.

We used WordNet lexical database [6] to provide lexical information. WordNet's basic unit is the concept that is represented by the set of synonym words (a synset) that can be used to express that concept in language. Between synsets there are relations corresponding to the relations between the sense of the concepts.

There are several ways to compute lexical similarity between concepts in Wordnet [7,14]. Many similarity measures are path-based and the core idea is that two concepts are semantically close if they are close in the Wordnet ontology. Having identified two concepts, we used *path* similarity, *Leacock-Chodorow* and *Wu-Palmer* similarity to determine the similarity between them.

The **Path Similarity** is defined as:

$$sim_{shortestPath}(C1, C2) = \frac{1}{1 + path\_length(C1, C2)} \quad (4)$$

Leacock-Chodorow similarity also rely on the length of the shortest path between two synsets but it uses a non-linear function and scales the path length by the maximum depth of the taxonomy

$$sim_{LCh}(C1, C2) = -log\frac{path\_length(C1, C2)}{2 \times D} \quad (5)$$

Wu-Palmer similarity is based on the idea that concepts with more depth would be more similar because they are more specific. With the notation LCS for the Least Common Subsumer or closest common ancestor that is the most specific concept that is a shared ancestor of the two concepts, Wu-Palmer similarity is given by the formula:

$$sim_{WuP}(C1, C2) = \frac{2 * depth(LCS)}{depth(C1) + depth(C2)} \tag{6}$$

The similarity measures described above are defined over concepts that are synsets in WordNet. But we need the similarity between words. To compute the similarity between two words based on the similarity of the synsets they appear in, we used the maximum similarity between the synsets in which each word appears [16]:

$$sim(w_1, w_2) = \max_{C_1 \in synsets(w_1), C_2 \in synsets(C_2)} sim(C_1, C_2) \tag{7}$$

3.3   Experiments and Results

Keywords and Set-Based Similarity. Each category has a set of subcategories. Their names, category and subcategories, as text words, can be considered a representative description for the characteristics, or the keywords specific to that characteristic. The first approach is are based on these *keywords*. They form a set of distinct word forms. To compute similarity between categories we used the set based similarity measures that are presented in Sect. 3.1.

Table 3. Associating categories based on keywords and set-based similarity: association results and similarities

ISO25010 category	ISO9126 factor	Overlap	Dice	Jaccard
Performance efficiency	Efficiency	1.000	0.923	0.857
Reliability	Reliability	1.000	0.909	0.833
Portability	Portability	1.000	0.889	0.800
Usability	Usability	0.750	0.400	0.250
Maintainability	Maintainability	0.600	0.545	0.375
Functional Suitability	Functional	0.400	0.400	0.250
Compatibity				
Security				

The results of associating the model characteristic based on keywords and set-based similarity are presented in Table 3. This approach gives 100% accuracy (in the sense that for characteristics that are present in both models the associations and similarities are computed), for all the three set-based computation formula. All three methods shown that few changes exist between first 3 characteristics, namely Performance efficiency, Reliability and Portability. However, the *overlap* measure in this case is not well suited, since its value is 1, but the corresponding concepts do not have identical subcharacteristics (as shown in Table 2). If we look at the similarity measures for maintainability, they show a significant difference between the two SQ models, and this is due to the difference in the names of subcharacteristics (Modificability vs. Changebility).

Keywords and Lexical Similarity. Keywords are also words and carry lexical information. The second method used to compute the similarity between sets is based on the lexical similarity between keywords. The similarity between two sets is computed as the average of the similarities of their keywords.

In this approach, a problem is that among the words used to name the categories and subcategories, there are word forms that don't appear in any WordNet synset. An example is *maintainability*. But, we expect that there are related words (like *maintainable, maintain*) that do appear. In order to associate some concepts to all the keywords, we get their stem and then the list of words that matches the stem and that have synsets in Wordnet, that means that we used a process of stemming - unstemming for each word. Porter stemmer is used, with some new rules added in order to handle for words like *co-existence* or *non-repudiation*, because *co* and *non* are prefixes that are not integrated in Porter stemmer (in NLTK).

With the use of stem-unstem process, we are able to associate close related concepts (synsets in WordNet) to each word. For example, for *maintainability* we go from not having any associated WordNet synset to getting 24 synsets.

By using the path similarity and Leacock and Chodorow similarity, we get 100% accuracy (see Table 4), while by using Wu and Palmer similarity there are 6 of 7 correctly matched categories.

Table 4. Associations of categories based on keywords and lexical information (using path similarity and Leacock-Chodorow similarity)

ISO25010 category	ISO9126 factor	Path	LCh
Functional Suitability	Functional	0.692	2.846
Performance efficiency	Efficiency	0.952	3.559
Reliability	Reliability	0.938	3.490
Usability	Usability	0.649	2.984
Maintainability	Maintainability	0.783	2.854
Portability	Portability	1.000	3.600
Compatibility			
Security			

Based on Description. Each characteristic has a *description* associated to it. The description should be specific enough to clarify the meaning of each characteristic.

A description is a short text. The similarity between the texts is computed based on the synsets of the words in the two text, and it is similar (but not the same) with the formula used in [14] which is based on word similarity.

$$simLeft(T_1, T_2) = \frac{\sum\limits_{ss_1 \in synsets(T_1)} \max\limits_{ss_2 \in synsets(T_2)} sim(ss_1, ss_2)}{dimension(synsets(T_1))} \quad (8)$$

$$sim(T_1, T_2) = (simLeft(T_1, T_2) + simLeft(T_2, T_1))/2 \quad (9)$$

Having words in context, we can determine their Part Of Speech (POS) and for each word we select only the synset of the words that satisfy also the POS restriction. We want to consider only words that are semantically relevant and we use just noun, verb, adjective, adverb. That means that implicit stop list are words with other POS, like conjunction, wh-pronoun, etc. such that words like *the, a, to, or*, etc. are not considered.

The results for this approach are weak and very different from one similarity formula to another, as we can see in Table 5. We also performed experiments with not using the constraint of POS and the results are similar: we get from 2 to 4 correct assigned categories. We want to further investigate this problem in the future and to use different other methods to compute text similarity.

Table 5. Associations of categories based on description; use lexical similarity of words for same POS

ISO25010 category	ISO9126 factors		
	Path similarity	LCh similarity	WuP similarity
Functional Suitability	Functional	Functional	
Performance efficiency	Reliability, Efficiency	Reliability, Efficiency	Reliability, Efficiency
Reliability			
Usability	Usability	Usability	Usability, Portability, Maintainability, Functional
Maintainability		Portability, Maintainability	
Portability	Portability, Maintainability		
Compatibility			
Security			

The conclusions of our study are the following. Set-based similarity, computed based on Dice measure can be used to detect if there is no change between SQ models. Path similarity measure can be used to detect when there is a change and how much had changed (values closer to 1 indicate a small change). Description-based similarity will take into consideration the other characteristics from the model that need to be studied in case of a change (renaming of characteristics, move of a subcharacteristic within model).

An overview of the results obtained by our approaches is presented in Table 6. We can see that better results are achieved by using keywords. The detailed results are available at https://softwareengubb.wordpress.com/page/.

Table 6. Associations of categories. An overview of the results

		Similarity computation method	No. of correctly matched categories
keywords	set-based:	overlap	6 (from 6)
		Dice	6 (from 6)
		Jaccard	6 (from 6)
keywords	lexical similarity:	path-based	6 (from 6)
		Leacock Chodorow	6 (from 6)
		Wu-Palmer	5 (from 6)
description (use POS)	lexical similarity:	path-based	4 (from 6)
		Leacock Chodorow	4 (from 6)
		Wu-Palmer	2 (from 6)
description (don't use POS)	lexical similarity:	path-based	4 (from 6)
		Leacock Chodorow	3 (from 6)
		Wu-Palmer	2 (from 6)

4 Related Work

As stated in the paper, there is currently no common standard in the domain of software quality to adhere to. Several software quality models and standards have been used over the past decades. They involve terminology and concepts with a certain degree of variation between the models. However, there is currently no unique set of concepts commonly agreed on by the software quality community to refer to when assessing the software quality.

Several efforts have been done by the research community to propose a common set of concepts using existing software quality models and standards. We will cite the most noticeable ones here. Kayed et al. [11] conducted an experiment in order to extract a condensed model for software product quality attributes.

They proposed, based on the analysis of the frequency and association of terminology and concepts in various documents, models and standards related to software quality, an ontology that formalizes the semantic of the attributes. The proposed ontology was the starting point for other efforts and research for trying to find a common understanding and agreed models to be used by software engineers, researchers, stakeholders and practitioners. Ciancarini et al. [5] proposed a three-dimensional ontology model, named SQuAP-Ont (https://w3id.org/squap/), based on existing standards for software quality, software process and software architecture. SQuAP is based on the latest software quality standard (ISO25010 [9]) and is easily extendable. A noticeable work was done by Kara et al. [10] in which a generic software quality model based on existing standards and an instantiation algorithm, based on fuzzy logic are proposed.

5   Conclusions and Future Work

The paper proposes a method to compare two SQ models using NLP techniques, namely: word based similarity, lexical similarity of keywords, respectively lexical similarities of descriptions. Several measures have been applied in order to determine the evaluation that identify as precisely as possible the changes between SQ models. ISO25010 and ISO 9126 models were used as case study and the similarity measures where checked against observations of the two models. As a conclusion, these types of similarities can be applied to SQ model to compare them, and determine how much change exists between them.

The results of this approach represent the basis for two future investigations. First, we think about making a complete survey of the SQ models proposed so far, that will lead to tracing of characteristics and subcharacteristics more precisely between models, with the final purpose of building an ontology of the domain. Comparing all SQ models needs an automated approach since the amount of data will be large. The second would be to extend the set of similarity measures that are used with corpus-based methods, and to conduct a comparison between them.

A tool that will incorporate this approach will be a useful method for SQ standard compliance. Imagine the situation in which a new standard is proposed (which is very possible since the last one was issued in 2011), and software products should comply the new standard. Instead of fulfilling all characteristics from scratch, our approach can be used to indicate which characteristics and subcharacteristics need to be changed/added/moved or removed in order to comply the new standard.

References

1. ISO 9126-1: Software Engineering - Product Quality (2001). https://www.iso.org/standard/22749.html. Accessed 2015
2. Agirre, E., Cer, D.M., Diab, M.T., Gonzalez-Agirre, A.: SemEval-2012 task 6: a pilot on semantic textual similarity. In: SemEval@NAACL-HLT (2012)

3. Bird, S., Klein, E., Loper, E.: Natural Language Processing with Python, 1st edn. O'Reilly Media Inc., Newton (2009)
4. Choi, S.S., Cha, S.H.: A survey of binary similarity and distance measures. J. Syst. Cybern. Inform. **8**, 43–48 (2010)
5. Ciancarini, P., Nuzzolese, G.A., Presutti, V., Russo, D.: An ontology of software quality relational factors from banking systems. In: Proceedings of the 15th European Semantic Web Conference, ESWC 2018 (2018)
6. Fellbaum, C.: WordNet - An Electronical Lexical Database, vol. 25 (1998)
7. Gomaa, W.H., Fahmy, A.A.: Article: a survey of text similarity approaches. Int. J. Comput. Appl. **68**(13), 13–18 (2013). Full text available
8. Harris, Z.: Distributional structure. Word **10**(23), 146–162 (1954)
9. ISO/IEC 25010:2011: Systems and Software Engineering (2011). http://www.iso.org. Accessed 2015
10. Kara, M., Lamouchi, O., Ramdane-Cherif, A.: Ontology software quality model for fuzzy logic evaluation approach. Procedia Comput. Sci. **83**, 637–641 (2016). http://www.sciencedirect.com/science/article/pii/S1877050916301739, The 7th International Conference on Ambient Systems, Networks and Technologies (ANT 2016)/The 6th International Conference on Sustainable Energy Information Technology (SEIT-2016)/Affiliated Workshops
11. Kayed, A., Hirzalla, N., Samhan, A.A., Alfayoumi, M.: Towards an ontology for software product quality attributes. In: Proceedings of the 2009 Fourth International Conference on Internet and Web Applications and Services, ICIW 2009, pp. 200–204. IEEE Computer Society, Washington (2009). https://doi.org/10.1109/ICIW.2009.36
12. McCall, J., Richards, P., Walters, G.: Factors in software quality. Technical report, National Technical Information Service 1 (1977)
13. McInnes, B.T., Pedersen, T.: Improving correlation with human judgments by embedding second order vectors with semantic similarity. CoRR abs/1609.00559 (2016)
14. Mihalcea, R., Corley, C., Strapparava, C.: Corpus-based and knowledge-based measures of text semantic similarity. In: Proceedings of the 21st National Conference on Artificial Intelligence, AAAI 2006, vol. 1, pp. 775–780. AAAI Press (2006)
15. Mikolov, T., Sutskever, I., Chen, K., Corrado, G., Dean, J.: Distributed representations of words and phrases and their compositionality. In: Proceedings of the 26th International Conference on Neural Information Processing Systems, NIPS 2013, vol. 2, pp. 3111–3119. Curran Associates Inc., USA (2013)
16. Resnik, P.: Semantic similarity in a taxonomy: an information-based measure and its application to problems of ambiguity in natural language. J. Artif. Int. Res. **11**(1), 95–130 (1999)
17. Rijsbergen, C.J.V.: Information Retrieval, 2nd edn. Butterworth-Heinemann, Newton (1979)
18. Yu, Z., Wallace, B.C., Johnson, T.R., Cohen, T.: Retrofitting concept vector representations of medical concepts to improve estimates of semantic similarity and relatedness. CoRR abs/1709.07357 (2017)

Automatic Query Translation Disambiguation Using Bilingual Proximity-Based Approach

Wiem Ben Romdhane[1], Bilel Elayeb[1,2(✉)],
and Narjès Bellamine Ben Saoud[1]

[1] RIADI Research Laboratory, ENSI, Manouba University, Manouba, Tunisia
br.wiem@yahoo.fr, Bilel.Elayeb@riadi.rnu.tn,
narjes.bellamine.bensaoud@ensi-uma.tn
[2] Emirates College of Technology, Abu Dhabi, United Arab Emirates

Abstract. In this paper, we propose a new automatic query translation disambiguation using bilingual proximity-based approach. This approach combines a traditional bilingual dictionary and parallel bilingual corpus to build a bilingual semantic dictionary of contexts (BSDC) and identify the suitable translation of a word using a proximity matching model. Besides, it uses and extends an existing probabilistic semantic distance to compute similarities between words using a bilingual semantic graph of the traditional bilingual dictionary and the BSDC. We experiment and compare this approach using the French-English parallel text corpus Europarl and the CLEF-2003 French-English CLIR test collection. Our experiments highlighted the performance of our bilingual proximity-based approach compared to both the known efficient probabilistic and the possibilistic ones, for both long and short queries and using different assessment metrics.

Keywords: Cross-language information retrieval (CLIR) ·
Query translation disambiguation · Bilingual semantic dictionary of contexts ·
Probabilistic model · Possibilistic model · Proximity

1 Introduction

Nowadays, the dictionary-based query translation techniques in CLIR systems still lacked by the problem of translation ambiguity [1, 8]. In any QT process, the context is relevant to find the suitable translation for each source query term, thus a word-by-word QT technique is not sufficient in this case. However, and in spite of their advantages, the traditional bilingual dictionaries suffer from the lack of accurate information useful for QT. Furthermore, there exists a lack of high-coverage parallel bilingual corpus on which methods of learning could be trained.

For these multiple reasons, we suggest in this paper the definition of a new linguistic resource, namely the bilingual semantic dictionary of contexts (BSDC), useful to support and ensure the machine learning in a semantic platform of QT. Indeed, the building of this BSDC is based on the combination of a parallel bilingual corpus and a traditional bilingual lexicon. Then, a proximity matching model, based on this BSDC, has been used to select the best translation corresponding to each polysemous source

© Springer Nature Switzerland AG 2019
C. Debruyne et al. (Eds.): OTM 2018 Workshops, LNCS 11231, pp. 218–229, 2019.
https://doi.org/10.1007/978-3-030-11683-5_25

query term. Indeed, we firstly model source query terms and their possible translations via a bilingual semantic graph of the traditional bilingual lexicon and the BSDC. Then, we compute similarities between words using an extended version of an existing probabilistic semantic distance in order to choose the best translation corresponding to each source query term. This approach has been tested using the CLEF-2003 French-English CLIR test collection and the French-English parallel text corpus Europarl (http://www.statmt.org/europarl/). Our experiments have showed the performance of the QT-based bilingual proximity compared to both the known efficient probabilistic and possibilistic approaches [2], for both long and short queries and using different assessment metrics.

The remaining of this paper is organized as the following. The BSDC is presented in Sect. 2. Section 3 details the bilingual proximity-based approach for QT disambiguation. Section 4 presents our experimentations and discusses a comparative study between our QT disambiguation approaches. Section 5 concludes our work in this paper and suggests some perspectives for future research.

2 The Bilingual Semantic Dictionary of Contexts (BSDC)

We suggest here a generic solution based in graphs in order to model knowledge required for QT as a BSDC. However, the automatic building and representation of the graph $G = (T, E)$ associated to a given set of source query terms and their possible translations require the definition of the set of nodes T as well as the set of edges E. During the training step of our approach, these edges and nodes are learned from both the traditional bilingual lexicon and the parallel bilingual corpus [7].

2.1 The Bilingual Set of Nodes

The nodes of the graph are the source query (SQ) terms and their possible translations existing in the bilingual dictionary. It will be considered as polysemous query term if it has more than one possible translation. The inputs of the BSDC are the context of the polysemous word and the inputs of the traditional bilingual lexicon. We model in the following by: (i) **Polysemy(SQ)**: Set of polysemous terms in the source query SQ: p_1, p_2, ..., p_k. This set includes source query terms having more than one possible translation. (ii) **Significant(SQ)**: Set of significant terms, which are not polysemous in the source query SQ: m_1, m_2, ..., m_i. (iii) **Context(p, SQ)** = {$Significant(SQ) \cup Polysemy(SQ)$}\{$p$}; with p is a significant term $\in SQ$. (iv) **Context(SQ)** = {$Significant(SQ) \cup Polysemy(SQ)$}. (v) **Translation($t_i$)**: Set of translations of a significant source query term t_i in the traditional bilingual dictionary d_{ti} if the term t_i is not a polysemy one; and p_i^1, p_i^2, ..., p_i^a if the term t_i is a polysemous one. This set includes only translations which are really used in the training set (i.e. in the BSDC).

2.2 The Set of Edges

According to the nature of the semantic relations which define the edges of the bilingual graph (nodes representing the lexemes of the language), we can distinguish many kinds of lexical networks. We used in the building of our BSDC graph the following kinds of relations:

The Semantic Proximity Relations: We build context-independent links between all possible translations in the graph. Indeed, we build an edge between two translations t_i and t_j if t_j appears in the translation definition of t_i. We formalized this relation as the following: $\forall t_j \in Translation(t_i)$ if $i \neq j \rightarrow <t_j, t_i> \ \in E$.

The Translation Relations: We build an edge between a polysemous source query term t_i and t_j if t_j appears in the translation set of t_i. We formalized this relation as the following: $\forall t_i \in Polysemy(SQ), \forall t_j \in Translation(t_i) \rightarrow <t_j, t_i> \ \in E$.

The Syntagmatic Relations: They are also known as relations of co-occurrence. We build an edge between two words in the graph if they co-occur in the same context. These relations are formalized as follows:

$$\forall t_i, t_j \in Context(SQ) \text{ if } i \neq j \rightarrow <t_j, t_i> \ \in E$$

The Paradigmatic Relations: We focus here on synonymic relation between two nodes. We build an edge between two words if they maintain a synonymic relation between them. In other words, if they share common words in their translations:

$$\forall t_i, t_j \text{ if } \left\{ Translation(t_i) \cap Translation(t_j) \right\} \neq \emptyset \rightarrow <t_j, t_i> \ \in E.$$

We assign weight to each edge in the bilingual semantic graph using formulae detailed in the following sections.

3 The Bilingual Proximity-Based Approach for QT Disambiguation

We present in this section our bilingual proximity-based approach for QT disambiguation. In fact, we have extended in Elayeb et al. [3] an existing proximity function (PROX) initiated by Gaume et al. [4] in order to apply it in the context of semantic query disambiguation. We more investigated this technique here in the field of QT disambiguation. We present in the following the semantic calculus. Firstly, we generate the matrix of transition from the graph of the BSDC. Secondly, we transform this adjacency matrix into a Markov one having the nodes of the graph as states and the possible transitions as edges. Finally, we apply the dynamic translation sense calculation in order to select the best translation.

Building the Adjacency Matrix. The adjacency matrix is generated from the graph $G = <T, E>$. We note $[G]$ the square matrix $n \times n$ defined as the following:

$$\forall r, s \in T, [G]_{r,s} = |<s,r>| \text{ if } (r,s) \in E \text{ and } [G]_{r,s} = 0 \text{ if } (r,s) \notin E \qquad (1)$$

We note $[G]$ the transition matrix of G. Since G is not directed, so $[G]$ is a symmetric matrix. In addition, G is a reflexive graph, so:

$$\forall r \in T, [G]_{r,r} = 1 \qquad (2)$$

Building the Markov Matrix. The Markov matrix is generated from the adjacency matrix. Let us note $\left[\widehat{G}\right]$ the Markov matrix corresponding to the graph $G = <T, E>$ defined as the following:

$$\forall r, s \in T, \left[\widehat{G}\right]_{r,s} = \frac{[G]_{r,s}}{\sum\limits_{x \in T} [G]_{r,x}} \qquad (3)$$

Gaume et al. [4] have defined $PROX(G, i, s, r)$ as the probability while the particle passing from the node r, at the moment $t = 0$, to the node s at the moment $t = i$:

$$PROX(G, i, s, r) = [\widehat{G}]^i_{r,s} \qquad (4)$$

Where M^i is the matrix M multiplied i times by itself.

Definition 1: The Dynamic Translation Sense Calculation. We propose here a dynamic technique computing the translation senses' scores corresponding to a polysemous source query term in its context using the BSDC graph. The best translation has the best score among all possible translations existing in the graph. We are based here on the principle of the PROX method, which computes a score of semantic similarity (proximity) between nodes of the BSDC graph in an original and innovative manner as the following. Given the polysemous source query t_i; having more than one possible translation in the bilingual lexicon. We note by:

(i) t_i is a node of the graph G.
(ii) *Translation* $(t_i) = p_i^1, p_i^2, \ldots, p_i^a$

$$G^\infty = \lim_{z \to \infty} \left[\widehat{G}^z\right] \text{ So, } G^\infty \text{ is a vector of } \mathbb{R}^a. \qquad (5)$$

$$f_\infty(r, s) = \lim_{z \to \infty} PROX(G, z, s, r) \qquad (6)$$

The function f_∞ indicates the semantic proximity between polysemous source query terms and their possible translations' definitions in the BSDC. So, we have the following property:

Property 1. Since the graph G is reflexive and strongly related, then:

$$\forall a \in T, \lim_{z \to \infty} PROX(G, z, s, r) = \lim_{z \to \infty} PROX(G, i, a, r) \tag{7}$$

That means the probability for a rather long time z to reach a node s does not depend on the node of departure (s or a). We note that α is strongly related to α^i if and only if: $\forall j \in \mathbb{N}\backslash\{i\}, f_\infty(\alpha, \alpha^i) > f_\infty(\alpha, \alpha^j)$. In this case, the suitable translation of α is α^i.

The word β carrying information checks the following properties: (i) $\beta \in Context$ (α, SQ); (ii) $\forall \delta \in Context(\alpha, SQ)\backslash\{\beta\}, f_\infty(\alpha, \beta) = max_\delta(f_\infty(\alpha, \delta))$; where β is the definition of α. In this case, β is the semantic definition of α in the BSDC.

4 Experiments and Discussion

4.1 Evaluation Using the Recall-Precision Curves

We present in Fig. 1 the recall-precision curves comparing the proximity-based, the probabilistic, the possibilistic [2] and the monolingual runs (English queries provided by CLEF-2003) using different combinations of source query's parts. Our goal is to assess the sensitivity of our approach to the contextual information provided by these parts. Indeed, if we run only the *title* of the source query the context will be limited to a small set of terms. Therefore, the probabilistic approach has a lack in the identification and translation of Noun Phrases (NPs) and it will be limited to a word-by-word translation process. That's why our proximity-based approach outperformed the probabilistic and the possibilistic ones starting from the point of recall 0.2. However, it is slightly under the probabilistic and the possibilistic ones especially in some low-levels points of recall (0 and 0.1). Between the points of recall 0.3 and 0.6, the proximity-based approach outperformed the probabilistic and the possibilistic runs with a significant gap between them. From the point of recall 0.7, this superiority becomes slight and the gap between the proximity and the possibilistic approaches is limited to these high-levels points of recall. In addition, the monolingual run outperformed the proximity-based, the probabilistic and the possibilistic ones in all points of recall. But, the gap between the monolingual run and our proximity-based approach is increasingly reduced starting from the point of recall 0.5. This achievement may be explained by the extra contextual information provided by the BSDC, which overcomes the lack of context caused by the source query *title* (cf. Fig. 1(e)). When we have run the *description* part of the source query, the context is slightly enlarged and the probabilistic and the possibilistic approaches can find and translate more NPs. Therefore, the possibilistic can outperform both the probabilistic and the proximity-based approaches especially in the point 0.6 and in some low- (from 0 to 0.2) and high-levels points of recall (0.9 and 1), while the probabilistic seems better in the points 0.3 and 0.4. Nonetheless, the proximity-based approach slightly outperformed the probabilistic and the possibilistic ones in some points of recall (0.5 and 0.7). Besides, the gaps between the monolingual run and the other approaches are more reduced starting from the recall point 0.7 (cf. Fig. 1(f)). Moreover, the context of the source query is more improved due to its *narrative* part, which is more suitable for both the probabilistic and the possibilistic approaches in their identification and translation of more frequent NPs. That's why they achieved almost equivalent performances with the proximity-based approach in the point of recall 0.5 and outperformed it in the point 0.7. They are also slightly under the proximity-based approach in some high-levels points of recall (0.8, 0.9 and 1). However, the proximity-based approach outperformed both of them, particularly in some low-levels points of recall (from 0 to 0.4). The gaps between the monolingual run and all the other approaches are more compacted starting from the point of recall 0.8 (cf. Fig. 1(g)). The superiority of the proximity approach may be explained by the extra contextual information issued from both the *narrative* part of the source query on the one hand, and the BSDC on the other hand. The running of the full source query parts (*title* & *description* & *narrative*) has been the most popular in the CLIR tools' assessments. In this case, each approach can benefit from the full contextual information. However, the proximity-based approach outperformed the probabilistic and the possibilistic ones, especially in some low-levels points of recall (from 0 to 0.3). These two approaches are under or equal to the proximity-based one starting from the point of recall 0.4. We also register the same performance of the proximity-based run as the monolingual one in some high-levels points of recall (from 0.7 to 1). The gaps of performance become narrower between all of these approaches compared to the first three cases (cf. Fig. 1(a)). We need also to investigate on the other possible combinations of the source query parts.

When we focus on both *title* & *narrative* parts, the proximity approach significantly outperformed both the probabilistic and the possibilistic ones, especially in the low-levels points of recall (from 0 to 0.5), and it is slightly upper them and under the monolingual run in some high-levels points of recall (from 0.8 to 1). But, the gaps between all of them are progressively reduced starting from the point of recall 0.6 (cf. Fig. 1(b)). We note also that the monolingual run is regularly upper bound of the CLIR performance. This's because we haven't involved in our tests any query expansion processes during the translation task and no close words/phrases have supported our source or/and target queries before retrieving documents.

However, *title* & *description* seem less suitable for the proximity-based approach when its performance slightly exceeds the probabilistic one and equal to the possibilistic approach in some points of recall (from 0.5 to 0.8). The proximity-based approach is slightly under both the probabilistic and the possibilistic ones in some low- (from 0 to 0.2) and high-levels points of recall (from 0.8 to 1), but they are equal between 0.4 and 0.5 (cf. Fig. 1(c)). Moreover, the *description* & *narrative* run provides more contextual information for the proximity-based approach to achieve better performance compared to its competitors, especially in some low-levels points of recall (from 0 to 0.4). But, this superiority is significantly reduced starting from the point of recall 0.6 until the point 1 (cf. Fig. 1(d)). This performance disruption of the proximity-based approach in both of these two last combinations may be caused by the *description* part of the source query in the standard CLEF-2003, which includes some recurrent expressions such as "Trouvez des documents qui…" (find documents that…), reducing the CLIR efficiency.

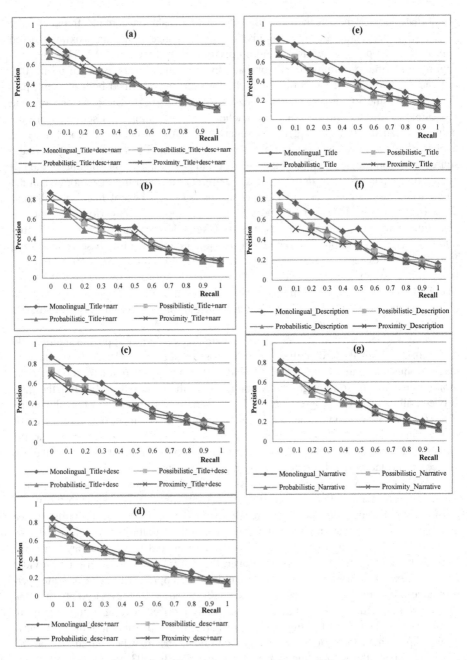

Fig. 1. Recall-precision curves of the four QT runs

4.2   Evaluation Using the Precision Values at Different Top Documents

We compare in Fig. 2 the overall performance of the monolingual, the proximity-based, the probabilistic and the possibilistic runs using the precision at different top documents (P@5, P@10,..., P@1000). When we focus on the precision at different top documents, we remark that the precision decreased when the number of returned documents has increased. When we run the full context of the source query (*title & description & narrative*), the proximity-based approach outperformed both the probabilistic and the possibilistic ones in terms of precision at all different top documents; except in some rare cases such as: (i) in P@100 and P@1000 when the probabilistic approach is slightly better than the proximity-based one; and (ii) in P@15, P@20 and P@30 when the possibilistic approach slightly outperformed the proximity-based one. Moreover, when the context of the source query is progressively decreased (using *narrative* or *title & narrative* or *description & narrative*) the proximity-based approach achieved better precision at all different top documents than the probabilistic one, except in some cases such as in P@50, P@100 and P@1000 using *narrative*, in P@100 using *description & narrative* and in P@1000 using *title & narrative* or *description & narrative* in which the probabilistic approach slightly outperformed the proximity-based one. In addition, the proximity-based is also the best one using *title & narrative*, while the possibilistic is the best one using *title & description*. Nonetheless, we can notice some exceptions in which the proximity-based is still slightly under the possibilistic approach such as in P@20, P@30, P@50, P@100 and in P@1000 using *narrative* or *description & narrative*.

4.3   Evaluation Using the MAP and the R-Precision Metrics

The proximity-based approach is the best one, in terms of MAP and the R-Precision metrics (cf. Fig. 2), using all source query parts' combinations. But, there are some exceptions when we run *description* or *title & description* where the possibilistic is slightly better than the proximity, which confirms our conclusions made above. In general, the proximity-based approach achieved better results than the probabilistic one for long queries using *title & description & narrative* or *title & narrative* or *description & narrative* and for short queries using *narrative*. Compared to the possibilistic one, the proximity-based has achieved the best results for long queries using *title & narrative* and short queries using *narrative*. But, it has some weaknesses with the *description* part of the source query as we explain above. Globally, when the context of the run is larger due to the double support coming from both the maximum context of the source query and the BSDC, the performance of the proximity-based approach is closer to the monolingual run. Besides, the proximity-based approach is often better than both the probabilistic and the possibilistic ones with a clear gap for the first values of recall corresponding to the first selected documents (except using *description* or *title & description*).

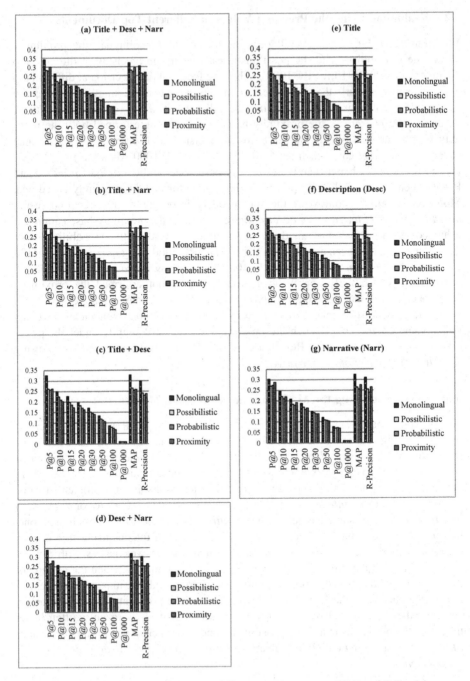

Fig. 2. Results using the precision at different top documents, MAP and R-Precision

4.4   Evaluation Using the Improvement Percentage

We show in Table 1 the improvement percentage of the proximity-based approach compared to both the probabilistic and the possibilistic ones, using the precision at different numbers of top documents, MAP and R-Precision for long and short queries. We remark that there is a significant improvement of the proximity-based approach, especially for the documents returned at the top of the list such as P@5, ..., P@30 using long queries (except the combination *title & description*) or using the part *narrative* of short queries. Firstly, and compared to the probabilistic, the proximity-based has achieved an improvement of more than 10.6% for P@10 for long queries using *title & description & narrative*. Besides, the average improvement percentage in terms of precision at different top documents is about 3.77% using *title & description & narrative*, 7.05% using *title & narrative* and 1.64% using *description & narrative*. For long queries, the average improvement percentage of the MAP is about 7.87% and of the R-Precision is about 5.43%. On the other hand, the proximity-based approach achieved a significant improvement percentage for the short queries, especially using the *narrative* part providing the maximum contextual information. For example, we achieved more than 5% for P@5 and almost 7% for P@15 using *narrative*. Besides, the average improvement percentage in terms of precision at different top documents is about 1.47% using *narrative*. But, the average improvement percentage of the MAP is about 3.07% and of the R-Precision is about 1.94% using short queries. Secondly, and compared to the possibilistic, the proximity-based approach has exceeded 14% for P@5 and almost 7% for P@10 for long queries using *title & narrative*. Besides, the average improvement percentage in terms of precision at different top documents is about 3.8% using *title & narrative*, while this average is about 3.83% for the MAP and 2.06% for the R-Precision using long queries. However, when we focus on short queries using *narrative*, the proximity-based approach achieved an improvement of more than 6.8% for P@5 and more than 4% for P@15. These results showed and confirmed the effectiveness of the proximity-based approach compared to both the probabilistic and the possibilistic ones for both long queries using *title & narrative* and short queries using *narrative* for all different assessment metrics and scenarios.

4.5   Statistical Evaluation

It is also relevant to investigate on the statistical significance of the proximity-based approach results compared to both the probabilistic and the possibilistic ones using the Wilcoxon Matched-Pairs Signed-Ranks Test. If we focus on the precision at different top documents, we notice that the improvements achieved by the probabilistic approach are statistically significant, especially in P@100 (*p-value* = 0.042 < 0.05) and in P@1000 (*p-value* = 0.013). Besides, the possibilistic approach has achieved statistically significant improvements, particularly in P@20 (*p-value* = 0.027), P@30 (*p-value* = 0.046), P@100 (*p-value* = 0.027) and P@1000 (*p-value* = 0.003). These results showed the weakness of the proximity-based approach in case of a great number of returned documents. In addition, the improvements of the proximity-based approach, compared to both the probabilistic and the possibilistic ones, are not statistically significant neither for the remaining precisions at different top documents, nor for the

Table 1. The improvement percentage of the proximity-based approach

Long queries	Precision metrics	% imp. Proximity vs. Probabilistic	% imp. Proximity vs. Possibilistic	Short queries	Precision metrics	% imp. Proximity vs. Probabilistic	% imp. Proximity vs. Possibilistic
Title + desc + narr	P@5	7.99	6.57	Title	P@5	-10.44	-13.07
	P@10	10.61	5.95		P@10	-13.52	-15.77
	P@15	2.68	-3.72		P@15	-9.13	-12.23
	P@20	1.65	-5.59		P@20	-8.68	-12.71
	P@30	4.43	-2.9		P@30	-9.08	-12.5
	P@50	5.09	2.03		P@50	-5.61	-9.25
	P@100	-0.27	-2.02		P@100	-11.9	-14.36
	P@1000	-1.98	-3.88		P@1000	-7	-9.71
	MAP	8.06	5.24		MAP	12.77	7
	R-Precision	3.17	1.44		R-Precision	5.36	4.5
Title + desc	P@5	1.43	0	Description (desc)	P@5	-8.48	-13.35
	P@10	-3.54	-9.91		P@10	-9.41	-10.93
	P@15	-7.3	-12.51		P@15	-11.65	-13.33
	P@20	-4.85	-10.64		P@20	-10.74	-12.62
	P@30	-3.45	-7.77		P@30	-5.15	-6.77
	P@50	-6.53	-10.63		P@50	-8.01	-7.45
	P@100	-9.38	-15.08		P@100	-9.92	-12.8
	P@1000	-2.91	-3.85		P@1000	-4.81	-4.81
	MAP	1.29	-2.15		MAP	-11.26	-11.68
	R-Precision	3.43	-1.32		R-Precision	-9.6	-11.13
Title + narr	P@5	12.49	14.07	Narrative (narr)	P@5	5.4	6.84
	P@10	12.6	6.83		P@10	4.41 *	-0.81
	P@15	7.55	4.64		P@15	6.93	4.02
	P@20	9.81	1.09		P@20	4.02	-2.76
	P@30	9.79	2.49		P@30	0	-3.42
	P@50	4.39	2.33		P@50	-2.71	-5.02
	P@100	0.82	0.82		P@100	-3.32	-1.13
	P@1000	-0.98	-1.94		P@1000	-2.94	-3.88
	MAP	13.64	7.42		MAP	7.7	4.08
	R-Precision	10.81	8.36		R-Precision	10.07	3.89
desc + narr	P@5	5.55	0				
	P@10	5.17	0.8				
	P@15	-0.64	-4.38				
	P@20	0.59	-4.64				
	P@30	6.22	0				
	P@50	2.73	0				
	P@100	-2.49	-3.68				
	P@1000	-3.96	-5.83				
	MAP	8.52	4.82				
	R-Precision	4.32	-0.23				

MAP and the R-precision. However, the proximity-based approach has showed its statistical significance compared to the probabilistic approach, especially for long queries using: (i) *title & description & narrative* when the *p-value* = 0.012 < 0.05; (ii) *title & narrative* when the *p-value* = 0.006; and (iii) *description & narrative* when the *p-value* = 0.046. Besides, and using the *description* part of the source query, the improvements obtained by the probabilistic approach are statistically significant with a *p-value* = 0.004. Finally, and compared to the possibilistic approach, the proximity-based one has showed its statistical significance, particularly for long queries using *title & narrative* when the *p-value* = 0.006 < 0.05. Whereas, the possibilistic approach has achieved statistically significant improvements for long queries using *title & description* (*p-value* = 0.007) and short queries using *title* (*p-value* = 0.036) or *description* (*p-value* = 0.005).

5 Conclusion and Future Work

The results have showed that the enhancement of our proximity-based approach is statistically significant, when we have compared its performance to the probabilistic approach and to the probability-to-possibility transformation based approach, especially when we have used large contextual information issued from long source queries. Unfortunately, our proximity-based approach has some weaknesses in the translation of domain-specific queries. This requires both a language model and a domain-specific translation process [6]. Besides, our new technique should be assessed in real contexts by involving the user in the evaluation process (e.g. BLEU [5]).

References

1. Elayeb, B., Bounhas, I.: Arabic cross-language information retrieval: a review. ACM Trans. Asian Low-Resour. Lang. Info. Proc. **15**(3), 18:1–18:44 (2016)
2. Elayeb, B., Ben Romdhane, W., Bellamine Ben Saoud, N.: A new possibilistic query translation tool for cross-language information retrieval. Multimed. Tools Appl. **77**(2), 2423–2465 (2018)
3. Elayeb, B., Bounhas, I., Ben Khiroun, O., Evrard, F., Bellamine Ben Saoud, N.: A comparative study between possibilistic and probabilistic approaches for monolingual word sense disambiguation. Knowl. Inf. Syst. **44**(1), 91–126 (2015)
4. Gaume, B., Hathout, N., Muller, P.: Word sense disambiguation using a dictionary for sens similarity measure. In: Proceedings of ACL, pp. 1194–1200 (2004)
5. Papineni, K., Roukos, S., Ward, T., Zhu, W.J.: BLEU: a method for automatic evaluation of machine translation. In: Proceedings of ACL, pp. 311–318 (2002)
6. Ture, F., Boschee, E.: Learning to translate: a query-specific combination approach for cross-lingual information retrieval. In: Proceedings of EMNLP, pp. 589–599 (2014)
7. Vidhu Bhala, R.V., Abirami, S.: Trends in word sense disambiguation. Artif. Intell. Rev. **42**(2), 159–171 (2014)
8. Xu, J., Fraser, A., Weischedel, R.: TREC 2001: cross-lingual retrieval at BBN. In: Proceedings of TREC, pp. 68–77 (2002)

Related Terms Extraction from Arabic News Corpus Using Word Embedding

Amina Chouigui[1,2(✉)], Oussama Ben Khiroun[1,2],
and Bilel Elayeb[1,3]

[1] RIADI Research Laboratory, ENSI, Manouba University, 2010 Manouba, Tunisia
`aminachouigui@gmail.com, oussama.ben.khiroun@gmail.com,`
`Bilel.Elayeb@riadi.rnu.tn`
[2] National Engineering School of Sousse, ENISO, Sousse University,
4002 Sousse, Tunisia
[3] Emirates College of Technology, P.O. Box: 41009,
Abu Dhabi, United Arab Emirates

Abstract. Different techniques are used in text mining to analyze data, extract knowledge, information and relations. We aim in this work to extract related terms for specific keywords. In the first step, we extract Arabic keywords from news articles titles using the TF-IDF terms weighting measure. In the next step, we extract the related terms, from both titles and main texts, using Word2Vec model as a word embedding technique. In order to evaluate our proposed approach, we compute the precision values of the extracted terms that are present in Wikipedia articles. The experiments results perform better for the extracted terms from the articles main texts than titles and the international news category has the highest precision value.

Keywords: Text mining · Word embedding · Word2Vec ·
Arabic language · Terms weighting · DL4J · Cosine similarity

1 Introduction

Text Mining is one of the trending research fields nowadays since the amount of available textual data is huge on the web. It is linked to many research areas such as computational linguistics and Information Retrieval (IR). Text mining can be used for unstructured or semi-structured data like emails, HTML files, textual documents and others. Therefore, text mining is mainly used to extract, briefly, interesting and non-trivial data from these texts [1].

Arabic language is considered as one of the most popular languages. It is used by 280 million people as a first language and by more than 250 million people as a second language [2]. Besides, Arabic language is categorized between the difficult languages to analyze. Indeed, it has special characteristics and complicated grammar rules which presents ambiguity problems [3,4]. So, for one word, we can get different morphological Part-Of-Speech (POS) tags. We mention as example

© Springer Nature Switzerland AG 2019
C. Debruyne et al. (Eds.): OTM 2018 Workshops, LNCS 11231, pp. 230–240, 2019.
https://doi.org/10.1007/978-3-030-11683-5_26

the word "علم" which has different morphological forms and the right POS tag depends on the diacritic marks [5]: the word "عَلِمَ" (he knew) is a verb while "عِلْم" (knowledge) is a noun.

We present our work as follows: Sect. 2 contains some related works. The Sect. 3 is about the proposed related terms extraction process. Then, in Sect. 4, we present the data analysis and experimental results. Finally, we conclude our work and present some perspectives.

2   Related Work

The research papers about text mining techniques can be classified according to different study domains [6]. For this state of the art, we present 4 domains: Islamic studies, Social networks/media, opinion mining and web pages.

Most Islamic studies researches for Arabic language use the Holy Quran (words of revelations) and Hadiths (the prophetic narrations texts) as corpora for knowledge and information extraction.

Alhawarat et al. [7] proposed an approach to analyze Arabic texts. Authors pre-processed the Quran text and considered the different possible partitioning. They used the term frequency (TF) and term frequency-inverse document frequency (TF-IDF) measures. Depending on the partitioning method, the terms of the holy Quran frequencies vary. Indeed, the terms frequencies depends on the chapter size if chapters are used as a partitioning method. The terms frequencies are almost equal once they used the parts. The calculated terms using TF measure might give good for semantic search and clustering. However, the calculated terms using TF-IDF are suitable to be used for topic modeling.

Harrag [8] used Sahîh of Bukhari as a corpus to extract the surface information. He used named entity extraction techniques to extract the entities containing relevant information from the corpus texts. So, he developed a system that must detect the relevant text areas and assign a label to it. The proposed labels are: Num-Kitab, Title-Kitab, Num-Bab, Title-Bab, Num-Hadith, Saned, Matn, Taalik, and Atraf. The named entities Num-Kitab, Num-Bab and Num-Hadith has the best F-measure results of 0.67, 0.67 and 0.54 respectively. The mean precision and recall values are 71% and 39% respectively.

For social networks and social media domain, we mention the work of Al-Horaibi et al. [9] who used a dataset containing 2 000 Arabic tweets for sentiment analysis. After manually annotating the dataset, they used machine learning algorithms for the classification: Naïve Bayes (NB) and Decision Tree (DT). Al-Horaibi et al made different combinations of text-processing functions to check the performance of using these algorithms. They developed functionalities that helped them improve the results. The experiments give an accuracy 64.85% for the NB classifier and 53.75% for the DT classifier. Sentiment analysis in Arabic language needs more work on the lexicon side.

Chan et al. [10] collected data from the social media web site Facebook. The downloaded data was comments written in English in the Samsung mobile Facebook page. Authors presented how to exploit social media data. So, they proposed a structured approach that analyze the social media comments and analyze the statistical cluster. Then, authors identify the relational analysis by analyzing inter-relationships among different factors.

Cherif et al. [11] presented their work in the opinion mining domain. In this paper authors, used a collection containing 625 Arabic reviews and opinions collected from Trip Advisor's official website. They proposed an approach based on sentiment classification, using Support Vector Machine (SVM), to analyze the Arabic reviews and comments. They evaluated the influence of Arabic grammatical richness on opinion mining accuracy.

Rushdi-Saleh et al. [12] collected a new Arabic corpus for the opinion mining. Their corpus has 500 movie reviews extracted from web pages and blogs in Arabic. 250 of the reviews are labeled as positive ones and the others as negative ones. Authors used machine learning algorithms such as SVM and NB to experiment this corpus. The SVM algorithm gives the best result (0.90) comparing by using trigrams with Pang corpus.

In the web pages domain, Atlam et al. [13] defined a new method to construct a comprehensive Arabic dictionary. Authors used the POS, pattern rules, and corpora in Arabic language to construct the dictionary. They used 251 MB corpora collected from the Arabic Wikipedia data and Alhayah newspaper online website. Atlam et al. proposed a text classification approach, on 5 959 documents, using Arabic Field Association terms compared to the machine learning algorithms: NB and KNN. The proposed approach gave the highest precision value 80.65% followed by NB with 72.79% and finally KNN with a precision 36.15%.

In the work of Wahsheh et al. [14], authors collected a new Arabic spam corpus. Using this corpus, authors analyzed the spammers behaviors in Arabic web pages. They analyzed the weights of the most popular words used by Arab users in their queries. The experiments revealed that the behavior of spammers is unique in Arabic web pages. They used the Decision Tree algorithm to evaluate the spammers' behavior and the accuracy was 90%.

3   The Related Terms Extraction Process

In this section we detail the process of extracting the related terms as presented in Fig. 1. Starting from an Arabic news text corpus, we extract, in the first step, a set of keywords from news titles. The process consists in classifying the titles by month and annotating them using the Arabic POS tagger Open NLP[1]. We apply the Arabic light stemmer [15], as well, to remove the prefixes and suffixes from each word and the stop words are also removed from the titles. Finally, we calculate the TF-IDF terms weighting measure [16]. This measure is about the weight of a specific word in the corresponding title for a specific month.

---

[1] http://www.arabicnlp.pro/.

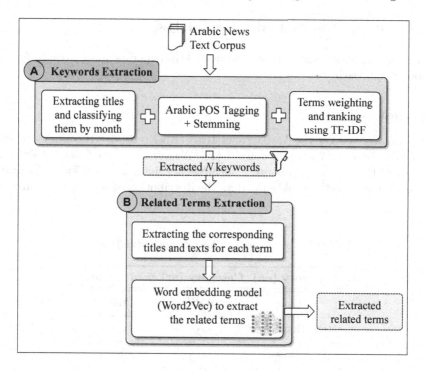

Fig. 1. Related terms extraction process

As a second step, the set of extracted terms is used to extract related words of news articles from both news titles and texts. We use the Word2Vec [17], a two-layer neural net that processes texts, in order to group the vectors of similar words in the same vector space. Word2Vec detects similarities mathematically and returns a set of vectors with numerical representations of the words. So, the extracted related terms are chosen by calculating the cosine similarity between the vectors. The cosine similarity is a measure that calculates the cosine of the angle between the two vectors K and T as shows the formula 1:

$$Cos\theta = \frac{K.T}{||K||.||T||} \tag{1}$$

where:

- K is the corresponding vector for the keyword
- and T is the corresponding vector for each extracted term.

For the related terms extraction process based on Word2Vec and cosine similarity, we use the Deep Learning 4J (DL4J) project[2].

---

[2] https://deeplearning4j.org.

4   Experimentation and Data Analysis

In this section, we present the used corpus and the experimentation results for our proposed approach.

4.1   Test Collection

We use, as a collection, the Arabic News Texts (ANT) corpus[3]. It contains articles collected from a tunisian radio web site [18]. We worked on the following six categories from this corpus: "economy", "localNews", "internationalNews", "politic", "society" and "sport". Table 1 presents the distribution of ANT Corpus articles by category.

Table 1. Number of articles in "ANT Corpus" (v1.1) per category

Category (en)	Category (ar)	# of articles
economy	اقتِصَاد	326
internationalNews	دولية	1 260
localNews	وطنية	4 832
politic	سيَاسة	514
society	مجتمع	1 087
sport	ريَاضة	1 460
Total		9 479

4.2   Terms Extraction

We classified the titles by month to extract the terms for each month and see the difference between the extracted related terms for the same term but for different months. For each month and each category, we extract the first N terms according to the TF-IDF measures. So, we choose the first 20 terms for each category, except the category "economy", since it contains generic words and the number of its articles is limited. So, we chose the terms that appear in at least 3 titles in this category. Among the extracted keywords, we notice some terms repeated almost each month for each category as presented in Table 2.

Moreover, we notice that there are common terms usually used almost each month. For example, the term "تونس" (Tunisia) appears in three categories by referring to Table 2. The society category also contains news from Tunisia but most of the titles in this category follows the format "event's location (Tunisian

---

[3] https://antcorpus.github.io/.

Table 2. Most repeated words per category

Category	Keywords
Economy	"تونس" (Tunisia), "بنك" (bank), "أسعار" (prices)
InternationalNews	"هجوم" (attack), "ترامب" (Trump), "نار" (fire)
LocalNews	"تونس" (Tunisia), "يوم" (day), "ايقاف" (arrest)
Politic	"تونس" (Tunisia), "انتخاب" (election), "رئيس" (president)
Society	"حجز" (detention), "حادث" (accident), "قبض" (catch)
Sport	"كرة" (ball), "نجم" (star), "بطولة" (championship)

state): event's description". The sport category contains both Tunisian and international sport news, the same for the "internationalNews" category. The existence of the term "يوم" (day) in the "localNews" category is explained by daily weathercast publication in the website. This term is ranked in the second position for four months. We present in Fig. 2 the word cloud of the most important keywords for all categories.

Fig. 2. Word cloud of most occurring terms in different categories

Nevertheless, there are some terms that appear in only one or two months. Indeed, these terms are related to specific news that appear and last for a limited period. We present in the Table 3 some terms that appear for the first time on April for some categories.

We notice that the term "تطاوين" (Tatwin: a state in Tunisia) appears on April in both "localNews" and "politic" categories. It is related to an event "الكامور" (Al-Kamour) in Tunisia for this period. This event belongs to the "localNews" category but it affects the "politic" category as well. So, an event in one category can affect other categories and we can deduct some inter-categories correlations, as represented in Fig. 3.

Table 3. Examples of terms that appear for a limited period

Category	Keywords	Duration
Economy	"النقد", "صندوق" (Monetary Fund)	only April
InternationalNews	"كوريا", "الشمَالية" (North Korea)	April and May
LocalNews	"تطاوين" (Tatawin), "احتجاج" (protest)	only April
Politic	"تطاوين" (Tatawin), "المصَالحة" (Reconciliation)	1st term only on April 2nd lasts for April and May

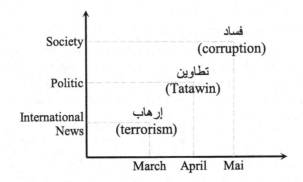

Fig. 3. Correlation inter-categories: A set of keywords that appear in "localNews" and other categories in the same months

Referring to Fig. 3, the term "ارهاب" (Terrorism) appears in both "localNews" and "internationalNews" categories on March. As well, the term "فساد" (Corruption) appears in "society" and "localNews" on Mai.

4.3   Related Terms Extraction

For each extracted term, we search the 10 nearest similar words using DL4J. We extract the related terms from both articles main texts and titles. For the same keyword, the related terms vary from month to another depending on the news in this period. As an example, we present in Table 4 the extracted related terms, from the main texts, for the word "ترامب" (Trump) on January and February.

We notice that the extracted related terms, on January, are semantically related to the presidential elections in the United States of America (USA). We mention for instance the terms "تنصيب" (nomination) and "رئيس" (president) as near terms to the elections context. Meanwhile, the extracted related terms from the month of February belongs to a different context. In fact, they are related to the decision of restrict immigration to USA from some Arabic countries. Hence, the extracted related terms depends strongly on the studied period.

Table 4. Extracted related terms, from the main texts, for the term "ترامب" (Trump)

Month	related terms
January	"رئيس" (president), "دونالد" (Donald), "وسط" (middle), "تنصيب" (nomination), "واشنطن" (Washington)
February	"وقف" (stopping), "تأشيرة" (VISA), "تفعيل" (activation), "عديد" (numerous), "معالجة" (treatment)

4.4 Experimental Results

To evaluate the related terms extraction process, we search the terms in an article dealing with the main term. We chose the Arabic Wikipedia[4] for searching such articles. Wikipedia contains articles from different categories and we chose it for the evaluation because of the lack of standard test collection. For the best of our knowledge, the resources are limited too and the available text mining standards are not suitable to our case study.

The nature of the used test corpus, as a news corpus, explains the presence of many proper nouns among the extracted keywords. The extracted keywords contain the first or last name but that's not enough to get the suitable article in Wikipedia. Taking as example, the keyword "يوسف" (Youssef) (the first name of the Tunisian prime minister), matches to an article about the means and the origin of this name. Meanwhile, we get the suitable article if we add the last name "يوسف الشاهد" (Youssef Chahed).

Therefore, there are some ambiguous terms from the extracted keywords. As an example, we mention the keyword "صندوق" which has two different meanings according to the context (box or fund). However, if we search Wikipedia articles about "صندوق", we find only an article about the box meaning. Meanwhile, this term appears frequently in conjunction with the words of "صندوق النقد الدولي" (international monetary fund).

So, to disambiguate these terms and get the relevant Wikipedia articles, we search the corresponding named entity (NE) that appears in the maximum number of titles. Each extracted related term that appears in the corresponding Wikipedia article is considered as a relevant term. The precision for the extracted related terms of a keyword is detailed in the formula 2.

$$PrecisionKeyword(k) = \frac{\sum_{i \in relatedTerms(k)} t_i}{T} \qquad (2)$$

Where:

- *PrecisionKeyword* is the precision of the extracted related terms of a keyword k.
- t_i is a related term that is available in Wikipedia article matching to k keyword.
- The T is the total number of extracted related terms for the keyword.

---

[4] https://ar.wikipedia.org.

In each category, the precision for each month is computed as follows:

$$MeanPrecisionMonth = \frac{\sum\limits_{j \in listOfKeywords} PrecisionKeyword(k_j)}{K} \tag{3}$$

Where:

- $MeanPrecisionMonth$ is the precision of the extracted related terms, in one category, for a month.
- $PrecisionKeyword(k_j)$ is the precision of a keyword on the month.
- K is the total number of keywords on that month.

The mean precision results from titles and main texts for the 6 categories are presented in Table 5. Results show that the related terms extracted from the articles texts have better precision values, for all the categories, comparing with those extracted from titles. In fact, titles are composed of few words that represent main terms for specific news which leads to a poor context. On the other side, texts presents a richer context and more words co-occurrences that are necessary for an accurate word embedding computation.

Table 5. The precision values per category

Category	texts	titles
economy	0.35	0.29
internationalNews	0.43	0.38
localNews	0.30	0.23
politic	0.30	0.30
society	0.25	0.23
sport	0.34	0.31

According to the precision values, we notice that the "internationalNews" category has the best values for both texts and titles. The Fig. 4 represents more details about the precision values for each month for this category.

As an interpretation of these results, the "internationalNews" category contains articles about international news so the articles in Wikipedia for this category are available with more details. Meanwhile, the articles in the "society" or "localNews" category are about local and daily events in Tunisia, that are not available Arabic Wikipedia. The "society" category has the lowest precision value. In this category, most of the extracted terms are names of Tunisian states. So, the related terms are about the news in these states for this period. Meanwhile, in Wikipedia we find articles describing the place and not the daily events.

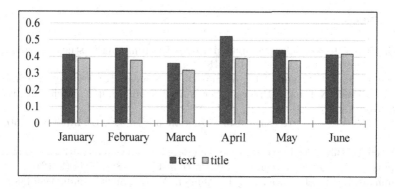

Fig. 4. The precision values by month for the "internationalNews" category

The "economy" category has the second highest value for the texts. This value could be explained by the small number of the extracted keywords in this category. Besides, the extracted keywords in the "economy" category are domain specific terms such as "بنك" (bank) so the related terms in the Tunisian context or international context is almost the same.

We can interpret the precision values for each keyword as well. So, for the keywords that appear in more than one month, we notice that the precision value vary from one month to another. As an example, we mention the precision values for the term "ترامب" (Trump) on each month from January to June are 0.7, 0.5, 0.5, 0.3, 0.5 and 0.6 respectively. On January, the precision value is the best since the related terms in this period are about the American elections.

5   Conclusion and Future Work

We presented in this paper an approach for text mining and related terms extraction based on word embedding. In fact, we extracted the keywords from the news articles titles by calculating the TF-IDF terms weighting measure for each word in the title. For the extracted words, we search their related terms using Word2Vec model, from both articles titles and texts. To experiment the approach, we search the extracted related terms in an article about the main term in Wikipedia website. Results show that the extracted related terms from main texts give better precision values than from the articles titles. The results vary with the categories and perform well for international news having 0.43 mean precision.

As a future work, we aim to study conceptual related terms extraction based on rich knowledge resources such as Arabic WordNet. Other Arabic news sources can be studied in order to analyze the dependencies with different texts sources. Besides Word2Vec model, other neural networks based approaches for Natural Language Processing could be also adopted as future perspectives.

References

1. Gök, A., Waterworth, A., Shapira, P.: Use of web mining in studying innovation. Scientometrics **102**(1), 653–671 (2015)
2. Salloum, S.A., AlHamad, A.Q., Al-Emran, M., Shaalan, K.: A survey of Arabic text mining. Intell. Nat. Lang. Process. Trends Appl. Stud. Comput. Intell. **740**, 417–431 (2018)
3. Elayeb, B.: Arabic word sense disambiguation: a review. Artif. Intell. Rev. **50**, 1–58 (2018)
4. Elayeb, B., Bounhas, I.: Arabic cross-language information retrieval: a review. ACM Trans. Asian Low-Resour. Lang. Inf. Process. **15**(3), 18:1–18:44 (2016)
5. Bounhas, I., Elayeb, B., Evrard, F., Slimani, Y.: Organizing contextual knowledge for Arabic text disambiguation and terminology extraction. Knowl. Organ. **38**(6), 473–490 (2011)
6. Al-Mahmoud, H., Al-Razgan, M.: Arabic text mining: a systematic review of the published literature 2002–2014. In: Proceedings of ICCC, pp. 1–7 (2015)
7. Alhawarat, M., Hegazi, M., Hilal, A.: Processing the text of the Holy Quran: a text mining study. Int. J. Adv. Comput. Sci. Appl. (IJACSA) **6**(2), 262–267 (2015)
8. Harrag, F.: Text mining approach for knowledge extraction in Sahîh Al-Bukhari. Comput. Hum. Behav. **30**, 558–566 (2013)
9. Al-Horaibi, L., Khan, M.B.: Sentiment analysis of Arabic tweets using text mining techniques. In: First International Workshop on Pattern Recognition (2016)
10. Chan, H.K., Lacka, E., Yee, R.W., Lim, M.K.: A case study on mining social media data. In: Proceedings of 2014 IEEE International Conference on Industrial Engineering and Engineering Management, pp. 593–596 (2014)
11. Cherif, W., Madani, A., Kissi, M.: A new modeling approach for Arabic opinion mining recognition. In: Proceedings of Intelligent Systems and Computer Vision (ISCV), pp. 1–6 (2015)
12. Rushdi-Saleh, M., Martín-Valdivia, M.T., Ureña-López, L.A., Perea-Ortega, J.M.: OCA: opinion corpus for Arabic. J. Am. Soc. Inf. Sci. **62**(10), 2045–2054 (2011)
13. Atlam, E.S., Morita, K., Fuketa, M., Aoe, J.I.: A new approach for Arabic text classification using Arabic field-association terms. J. Am. Soc. Inf. Sci. **62**(11), 2266–2276 (2011)
14. Wahsheh, H.A., Alsmadi, I.M., Al-Kabi, M.N.: Analyzing the popular words to evaluate spam in Arabic web pages. Res. Bull. Jordan ACM **11**(11), 22–26 (2012)
15. Larkey, L.S., Ballesteros, L., Connell, M.E.: Light stemming for Arabic information retrieval. In: Soudi, A., Bosch, A., Neumann, G. (eds.) Arabic Computational Morphology. Text, Speech and Language Technology, vol. 38, pp. 221–243 (2007). Springer, Dordrecht. https://doi.org/10.1007/978-1-4020-6046-5_12
16. Chowdhury, A., Aljlayl, M., Jensen, E.C., Beitzel, S.M., Grossmanand, D.A., Frieder, O.: IIT at TREC 2002 linear combinations based on document structure and varied stemming for Arabic retrieval. In: Proceedings of TREC 2002, pp. 299–310 (2002)
17. Mikolov, T., Sutskever, I., Chen, K., Corrado, G., Dean, J.: Distributed representations of words and phrases and their compositionality. In: Proceedings of NIPS 2013, pp. 3111–3119 (2013)
18. Chouigui, A., Ben Khiroun, O., Elayeb, B.: ANT corpus: an Arabic news text collection for textual classification. In: Proceedings of AICCSA 2017, pp. 135–142 (2017)

Green Map - An Application for Air Quality Monitoring in the City

Diana Soponar and Ioana Ciuciu[(✉)]

Computer Science Department, University Babes-Bolyai, Cluj-Napoca, Romania
soponar.diana@gmail.com, ioana.ciuciu@cs.ubbcluj.ro

Abstract. This paper presents an approach and its corresponding application to monitor the air quality from a city, to collect air quality data and use it to provide information to the public. This study focuses on detecting the small particulate matter (PM 2.5) in the air and it considers two approaches in order to determine the air pollution levels: the users' opinion and a technical sensor.

Keywords: Air quality · Sensor data · Particulate matter · Social sensors

1 Introduction

Air pollution is a major threat to our health and to the environment. The World Health Organization (WHO[1]) claims that 9 out of 10 people worldwide breathe polluted air. More than 80% of people who are living in the urban areas are exposed to high levels of air pollution, leading to dangerous disease such as stroke, heart disease or cancer. This approach proposes to raise awareness of the air pollution problem by offering a device to detect and monitor the small particulate matter (PM 2.5) in the air. Particulate matter are inhalable particles that come from vehicle exhausts or from burning of fuels such as wood, or heating oil. A mobile application implemented for the users to be informed about the pollution in the city is also proposed here. The application comes with the possibility for users to participate in monitoring the pollution by rating the quality of air or submitting the pollution levels registered by their own devices. The proposed device could be used both indoors and outdoors, depending on the need.

The results collected from the sensors, but also from the users, can build a set of data consisting of pollution levels and air quality of a city from a user point of view. With these data a user can visualize the green and polluted areas from a city or region.

2 Related Work

Air quality monitoring has been extensively studied, with case studies ranging from indoor environment monitoring [1, 2], to farm monitoring [3], industrial sites [4], vehicular emissions [5], cities [6], to highly polluted areas on the Globe. The work in [7] proposes P-Sense, a participatory approach to air pollution monitoring that provides

---

[1] http://www.who.int/.

C. Debruyne et al. (Eds.): OTM 2018 Workshops, LNCS 11231, pp. 241–245, 2019.
https://doi.org/10.1007/978-3-030-11683-5_27

large amounts of air pollution data in time and space with different granularities. In [8], an Arduino-based device for air quality monitoring aiming at maximizing the number of air pollutants monitored is presented. An Arduino-based approach for low-cost and portable devices, with real-time data visualization is introduced in [9]. AirCasting[2] is an open platform that allows users to record and share health and environmental data using their smart phones. The European Environmental Agency developed a GIS Map Application, named Air Quality Index[3] which allows users to understand more about air quality. However, from their side, there is very few data about Romania (our case study region) regarding air pollution.

This paper proposes a low-cost Arduino-based device to measure the pollution from the air and an Android mobile application with a friendly user interface. The main contribution of the paper is a social approach to air quality monitoring. Citizens are involved as active contributors to the air quality monitoring of their city/region.

3 Air Quality Monitoring in Smart Cities

A *smart city*[4] is an urban area that uses information and communication technologies to reduce waste, improve infrastructure and efficiency for energy use. It also focuses on environmental concerns such as climate change and air pollution by using sensors to measure the quality of drinking water or the quality of the air.

Particulate Matter[5] is an air pollutant defined as a mixture of solid particles and liquid droplets found in the air. It includes aerosols, smoke, fumes, dust, ash and pollen. It is one of the deadliest form of air pollution. Created by both natural and man-made causes, like construction sites, unpaved roads, fields, smokestacks or fires. These particles impact the climate, precipitation level and has significant effects on humans' health. They come in many sizes and shapes and can be made up of hundreds of different chemicals. Particles, such as dust, dirt, or smoke, are large or dark enough to be seen with the naked eye. Others are so small they can only be detected using an electron microscope. They are often separated into two main groups based on their size: Inhalable coarse particles (PM 10) found near roadways and dusty industries with a diameter between 2.5 micrometres (μm) and 10 micrometres (μm); and fine particles (PM 2.5) with a diameter up to 2.5 micrometres (μm) found in smoke and haze, gases emitted from power plants, industries and automobiles react in the air. *Fine Particles*[6] (PM 2.5) are tiny particles in the air that reduce visibility and cause the air to appear hazy. These are present outdoor and indoor.

---

[2] http://aircasting.org/.

[3] http://airindex.eea.europa.eu/.

[4] https://internetofthingsagenda.techtarget.com/definition/smart-city.

[5] https://www.epa.gov/pm-pollution.

[6] https://www.health.ny.gov/environmental/.

4 Use Cases

The Android mobile application follows **three directions** for the application usage. On the **first view** (Fig. 1(a)), the user is able to rate his current location, to view a list with the nearby sensors and its pollution levels. When taping on one of the sensors an analysis by time of the recorded data will be showed to the user. Also, a user will be able to see the best rated locations by the users in a bar chart. The value of the pollution level index is determined according to the EU Air Quality Standards[7].

The **second view** (Fig. 1(b)), a map is displayed to the user. A heatmap of the air quality ratings is placed on top of the city map that can be activated and deactivated. On the city map, the user can add a location to rate. Two types of markers are placed: one for ratings and one for fixed sensor devices. When selecting any of the markers, an info window pops up with details about the location. For the second type of marker, the one that represents the sensors, when taping on the pop-up window, statistics of the pollution levels from the sensor are available. On the **third view** (Fig. 1(c)), the data collected from the device is available to the user. This way a user can determine and publish the level of (outdoor) pollution from his location.

5 Application Development

In the development of the Air Quality Monitor the basic used components are: Arduino Uno, Wi-Fi Module ESP8266 and the Grove – Dust Sensor (PPD42NS).

Arduino Uno[8] consists of a physical programmable circuit board (or the microcontroller) and a piece of software, or IDE (Integrated Development Environment) that runs on your computer, used to write and upload computer code to the physical board. The microcontroller comes preprogrammed with a bootloader that allows to upload new code to it without the use of an external hardware programmer.

The *ESP8266*[9] is a low-price Wi-Fi module useful for easily controlling devices over the Internet. It allows microcontrollers to connect to a Wi-Fi network and comes with factory installed firmware allowing simple TCP/IP connections.

The Grove-*Dust Sensor*[10] measures the dust concentration in an environment, giving a good indicator about the air quality. It is sensitive to dust particles and cigarette smoke which can trigger many allergic symptoms. The PM level in the air is measured by counting the Low Pulse Occupancy time (LPO time) in a given time unit. LPO time is proportional to PM concentration. The sensor uses the counting method to measure dust concentration, not weighing method, and the unit is pcs/L or pcs/0.01cf. The sensor sends the PM concentration using pcs/0.01cf as a counting method and according to the European Air Quality Standards, which refers to PM using $\mu g/m^3$. An approximate transformation was made for the pollution levels to correspond to these

---

[7] http://ec.europa.eu/environment/air/quality/standards.htm.

[8] https://www.arduino.cc/.

[9] https://en.wikipedia.org/wiki/ESP8266.

[10] http://wiki.seeedstudio.com/Grove-Dust_Sensor/.

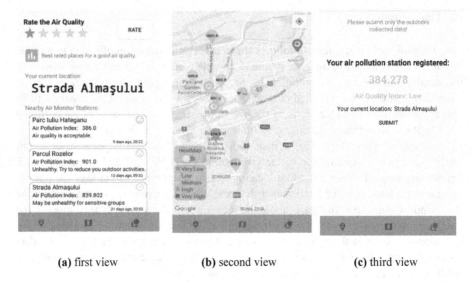

(a) first view   **(b)** second view   **(c)** third view

Fig. 1. Use cases – three views of the application

standards (Very Low: <300 pcs/0.01cf; Low: 301–600 pcs/0.01cf; Medium: 601–900 pcs/0.01cf; High: 901–1200 pcs/0.01cf; Very High: >1200 pcs/0.01cf). The application uses Firebase[11], a cloud-hosted NoSQL database. Data is stored as JSON[12] and synchronized in real time. The circuit design in Fig. 2 was realized in the context of this work. For this, only one sensor was configured, but it can be expanded to more sensors and devices.

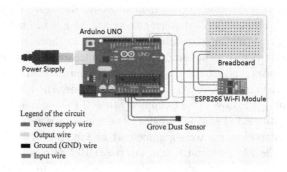

Fig. 2. Circuit structure

---

[11] https://firebase.google.com/.

[12] https://www.json.org/.

6   Conclusion and Future Work

This paper addresses one of the problems we all have to face every day, air pollution. One of the main contributions of our work to this domain is to consider people as social sensors and let them interpret and express how they perceive the air quality, and furthermore share their vote to others who are likely to stay informed about the air quality of their city or neighborhood.

Future work includes a recommendation section, for personalized locations according to specific user activity; also, placing sensors all over the city in order to collect real-time data and to compare the results to the ones coming from the social sensors. The final aim is to have an open environment for air pollution monitoring enabling wide citizen participation and awareness.

References

1. Pitarma, R., et al.: Monitoring indoor air quality for enhanced occupational health. J. Med. Syst. **41**, 23 (2017)
2. Preethichandra, D.M.G.: Design of a smart indoor air quality monitoring wireless sensor network for assisted living. In: IEEE International Instrumentation and Measurement Technology Conference (2013)
3. Jindarat, S., Wuttidittachotti, P.: Smart farm monitoring using Raspberry Pi and Arduino. In: IEEE International Conference on Communication and Control Technology (2015)
4. Vadlamudi, M.K., Brindha, G.S.: Monitoring of green house gases using wireless sensor networks with Arduino board. Int. J. Sci. Eng. Technol. Res. **4**(4), 741–745 (2015)
5. Chaudhry, V.: ARDUEMISSION: vehicular emissions monitoring. Int. J. Adv. Res. Eng. Appl. Sci. **3**(7), 35–44 (2014)
6. Devarakonda, S., et al.: Real-time air quality monitoring through mobile sensing in metropolitan areas. In: Proceedings of ACM SIGKDD (2013)
7. Mendez, D., et al.: P-Sense: a participatory sensing system for air pollution monitoring and control. In: IEEE International Conference on Pervasive Computing and Communications Workshops (2011)
8. Husain, A.M., et al.: Air quality monitoring: the use of Arduino and Android. J. Mod. Sci. Technol. **4**, 86–96 (2016)
9. Chaudhry, V.: Arduair: air quality monitoring. Int. J. Environ. Eng. Manag. **4**(6), 639–646 (2013)

Local and Open ICH Archives: Developing Integration and Interaction Tools

Maria Teresa Artese[✉] and Isabella Gagliardi

CNR IMATI – Milano, Via Corti 12, 20133 Milan, Italy
{artese,gagliardi}@mi.imati.cnr.it

Abstract. The UNESCO Convention of 2003 has promoted the growth of online inventories containing multimedia data, even if usually developed as data silos and searchable with different and rigid criteria. We present here a work-in-progress that aims to overcome these limits, studying the implementation of a system that allows to query different inventories simultaneously in the same way, whether they are local or not, overcoming the limit represented by data different languages and providing intuitive and attractive search tools. The query criteria designed combine keywords semantic together with temporal and space information to create useful tools for intangible heritage data. The main points are: the use of MultiWordNet to structure the document keywords, the generation of thematic paths, the creation of table games.

Keywords: Terminological resources · MultiWordNet · ICH timeline · Open archives · Storytelling

1 Introduction

The growth of open archives available online favored by the UNESCO Convention of 2003 has given the opportunity to find useful information and to improve the knowledge about intangible heritage. Unfortunately still many archives are developed as data silos and need specific skills to be used. The aim of this work is twofold: on one hand to develop a system able to get data from different inventories at the same time, which may be local databases or open archives available on-line. On the other hand to study new storytelling tools based on keywords semantic, able to bring the inventories closer to people and facilitate the passage of intangible heritage from one generation to the next.

Multimodal and multimedia search will be operated both on local and on-line data: visual interactions, timelines, games, can reach a wider public, together with the archives connections to query them simultaneously as parts of a complex heritage.

The paper is structured as follows: after a brief description of local and on-line archives to be used in our experimentation, storytelling tools defined will be presented and explained. Finally some preliminary results will be discussed.

© Springer Nature Switzerland AG 2019
C. Debruyne et al. (Eds.): OTM 2018 Workshops, LNCS 11231, pp. 246–250, 2019.
https://doi.org/10.1007/978-3-030-11683-5_28

2 Local and Open ICH Archives

The following datasets - related to social or cultural heritage collections of images and multimedia data - have been used to define and test the integration and storytelling tools. One of the features of our approach is that many others, mainly online, may be added and tested, in a seamless way:

- **IntangibleSearch Archive** and **AESS archive**: the two ICH archives of the Lombardy Region [1–3].
- **Museum of Contemporary Photography** in Cinisello Balsamo, Milan: a significant cross-section of photography after World War II to the present day [4].
- **Europeana**: is the EU digital platform for cultural heritage [5].
- **Wikipedia**: for the pages belonging to the category "Popular traditions" and "Oral and intangible heritage of humanity". The extraction of data and integration of this inventory is under study [6].

At the base of navigation process there is the creation of a new layer dedicated to data extraction: a web service, based on REST API protocol, is needed to interact with the underlying local databases in a common and standard way, conforming to the data interaction methods provided by Europeana and Wikipedia [5, 6]. For external archives involved it is necessary to study and implement a proper layer where interaction with each single web service is defined.

3 Storytelling Tools

We present here some tools which, through automatic and semi/automatic data processes, can improve and increase the potential of available data. From the analysis of documents, present both in local and on-line archives considered here, we observed that some intrinsic information is common: localization, general information about the time, keywords related to very specific subjects. The tools studied analyze and combine this common data in different ways.

3.1 Semantic Hierarchy Between Keywords

Keywords associated to documents are usually chosen by expert catalogers and selected on the basis of specialized vocabularies, enriched by new words when necessary. Terms are organized as flat lists, neither structured nor linked together. We studied how to create a hierarchical structure to group terms on the basis of their semantic meaning. This operation is performed using the structured dictionary "MultiWordNet", which is available online [7] and give us the possibility to search both English and Italian terms. A specific search process, showed in Fig. 1, has been developed to search each keyword into MultiWordNet and, when found, tag it with the all unique codes related to the different retrieved meanings. Each retrieved code makes it possible to link each term with others of upper and lower level, and with the related translations, allowing to import the hierarchical structure taken from MultiWordNet into the query section of the system [8]. All the meanings of a searched key, together with the hierarchical structure for each of them are organized in a tree structure and are available to be used as new query keys, allowing to enlarge or restrict the set of retrieved data according to that specific meaning, to link documents from a semantic point of view, regardless of the language with which the term is used.

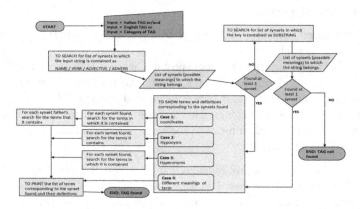

Fig. 1. Search process of a key within "MultiWordNet"

This process can also be applied to online open archives, often these data are accompanied by words that act as tags: in Europeana, for example, they are called "subject" and are expressed in various languages. It is interesting also to see how the keywords lists and structures extracted from a local archive can be generalized and used to search on others inventories, such as Europeana, where they become a valid entry point to navigate between such a large amount of data.

3.2   Itineraries and 'Themed' Routes

After the analysis of terms and keywords most used to query local archives we defined a hierarchical structure containing categories and sub-categories often recurring. Each of them is linked with keywords and terms of common use, when available, and an image to represent it. This structure is the input for a procedure able to group and extract data, to generate a series of guided tours among with the user can navigate, allowing him to explore and retrieve semantically similar documents. An example is shown in Fig. 2, where the main category is "Objects" and sub-categories found are shown, among them "Musical Instruments" is selected with all related documents found. This has given excellent results for the local archives used at first, but it is interesting to use these themed routes to search other inventories, allowing to quickly and easily query huge archives such as Europeana where it is not easy to understand at first glance what it contains and can be searched for.

The further step is the combination of data coming from 'themed' routes with those of the time period: this allows to show the retrieved documents in a timeline, grouping them by historical period. With the introduction of localization key, it is possible to

Fig. 2. Example of hierarchical structures made between keywords

generate thematic maps which are organized according to the historical period. This allows us to extract everything that is available in a certain place of interest for the period indicated related to a given theme, achieving a "Near to me now" extraction procedure. So, given for example the place where the user is, identified by the GPS and today's date taken from the phone, he could ask to view what is available to visit or events he can attend, for example processions, carnivals, rituals, museum collections, etc... that may be available near the place where the user is, getting data from all inventories available.

3.3 Games and Riddles

We tried to create new ways to navigate ICH contents, oriented to communicate with a wider audience and common people through play and discovery. We focused at first on the two AESS archives: the analysis of those inventories combined with a work of post-editing done with specialized experts gave hints on how to develop new tools and enrich the archives with a play section:

- Make a list of trivia or anecdotes extracted from document analysis and put them in a question/answer form, for example about different carnival characters and roles, traditional mask names, traditional foods recipes, musical repertoires and so on.
- Label each questions/answers with keywords, time and place information, a difficulty level and finally a score.
- Extract images to add graphic data to each entry in the list.

Such amount of new data added gradually to the system can be used to build different stage games, mixing data randomly. Taking inspiration from the snakes and ladders game, different tables can be created extracting questions and using associated keywords time and place also, to create connections between different questions of the game. The user can save his game and explore the archives to search the correct answers, to improve his score based on the number of correct answers given.

The process can be enlarged and applied to other inventories, by creating an incremental game structure containing data coming from all inventories, both local and on-line archives, where to store new questions/answers able to query and approach data in a different and funny way.

4 Preliminary Results and Conclusions

We have presented here a study concerning the implementation of tools that allows to query different inventories simultaneously, overcoming the problems given by data silos and different languages where the basic idea is to combine keywords semantics together with temporal and space information to create useful tools and games for the storytelling of the intangible heritage. This study is the basis for a prototype development, whose structure is shown in Fig. 3. A preliminary test phase made on the different types of data available has provided encouraging results, especially because search criteria, conceived and applied to one specific inventory, give excellent solutions once applied to all the archives involved.

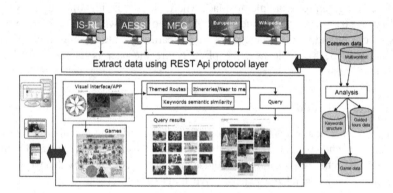

Fig. 3. Structure of the developing system

References

1. Intangible Search. http://www.intangiblesearch.eu. Accessed 12 July 2018
2. Lombardia Digital Archive (AESS). http://aess.regione.lombardia.it/ricerca. Accessed 12 July 2018
3. Artese, M.T., Gagliardi, I.: Inventorying intangible cultural heritage on the web: a life-cycle approach. Int. J. Intang. Herit. **12**, 111–138 (2017). Natl Folk Museum Korea-Nfmk, South Korea
4. Museo Fotografia Contemporanea. http://mfc.itc.cnr.it/home.htm. Accessed 12 July 2018
5. Europeana. http://www.europeana.eu. Accessed 12 July 2018
6. Wikipedia, Traditions. https://en.wikipedia.org/wiki/Category:Traditions. Accessed 12 July 2018
7. Multiwordnet. http://multiwordnet.fbk.eu/english/home.php. Accessed 12 July 2018
8. Artese, M.T., Gagliardi, I.: Multilingual specialist glossaries in a framework for intangible cultural heritage. Int. J. Herit. Digit. Era **3**(4), 657–668 (2014)

Unsupervised Automatic Keyphrases Extraction Algorithms

Experimentations on Paintings

Isabella Gagliardi[(✉)] and Maria Teresa Artese

CNR IMATI – Milano, Via Bassini 15, 20133 Milan, Italy
{gagliardi,artese}@mi.imati.cnr.it

Abstract. Massive volumes of images of museums or art collections, or made available by artists and photographers, more and more often, are available on the web, along with some metadata, essential for their characterization and retrieval. A set of (scored) keywords/keyphrases that characterize the semantic content of the documents should be, automatically or manually, extracted and/or associated. We present here a work-in-progress to evaluate different methods for the unsupervised keyword extraction to Italian and English datasets. In the paper datasets, algorithms and approaches are presented and discussed together with some preliminary results referred to relatedness of terms.

Keywords: Unsupervised Automatic Keyphrase Extraction · Evaluation · Information Retrieval · TextRank · RAKE · Tf-Idf · Latent Semantic Indexing

1 Introduction

Massive volumes of images of museum permanent collections are available for free usage on the web, along with some metadata, essential for their finding and retrieval. While the images may be processed without any further information - e.g. it is possible to automatically extract color information or low-level features, to allow retrieval based on semantic information that cannot be extracted from the image alone, it is essential to associate, manually or automatically, a set of (scored) keywords/keyphrases that characterize the semantic contents of the document and are useful in identifying relevant documents for a given query and/or in "suggesting" something related in some way. Keywords/keyphrases should, therefore, satisfy the following characteristics: (i) have a good coverage; (ii) be relevant; (iii) be consistent and (iv) be up-to-date. Manually identifying and associating words is a time-consuming job, requires specialized personnel both as a terminologist, as an expert in the subject and as a web specialist. Although the problem of extracting keywords able to represent the contents of texts in natural language has been faced since the first Information Retrieval systems appeared, the advent of new tools and techniques makes it still very actual [1, 2]. A large number of algorithms, categorized into supervised or unsupervised methods, have been developed to address the problem of automatic keyphrases extraction. Supervised methods typically consider this problem as a classification task, in which a model is trained on annotated data to determine whether a given phrase is a keyphrase

© Springer Nature Switzerland AG 2019
C. Debruyne et al. (Eds.): OTM 2018 Workshops, LNCS 11231, pp. 251–255, 2019.
https://doi.org/10.1007/978-3-030-11683-5_29

or not. These systems need a lot of training data, which can be unfeasible in the web scenario, and yet show a bias towards the domain on which they are trained. Keyphrase extraction task in unsupervised approaches is considered as a ranking problem and can be gathered into statistical-based, graph-based and cluster-based approaches. In statistical-based approaches, texts are usually represented as matrices in which the statistical techniques are applied to rank the words by using tf-idf term weighting metric [3]. The graph-based methods build a graph from the input documents, and each document is represented as a graph where vertices or nodes represent words, and edges are connected based on either lexical or semantic relations, such as a co-occurrence relation. Examples are TextRank [4], RAKE [5], SingleRank [6] or CollabRank [7]. Cluster-based methods extract terms, group them into clusters based on their semantic relatedness using Wikipedia and/or other co-occurrence similarity measures, and select phrases that contain one or more cluster centroids. Examples are KeyCluster [8], SemCluster [9] or the one proposed in [10].

We present here a work-in-progress, an experimentation done with the aim of evaluating algorithms for the automatic extraction of scored keyphrases from documents. The paper is structured as follows: after a short description of the Unsupervised keyword extraction methods used, our approach is presented together with some preliminary results, that are briefly discussed.

2 Unsupervised Keyphrases Extraction Algorithms

In the following, we present three classical unsupervised algorithms for keyword extraction – tf-idf, TextRank, and RAKE, together with Latent Semantic index algorithm used in our experimentation.

Tf–idf [3], short for term frequency–inverse document frequency, is widely used in Information Retrieval, and is able to measure the importance of a word in a document, within a collection or corpus: a tf-idf score is highest when a term occurs many times in a small number of documents, decreasing to 0 when the term occurs in all items.

TextRank [4] is a graph-based, domain-independent ranking model for text processing, and is based on the same assumptions of Google PageRank.

Rapid Automatic Keyword Extraction (RAKE) [5] is an unsupervised, domain-independent, and language-independent graph-based method for extracting keywords from individual documents.

LSI [11] is a technique able of analyzing relationships between a set of documents and the terms they contain by producing a set of concepts related to the documents and terms. The method is able to reduce the number of rows in the matrix while preserving the similarity structure among columns.

3 Our Approach

For our experimentations, we started from the 'paintings 91' [12, 13] database, which consists of well-known paintings by famous artists ranging from Vermeer to Chagall, from Bosch to Matisse. The original dataset consists of 4,214 paintings from 91 different artists with some metadata. We first associated to each painting its title (in Italian or in English), and then, in a completely automated way, we retrieved from the web descriptions of the painting, whose provenience is mainly from Wikipedia or the first results of a google search based on title + author query, in Italian and/or in English. Although 'painting 91' contains works by famous artists, some search has produced no results or results irrelevant to the paintings. So to ensure that the web pages retrieved are semantically related to the paintings, a similarity score based on co-occurrence of words in the web page title and painting title – in particular on cosine similarity of vectors of (unweighted) terms - has been computed and assigned.

We used, as texts associated with each item, those web descriptions scoring higher than 0.1, and a length greater than 500 characters. In Table 1 a summary of datasets used: the total number of documents, number of web descriptions (texts) per item (average, min, and max), similarity scores (average, min, and max), and length of texts in characters (average, min, and max).

Table 1. Datasets details: number of documents, number of texts per document, similarity scores, and length. Only English and Italian data have been used

Language	Tot. no. of documents	No. of texts/item Av. (min–max)	Similarity score Av. (min–max)	Length Av. (min–max)
All	23165	5.75 (1–19)	0.31 (0.10–1)	4661.30 (501–26238)
English	12792	3.61 (1–16)	0.30 (0.10–1)	5336.48 (501–26238)
Italian	9666	3.30 (1–12)	0.29 (0.10–1)	4255.35 (501–15863)

The first step of our approach is to harvest pieces of texts, from the web, either extracted from Wikipedia or considering the top-ranked results from google. On these texts, we applied RAKE, TextRank, tf-idf and LSI methods, in different implementations, considering each text as a single document and/or as part of a unique document. RAKE, TextRank, tf-idf algorithms extract a varying number of weighted keywords, while LSI groups documents assigning them a chosen number of topics.

Having more than a text for each item, a post-processing phase is required, in which the keywords extracted for each algorithm are integrated into a single (scored) set, and merged in several ways, according to different criteria, as union and/or intersection of all keywords, of top n keywords, of top-weighted keywords. In the end, the results obtained are evaluated on single or grouped results.

- For each piece of text:
  - Preprocess data: remove stopwords from the text, perform stemming, tokenize...
  - Create a list of candidate keywords/keyphrases using different algorithms,
  - Score each candidate keywords/keyphrases, according to different methods,
  - Select the first m keywords/keyphrases.
- Post processing: from n (pieces of texts) × m (keywords) extract the top k keywords for each element representing its semantic contents.
- Evaluate the results.

Designing evaluation metrics for automatic unsupervised keyphrase extraction algorithms is by no means an easy task. In general, the results are compared with the keywords chosen manually by experts or using gold standard datasets. Here our idea is to define a fully automatic evaluation method. In [14] we used Recall and Precision to evaluate the results, the same metrics used in SemEval contexts. Our results were not so clear, so in this paper, we use Sørensen–Dice (S) similarity coefficient. The coefficient measures the shared information (overlap) over the sum of cardinalities. In Table 2 a summary of evaluation results obtained applying RAKE, TextRank, tf-idf, LSI methods on the English and Italian datasets is shown. We report the best results obtained in the different runs with different options for the algorithms. Results for Single data are intended obtained for each document retrieved on the web, while in Grouped data, results are grouped on a per painting basis and considered as a unique item, and the keywords are merged. We report results computed on the top ten keywords extracted.

Table 2. Evaluation results obtained (limited to Sørensen–Dice measure) for RAKE, TextRank, tf-idf, LSI methods on the English and Italian datasets

Dataset	Data	TextRank	RAKE	tf-idf	LSI
En	Single	0.174	0.862	0.192	0.075
En	Grouped	0.282	0.549	0.255	0.134
It	Single	0.222	0.860	0.159	0.100
It	Grouped	0.320	0.545	0.256	0.131

The choice and the cardinality of keyword sets against which to evaluate the results influence greatly the evaluation: in this first test, we used all those extracted from the different algorithms, greater than 1 for Single or the number of texts for Grouped. Further normalization steps, able to take into account the different cardinality of the results, is being studied, both to select keywords and to create the evaluation sets, which also require more sophisticated merging/creation techniques.

TextRank, RAKE, and tf-idf confirmed as the more effective algorithms, validating the evaluation of [14]: RAKE extracts a large number of keywords, so its score is the highest. TextRank and tf-idf extract few terms and therefore obtain rather good results; while LSI, due to the difficulty of reaching the optimal number of topics, is struggling to achieve acceptable results. The various implementations of the algorithms and the different options in the runs lead to very different results, in terms of both (scored) keywords extracted and evaluations.

Grouping results bring opposite ratings for RAKE compared to TextRank and tf-idf: this is due to the different number of keywords extracted.

4 Conclusions

In the paper we have presented some experimentations related to unsupervised automatic keyphrases extractions methods, describing the algorithms chosen, the dataset characteristics, and discussing some preliminary results obtained in terms of Sørensen–Dice similarity measure. The work is still in progress, and future works should be oriented towards: (i) implementation and test of other algorithms and methods;

(ii) comparison of Italian vs English algorithms; (iii) normalization of results on the basis of the number of keywords extracted and length of texts; (iv) integration of best top keywords from different methods; (v) integration of word2vec, GloVe or WordNet to manage the synonyms and topic identification issues in a more efficient and effective way and (vi) more studies on the evaluation task, both testing different ways to create keyword sets for comparison/evaluation, as terms and numbers, and investigating other methods, borrowed also from information retrieval or image tagging.

References

1. Hasan, K.S., Ng, V.: Automatic keyphrase extraction: a survey of the state of the art. In: Proceedings of the 52nd Annual Meeting of the ACL, vol. 1, pp. 1262–1273. ACL Baltimore, Maryland (2014)
2. Siddiqi, S., Sharan, A.: Keyword and keyphrase extraction techniques: a literature review. Int. J. Comput. Appl. **109**(2), 18–23 (2015). https://doi.org/10.5120/19161-0607
3. Schütze, H., Manning, C.D., Raghavan, P.: Introduction to Information Retrieval, vol. 39. Cambridge University Press, Cambridge (2008)
4. Mihalcea, R., Tarau, P.: Textrank: bringing order into text. In: Lin, D., Wu, D. (eds.) Proceedings of EMNLP 2004, pp. 404–411. ACL (2004)
5. Rose, S., Engel, D., Cramer, N., Cowley, W.: Automatic keyword extraction from individual documents. In: Berry, M.W., Kogan, J. (eds.) Text Mining: Applications and Theory, pp. 1–20. Wiley, Hoboken (2010). https://doi.org/10.1002/9780470689646.ch1
6. Wan, X., Xiao, J.: Single document keyphrase extraction using neighborhood knowledge. In: AAAI-08, pp. 855–860. AAAI Press, Menlo Park, California (2008)
7. Wan, X., Xiao, J.: CollabRank: towards a collaborative approach to single-document keyphrase extraction. In: Proceedings of the 22nd International Conference on Computational Linguistics, vol. 1, pp. 969–976. ACL (2008)
8. Liu, Z., Li, P., Zheng, Y., Sun, M.: Clustering to find exemplar terms for keyphrase extraction. In: Proceedings of EMNLP 2010, vol. 1, pp. 257–266. ACL Cambridge, MA (2010)
9. Alrehamy, H.H., Walker, C.: SemCluster: unsupervised automatic keyphrase extraction using affinity propagation. In: Chao, F., Schockaert, S., Zhang, Q. (eds.) UKCI 2017. AISC, vol. 650, pp. 222–235. Springer, Cham (2018). https://doi.org/10.1007/978-3-319-66939-7_19
10. Bracewell, D.B., Ren, F., Kuriowa, S.: Multilingual single document keyword extraction for information retrieval. In: Proceeding of IEEE NLP-KE'05, pp. 517–522 (2015). https://doi.org/10.1109/NLPKE.2005.1598792
11. Dumais, S.T.: Latent semantic analysis. Ann. Rev. Info. Sci. Tech. **38**, 188–230 (2005). https://doi.org/10.1002/aris.1440380105
12. Khan, F.S., Beigpour, S., Van de Weijer, J., Felsberg, M.: Painting-91: a large scale database for computational painting categorization. Mach. Vis. Appl. **25**, 1385 (2014). https://doi.org/10.1007/s00138-014-0621-6
13. Artese, M.T., Ciocca, G., Gagliardi, I.: Evaluating perceptual visual attributes in social and cultural heritage web sites. J. Cultural Herit. **26**, 91–100 (2017). https://doi.org/10.1016/j.culher.2017.02.009
14. Artese, M.T., Gagliardi, I.: What is this painting about? Experiments on unsupervised keyphrases extraction algorithms. In: IOP Conference Series: Materials Science and Engineering, vol. 364, p. 012050 (2018). https://doi.org/10.1088/1757-899x/364/1/012050

Sentiment Analysis-Guided Cryptocurrency Investment

George Linut and Ioana Ciuciu[(⊠)]

Computer Science Department, University Babes-Bolyai,
Cluj-Napoca, Romania
george.linut@catalysts.cc, ioana.ciuciu@cs.ubbcluj.ro

Abstract. The paper presents an ongoing approach and experiment that proposes to apply sentiment analysis in the context of cryptocurrency investment. The approach performs sentiment analysis on user feeds from relevant social media communities (e.g., Reddit) and uses the results as input to a price reaction algorithm, together with live market prices. Our hypothesis is that taking into account human emotion and community dynamics enables better prediction of the trends in the field of cryptocurrency investment.

Keywords: Sentiment analysis · Cryptocurrency · Machine learning

1 Context and Motivation

Cryptocurrencies have been around since 2008 when the presumed pseudonymous Satoshi Nakamoto integrated many existing ideas from the cypherpunk community creating Bitcoin[1]; however they were only put into the spotlight in the fall of 2017. The main communication channels of the cryptocurrency community are Facebook, Twitter and Reddit. The impact of these social media platforms on the price of the cryptocurrencies has been observed more than once[2]. By studying relevant social media content, it is possible to infer the 'feeling of the market' and to predict how the price is going to shift. The community behind a cryptocurrency plays an important role in determining the market capital. Behavioral finance helps understand certain financial choices that people make. In line with this, the paper proposes to study how the community affects the cryptocurrency market trends. The approach considers human factors, going beyond traditional market analysis.

2 Approach

As shown in Fig. 1, the proposed approach considers **three main steps**, namely: (1) **data collection**; (2) **sentiment analysis**; and (3) **enhanced price reaction algorithm**. **Data is collected** from **two channels**: (1) the **social media data**, from

---

[1] www.bitcoin.org.

[2] https://fortune.com/2017/10/16/ibm-blockchain-stellar/.

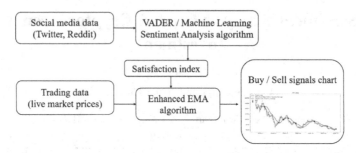

Fig. 1. Approach for sentiment analysis-guided cryptocurrency investment

relevant social media communities, such as Twitter and Reddit; and (2) **trading data**, collected as live market prices.

The **sentiment analysis** step is performed in two phases: first, the VADER[3] tool and lexicon are used to classify user feeds from social media channels. However, since the accuracy we obtained is 65% (tested against the Stanford Sentiment Analysis Corpus[4]), due to the specificities of the terms used by these communities, the results are only used as baseline for the second phase, the machine learning algorithm. A neural network was used, with an obtained accuracy of 81%.

The **enhanced price reaction algorithm** proposed takes in input both the price interpretation, using the Exponential Moving Average (EMA[5]) algorithm, and the result from the neural network, computed as a satisfaction index. The trained neural network was used to compute the sentiment for each day in the previous year, as the number of positive tweets over the total number of tweets. A zero value for a given day indicates a selling trend, while a value of 1 indicates a buying trend. The buy-sell strategy given by the EMA, takes into account the neural network by multiplying every day not only with the decay influence but also with the transposed value in the interval [−1,1] of the neural network result for that day. Thus, positive and negative days are amplified by the trend of that day. A buy/sell signal is issued when the price goes under or over the current trend (classic EMA), and also when the index obtained from the social media data has large variations.

3   Conclusion

The paper presents an ongoing study realized in the context of a student degree thesis. The verification of our hypothesis is work in progress. Several challenges that we faced could leave place to future innovation. First, the data processing could be optimized using big data technologies. A dedicated semantic lexicon for crypto trading will

---

[3] https://github.com/cjhutto/vaderSentiment.

[4] http://cs.stanford.edu/people/alecmgo/trainingandtestdata.zip.

[5] https://www.investopedia.com/terms/e/ema.asp.

provide more accurate sentiment analysis. The multilingual aspect is also to be considered. Finally, a community analysis tool would help to better understand human choices specifically in the field of cryptocurrency investment.

Author Index

Printed in the United States
By Bookmasters